Maggie Lane is a librarian and lives in Bristol with her son and daughter. Her other books include *Jane Austen's Family*, *Literary Daughters* and *A Charming Place: Bath in the Life and Times of Jane Austen*. She has published articles in the Annual Report of the Jane Austen Society and in *Persuasions*, the journal of the Jane Austen Society of North America. In a lighter vein she is the author of a series of literary quiz and puzzle books including *The Brontë Sisters Quiz and Puzzle Book* and *The Jane Austen Quiz and Puzzle Book*.

overleaf: Godmersham Park, Kent (1780)

JANE AUSTEN'S
ENGLAND

by

Maggie Lane

Robert Hale Limited
Clerkenwell House
Clerkenwell Green
London EC1R OHT

British Library Cataloguing in Publication Data
Lane, Maggie, *1947–*
Jane Austen's England.
1. Austen, Jane – Criticism and
interpretation
I. Title
823'7   PR4037

ISBN 0 7090 3709 0

Design by Katrina Restall

Photoset in Ehrhardt by
Rowland Phototypesetting Limited,
Bury St Edmunds, Suffolk
Printed in Great Britain by
St Edmundsbury Press Limited
Bury St Edmunds, Suffolk
Bound by Hunter & Foulis Limited

Contents

By the same author

Jane Austen's Family: Through Five Generations
Literary Daughters
A Charming Place: Bath in the Life and Times of Jane Austen

To R. A. C.
who loves Jane Austen
and England

List of Illustrations

Acknowledgements

The engravings chosen to illustrate this book, almost all of them contemporary with the adult years of Jane Austen, have been drawn from a wide variety of sources too numerous to mention individually, but it may interest readers to know that nearly half of them (those printed in bold below) come from *The Beauties of England and Wales* by J. Britton and E. W. Brayley, published in eighteen volumes between 1801 and 1815.

For permission to reproduce prints in their collections, I am grateful to: Avon County Libraries (illustrations no. 1, **2**, 4, **5**, 7, **8, 9, 10**, 13, **14, 15**, 17, 18, 19, 22, 23, 24, 26, 27, **29, 30, 31, 32**, 33, 34, **38, 39, 40, 41**, 43, 44, 45 and **46**); Bristol City Museum and Art Gallery (25 and 42); Devon Library Services (3, 20 and 21); Hamlyn Publishing Group (frontispiece); Hampshire County Libraries (Portsmouth) (6 and 36) and the Jane Austen Memorial Trust (12 and 35). To all the staff of the above organizations who helped me to locate appropriate engravings and provided copies for reproduction I would like to express here my deep gratitude.

I am grateful to the Jane Austen Memorial Trust too for permission to quote from the unpublished poems of James Austen kept at Jane Austen's house in Chawton, and to Mr and Mrs Lawrence Impey for allowing me to quote from the *Austen Papers*, long out of print and an invaluable source for any Austen scholar.

Publishers to whom my gratitude is due for permission to quote from their books are: Oxford University Press (*The Letters of Jane Austen* edited by R. W. Chapman); Batsford (*Cheltenham* by Bryan Little); Penguin (*The Buildings of England* series by Nikolaus Pevsner and others); and Macmillan (*Warren Hastings* by Keith Feiling).

Finally I would like to express my warmest personal thanks to all those fellow-Janeites who in correspondence or conversation generously shared ideas and information relevant to this book, and to Lesley Bellamy for typing the manuscript with remarkable efficiency and cheerfulness.

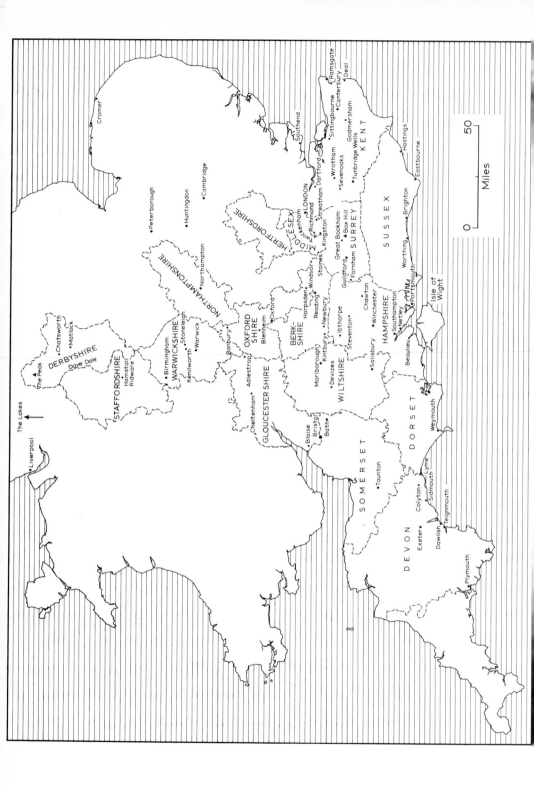

Introduction

Breathes there a man, with soul so dead,
Who never to himself hath said,
This is my own, my native land!
                                    Walter Scott,
                    The Lay of the Last Minstrel, 1805

'We have got the second volume of *Espriella's Letters*, and I read it aloud by candlelight. The man describes well, but is horribly anti-English. He deserves to be the foreigner he assumes', wrote Jane Austen in October 1808 of the book in which Robert Southey, posing as a Spaniard, offered a critical commentary on England.[1] She was intensely, and to me endearingly, xenophobic. 'The idea of a fashionable bathing place in Mecklenburg! How can people pretend to be fashionable or to bathe out of England!' she exclaimed in 1813 in reply to a letter from her brother Frank, then serving in the Baltic Sea. More seriously, perhaps, she wrote of an acquaintance the year after Waterloo, 'He is come back from France, thinking of the French as one could wish, disappointed in everything'.

Revolutionary France had not even the initial appeal for Jane Austen that it had for her contemporary, Wordsworth. In her view the stability of the English political, social and religious institutions offered the individual the safest degree of freedom within an ordered framework by which to live a satisfying and worthwhile life, without impinging on the rights of others.

Her affirmation of the superior sense and moderate behaviour of the English nation finds amused expression in *Northanger Abbey* when Catherine Morland compares 'the Alps and Pyrenees' with 'the Midland counties of England' and decides that in the latter, 'the laws of the land and the manners of the age' provide security against anything too terrible happening. Furthermore, 'among the English, she believed, in their hearts and habits, there was a general though unequal mixture of good and bad'.

Jane Austen pokes gentle fun at the naïve Catherine, but in *Emma*, a more mature heroine surely expresses her creator's thoughts as she surveys Donwell Abbey, with its surrounding woods, meadows, river and farms. 'It was a sweet view – sweet to the eye and to the mind. English verdure, English culture, English comfort, seen under a sun bright, without being oppressive.' Natural endowments and what man has, by taste and ingenuity, made of them, are bound up together and celebrated in a profound love of England, its 'prosperity and beauty'.

How much of England did Jane Austen know? Like Catherine Morland she was confessedly ignorant of 'the northern and western extremities'. But it is not true as some think that she rarely ventured beyond Hampshire and Bath. Her travels took her through fourteen counties, some of them repeatedly; she knew three cities intimately, and she was acquainted with many stretches of the English coastline. It can be said that the whole of southern England was her territory. Farms, villages, country estates, market and coaching towns and seaside resorts were known to her in great number. And this was at a time when every place had more local flavour – in terms of agricultural produce, building materials and the character and function of each town – than today. We cannot doubt that when travelling she took the same pleasure and interest as her own Fanny Price 'in observing all that was new, and admiring all that was pretty . . . in observing the appearance of the country, the bearings of the roads, the difference of soil, the state of the harvest, the cottages, the cattle, the children. . . .'

As Jane Austen knew and as her sister Cassandra once wrote, in this life 'there must be always something to wish for'[2], and even England was not perfection on earth. In the same novel that expresses delight in the Donwell scene, Emma, having paid a charity visit to a poor cottager, stops 'to look once more at all the outward wretchedness of the place, and recall the still greater within'. That was in a village; in the cities conditions for the poor were yet worse, and neither the 'noise and disorder' of Portsmouth, the bad smells of Bath nor the polluted atmosphere of London escape Jane Austen's censure. Yet visually, at least, even the cities presented little ugliness, in comparison with what they would become. In the novels of Jane Austen, towns offend almost every sense except the *sight*.

It is with Jane Austen's reaction to the visual world about her that this book is chiefly concerned. It is not a guidebook – that has been admirably accomplished already[3] – nor is it founded on speculation, on the amusing but in my view misguided game of identifying this village or that house as the original of some place in the novels. I firmly believe that Jane Austen was quite capable of inventing entire a Mansfield or a Barton, a Rosings or a Highbury, and that to try to match them up with real locations is as fruitless as it is insulting to her imagination.

Instead I have attempted to explore what her experiences of the English countryside, in all its component parts and all its regional variety, meant to her. She was indeed fortunate to live in an age when not only was England at the peak of its physical beauty, improved but not yet desecrated by human activity, but when cultured people were learning to appreciate the natural world after centuries of indifference or fear. During the course of her life, her ideas on landscape underwent subtle changes as she absorbed and responded to contemporary thinking, and as her reading was supplemented by personal knowledge. These ideas, and their influence on her novels, are the particular 'pattern in the carpet' that I have chosen here to trace.

My own understanding of the background to Jane Austen's work has been greatly enriched in the process of researching this book, as I have delved into the eighteenth-century attitude to the environment – a subject that, as Margaret Drabble too rightly says, 'engrosses those who become involved in it'[4] – and as I have endeavoured to evoke that environment itself. It takes a great effort of imagination to retrieve towns like Southampton or Portsmouth when they were still confined within their medieval city walls; or Cheltenham when it was little more than one long and airy village street; or even London, when each district had its own distinctive character. Jane Austen has helped me to visualize this lost, this lovely England – for that, as for so many other pleasures, I am greatly in her debt. This England is, after all, our common heritage; we are just unfortunate that intervening generations have allowed so much to slip away. *We* must be more vigilant over what remains. Happily, it is not so difficult to recapture Jane Austen's England in the countryside and the villages, so many of which remain largely unspoilt, or in Bath, which preserves in stone to a remarkable degree the aesthetics and values of her age.

1

The England of Jane Austen's Time

... look around
Upon the variegated scene of hills,
And woods, and fruitful vales, and villages
Half-hid in tufted orchards, and the sea
Boundless, and studded thick with many a sail.
William Crowe, *Lewesdon Hill*, 1788

The England that Jane Austen knew was the result of the profound change in man's attitude to himself and his environment which had begun some seventy or eighty years before her birth. The new way of thinking both shaped the landscape and offered the means to appreciate it. She grew to consciousness just as these processes reached their full development, so that not only was the countryside at its loveliest, but discussion of it at its most stimulating.

This revolution in thought was the first of the great revolutions which were to propel English life from medievalism to modernity, and the one on which all the others – agrarian, industrial, social and political – depended. It was also, perhaps, the happiest in its effect. It turned man from a miserable creature, dourly battling against the forces of nature, preoccupied by the state of his soul and reliant for his reward in the life hereafter, to one who came to believe that rational happiness was attainable on earth, through the cultivation of his mind and senses, and the educated enjoyment of the world's delights.

The birth of the Age of Reason coincided with a new national prosperity, but it was no coincidence: both were the result of the toleration and stability which took the place, perhaps first more through weariness than design, of the civil and religious strife of the preceding centuries – and each nourished the other.

The possibilities for the improvement of the human condition, both material and moral, seemed suddenly limitless. Guilt and superstition, which for generations had kept humanity in thrall, were shaken off. Living standards rose, and an ingenious race found scope for its inventiveness. There grew an insatiable demand for new experiences and new possessions. People became more sociable and more acquisitive, both of which characteristics, by creating the concept of fashion, were to influence the way the country looked.

At the same time, the way *they* looked at the country radically altered. As their inventions and their prosperity shielded them from the harsher aspects of nature, so they feared her less and admired her more. Their aesthetic faculties became highly developed, and their religion took the comfortable form of gratitude for the creation of the wonderful world they were discovering. In this spirit scientific enquiry leapt forward. To understand was to praise. John Ray, the botanist, expressed the view which was to prevail throughout the coming century when in 1691 he wrote, 'there is no occupation more worthy and delightful than to contemplate the beauteous works of nature and honour the infinite wisdom and goodness of God'.

The Georgian response to landscape was by no means a static thing, but evolved almost with each generation, each development being a reaction to the last. They began by admiring the proofs of their own ingenuity and control. Fields of ripening crops, well-fed beasts, harbours alive with trade and roads in good repair were what brought joy to the heart of Daniel Defoe as he journeyed about England in the 1720s.[1] He was close enough to the age of privation and discomfort to relish their subjugation. At this stage the great formal gardens of the aristocracy were regarded with complacency, for what could better display mastery over unruly nature than a vast complex of straight lines?

As their ability to control nature came to be taken for granted however, people began to perceive beauty where they had never thought to look for it before – in the natural landscape about them. Soon there was not an educated Englishman who did not sympathize with Shaftesbury's cry, 'I shall no longer resist the passion growing in me for things of a natural kind'.[2] With the help of the early landscape gardeners such as William Kent, they 'leapt the fence, and saw that all nature was a garden'.[3]

If one generation welcomed nature into the park palings, the next ventured beyond them to admire those portions of England that would never be cultivated, 'landscaped' or mown. The rage for travel in search of picturesque beauty gained ground. The concept of the picturesque was that to please the person of taste, a piece of scenery must be capable of forming a picture, with all the elements correctly balanced. This was a highly intellectual and exclusive view of nature, one which acquired its own jargon and was often carried to excess – and one with which Jane Austen had considerable fun. Or rather, it was with the people who took it up too enthusiastically, that she characteristically had fun. Nevertheless, the movement awakened people to the great variety of natural beauty to be found within the British Isles – and spread that beauty too, for if they were wealthy landowners, as many of them were, they were not content until they had improved whole estates, perhaps for a second time, to conform to picturesque principles.

It was the element of conformity, perhaps, that created the eventual dissatisfaction with this view. The next generation replaced it with the Romantic movement, in which the untaught response to nature of the individual soul was deemed more valuable than any amount of aesthetic appreciation learnt from books. The language of this movement was not jargon but poetry. In theory, though probably not often in practice – for the lower levels of society were as much preoccupied with sheer survival as ever – it was open to the peasant as well as the man of letters to glory in his world from a Romantic viewpoint, which certainly had not been the case with the picturesque. The Romantics sought the very scenery that had repelled their forebears – the wild, barren, mountainous country of the north, though for those who were confined to southern England, the grandeur of the coastline and the newly-discovered charms of the sea proved acceptable alternatives. Occurring towards the end of Jane Austen's lifetime, the Romantic movement interested and influenced her, as we shall see.

Through all these changes, which occupied a period of some hundred years, the vast body of educated thought in the nation kept pace. Among the cultured classes, from the aristocracy down to the 'middling people'[4] of England, there was a remarkable homogeneity of ideas and taste. This had two fortunate effects when they came not just to admire but to re-fashion their environment. Economically, their progress was unhampered by conflicting interests, and visually, their individual improvements wrought upon the landscape an exquisite harmony never achieved before or since.

Brighton (1810) Brighton was the first of many villages along the southern English coast to turn itself into a fashionable resort as travel became more popular. Lydia Bennet and Maria Bertram were among the visitors to Brighton

The three elements of a highly civilized but not yet industrialized landscape, such as was southern England in the late-eighteenth and early-nineteenth centuries, are the fields and farms that support it, the country estates that adorn it, and the towns and villages that punctuate the greenery of the rest.

The England of that period was lightly populated and predominantly rural. At the time of the first census in 1801, when Jane Austen was a young adult, England was inhabited by fewer than nine million people, of whom it is estimated about half were literate. Fewer still, of course, possessed the leisure to enjoy or the means to improve their surroundings. Only one-fifth of the population lived in towns, none of which, excepting London, was very large. The vast majority of people depended directly for their livelihood on the land – whether as owner, farmer or labourer.

The countryside was both more tranquil and less desolate than now, for the human figure was very much part of the scenery. Amongst the rural working classes most people, men, women and children alike, spent almost all the daylight hours out of doors. There was always a handy labourer at work from whom to enquire the way, as Henry Crawford found at Thornton Lacey. Gangs of women and children performed the various seasonal tasks about the fields, and the entire neighbourhood would turn out for haymaking and harvest. Their voices were all that broke the quiet. Wheat was still reaped by sickle or scythe and threshed by flail.

Even domestic chores were performed whenever possible outside the cottage door, for the sake of daylight, air and companionship. Children too small to work played within sight of their mothers, and poultry scratched for food at their feet. Animals, indeed, were much in evidence, not only grazing the meadows or grunting for windfalls in the orchard, but walking in droves to market. Creatures even as small as geese and turkeys were obliged to go thither on foot. Horses, carriages and wagons of every description gently animated the scene as the mobility, of both people and goods, steadily increased.

If all this seems more like the world of Thomas Hardy than of Jane Austen, it is only because he was recording a way of life whose demise he could foresee, whereas she took for granted this perpetual background to the lives of the leisured classes with whom she was concerned. But even those whose wealth or profession absolved them from the necessity of physical work were much closer to the countryside than their counterparts of Victorian England. The seasons, the weather and the state of the harvest were of real importance and interest to everybody when the production of food was a much more localized affair, for despite the steady improvement in transportation, communities and often households were still largely self-sufficient. Great landowners interested themselves in their estates and almost everybody, at every level of society, cultivated something. Cottagers grew vegetables and kept a pig, parsons had their glebe lands to farm, and we have only to think of the game and garden-stuff furnished by Barton Park, the fruit trees and stew-ponds of Delaford, and the greenhouse and poultry yard of Cleveland (to take examples from one novel alone) to realize that the production of food was a concern of all. Not only food and drink, but remedies and medicines also were home-produced, requiring a knowledge of and involvement in nature which largely vanished with the industrial age.

Foreign visitors saw Georgian England as a land of peace and plenty, and marvelled at both the quality and the quantity of the meat consumed. Never had food been so abundant, so varied, so cheap; even the lowly labourer ate better at this period than before or afterwards. 'All I can say is, that the poor do not look so poor here as in other countries; that poverty does not intrude on your sight; and that it is necessary to seek it. All human societies are full of it – here it does not overflow, certainly', wrote Louis Simond, a Frenchman who had emigrated to America and who spent the years 1810–11 travelling round England.[5]

That an increasing population could be adequately fed, that the countryside could produce enough surplus to supply the growing towns, was the result of several important innovations in agricultural practice, a subject which engaged some of the best – and most gentlemanly – brains of the day. (The Knightley brothers found it endlessly fascinating.) The newly developed science of stockbreeding produced better animals, while the introduction of turnips and other fodder crops enabled them to be overwintered. Crop rotation was an idea which revolutionized arable farming, obviating the need for the land to lie fallow one year in three and creating a more fertile soil and greater yields per acre: that of wheat, for example, was boosted by almost a third during the second half of the eighteenth century.[6]

But the most radical reform in agriculture, the one which made the greatest visual impact on the landscape, as well as on the economy and on men's lives, was enclosure.

This was the process, effected on a local basis sometimes by mutual agreement but more often by individual acts of parliament, whereby the medieval system of cultivating the land in strips, each person's holding consisting of a number of such strips scattered inconveniently throughout the parish within large, open, unfenced, straggling plots, was tidied up into the present pattern of regular fields, neatly bordered by hedges, each person being allocated a parcel of such fields in one piece.

It was logical, it made for much greater efficiency in producing food, and in accommodating progressive methods, and it was carried through with characteristic Georgian purposefulness – even ruthlessness. Eighty per cent of all enclosure acts were passed in the two periods 1760 to 1780 and 1793 to 1815 – almost exactly covering Jane Austen's lifespan. It was the high price of grain during the Napoleonic Wars which provided the incentive for bringing more land under cultivation. Norland Common is being enclosed during the action of *Sense and Sensibility*, written in the late 1790s. In *Northanger Abbey*, another novel of the same period, Henry Tilney talks of 'forests, the enclosure of them, wastelands, crown lands and government'. In fact one-third of the land enclosed in England had previously been either common, on which the villagers had traditionally enjoyed grazing rights, or waste – rabbit warrens, ant-hills, weeds, rocks or scrub.

If a person from the preceding century had been able to revisit England in Jane Austen's time this, indeed, would have been the greatest difference he would have noticed in the countryside – this fundamental reworking and recolouring of the very fabric of the landscape, whereby England became a lush green patchwork, stitched together by dark hedges and embroidered, here and there, with clumps of trees deliberately planted to give shelter and shade.

Before enclosure, yeoman farmers had lived in the centre of the village, walking out to the various locations of their strips to work. With their holdings all in one place however, it made sense to live on the spot, so numerous outlying farmhouses came to be built, to the great advantage of the landscape, for a farmhouse of Georgian design snuggled into a fold of the hills amid its cluster of barns, a light column of smoke ascending, gave to the scene an air of 'cheerful inhabitancy'.[7] Moreover, as the owners of these farmsteads grew in prosperity and gentility, so the custom of providing board and lodging for the labourers was discontinued, requiring new cottages to be built to accommodate them. Often these dwellings were mere hovels, but even when cramped and insanitary within, they could present a charming appearance to the casual passer-by; and that more and more were model cottages, provided by a benevolent landlord, the great increase in pattern-books for cottages around the turn of the century attests.

At the time of the enclosure of a parish or group of parishes and the re-drawing of the local map, the opportunity was taken to lay out a proper network of roads or lanes connecting village to village, and village to neighbouring town. This had a profound effect not only on the tidiness of the landscape but on the mental outlook of its inhabitants. Formerly, 'in the passages through lands under the open-field culture, not only the roads are bad, but the difficulty of discerning public roads from mere drift-ways, or from passages to lands of different proprietors is so great, that without a guide, some of them cannot be travelled by a stranger with safety'[8], it was reported to the Agricultural Board, who conducted a series of surveys into every county. These old tracks had sufficed when hardly anybody looked beyond the next parish, but the new road system opened up not only distant markets for produce, but wider mental horizons. Observers began to note the correlation between the degree of activity on the roads of any area and the general alertness of the population. 'Good roads are an infallible sign of prosperity' wrote one traveller in 1808, going on to extol 'the animation, vigour, life, and energy of luxury, consumption and industry, which flow with a full tide through this kingdom, wherever there is a free communication between the capital and the provinces'.[9]

With the planting of trees and hedgerows, the building of farms and cottages, the reclamation of waste land and the improvement of the roads it could take ten or fifteen years for the new landscape to mature.

The social repercussions of enclosure were less happy than the visual and economic ones – though taking even longer to manifest themselves, did not greatly impinge on the England Jane Austen knew. The loss of common grazing rights coupled with the cost of paying the legal fees of the transfer and hedging the new holdings forced many of the smaller owners to sell out, and the sturdy independence of the yeomen became too often the wretched dependence of the casually employed farm labourer. That was when he was not forced by want to emigrate altogether, to the new industrial towns or to the colonies. For a considerable period, however, the quantity of work generated by enclosure itself absorbed their labour, and a buoyant economy masked the deepening divisions between rich and poor. It was only after the peace of 1815 that grinding rural poverty became a large-scale problem, and later still that mass urban misery reached the consciousness of a perplexed nation. By that time, the old interdependence and self-sufficiency of country communities, perhaps under the type of enlightened, involved and benevolent landlord of whom, in George Knightley, Jane Austen gave such an admirable example, had been irretrievably lost.

If enclosure represented the Georgian triumph over the haphazard methods of their forebears, then the mania for building and gardening, by which whole country estates were transformed, proclaimed even more impressively the good sense, educated taste and great wealth of their owners – and of the nation to which they proudly belonged.

Beginning with a few aristocrats, the passion for 'improving' percolated down the social scale, so that first the great estates, then the medium, then the relatively humble, were made to fit the Georgian image of themselves. Those with extensive grounds and incomes to match worked on a large scale, spending vast sums of money and decades of labour shifting hills, damming streams and excavating lakes to create the perfect setting for

Chatsworth, Derbyshire (1802) One of the most magnificent of English country houses, with grounds improved by 'Capability' Brown, Chatsworth was included in the northern tour by the Gardiners and Elizabeth Bennet

their noble new mansions. People of more modest means had to be 'satisfied with rather less beauty and ornament', as Edmund Bertram put it, but there was no dispute as to what constituted beauty. In architecture it was founded on the classical orders; in landscaping, on the seeming artlessness of nature. The two sat well together, and suited the contours and the climate of England. Nothing jarred, in a land where green and tranquil parks provided the foil for perfectly proportioned buildings.

Rich and less rich alike, the landowners took a dynastic view of their improvements. Troubled by no doubts about the continuance of their way of life, they planted and planned not just for their own pleasure, but for the benefit of generations unborn. The family was more important than the individual; each inheritor held his land on trust, and was bound by duty to leave it in better shape, economically and aesthetically, than he had found it. Thus woods were preserved and replenished not only to provide cover for game and so contribute to the enjoyment of leisure, but to assure the estate of a future income from timber (and the nation a supply of its vital 'wooden walls'). The lovely deciduous woodland of southern England, the coppices of beech and oak thinly planted to admit the light and encourage the undergrowth of useful hazel, are Georgian bequests.

Within the agreed standards of beauty and seemliness, there was sufficient scope for allowing 'the genius of the place' to hold sway and sufficient subtle change as one generation reviewed the achievements of the last, to preclude monotony. Some people would be swept along with the latest trend, others, like Jane Austen herself, were more resistant to change and continued to perceive a certain charm in what was slightly old-fashioned.

The new style of gardening had its origins, some fifty or sixty years before Jane Austen's birth, in the discovery of the Italian landscape paintings of Claude Lorrain, Gaspar Poussin and Salvator Rosa by young English noblemen when they began to make the Grand Tour of Europe following the Treaty of Utrecht in 1713. The desire was awakened to create landscapes equally beautiful of their own grounds in England. There was also a political aspect of the question, the idea that as England had escaped the tyranny of the French political system, so she should throw off the rigidity and prescription of the existing Versailles-type layout and strike out something new for herself.

The movement began among aristocrats, landowners, poets and essayists, some of whom created their own revolutionary gardens as well as writing about the new theories. But the professional who brought the English landscape garden to its first peak of perfection was Lancelot 'Capability' Brown. His vision was exceptionally pure. He banished not only regularity but ornament of every kind, even the classical statues and Grecian temples with which the early improvers loved to adorn their grounds and display their erudition.

He it was who set the great English houses in their expanses of smooth undulating lawns, broken in the middle distance by carefully sited clumps of trees, and encircled, for privacy, by an irregular belt of woodland. He set paths and streams meandering and from the latter created the shining lakes in which the houses gazed in tranquillity and complacency at themselves. He, more than any other man, made the England Jane Austen knew and accepted as both beautiful and right.

Pemberley is her most perfect Brownian creation. 'It was a large, handsome, stone building, standing well on rising ground, and backed by a ridge of high, woody hills; and in front, a stream of some natural importance was swelled into greater, but without any artificial appearance. Its banks were neither formal, nor falsely adorned.' There is a bridge – a typical Brown touch – and between the water and the house, simply lawn.

Brown was active from 1740 until his death in 1783. 'I have not yet finished England', he had said, half-humorously, when offered a thousand pounds to look at the 'capabilities' of Ireland. Fortunately for

England, a second genius was on hand to continue the transformation. Humphry Repton began to practise the art of landscape gardening in 1788, and was thus the most famous 'improver' of Jane's lifetime (he died the year after her).

Ideas had moved inexorably on, and Repton knew what his age required. Though he himself had a profound professional respect for Brown's works, there were those who had begun to find them insipid and to criticize his 'never-ending sheets of vapid lawn'.[10] Repton, while remaining fluid and natural, brought greater variety and intricacy to the garden scene, both as a response to the demand for picturesqueness, and from his conviction that the house should be related more intimately to the garden, and that utility as well as beauty ought to be considered.

Horace Walpole, in his *History of Modern Taste in Gardening* (1771), had been among the first to sound the warning: 'The total banishment of all particular neatness immediately about a house, which is frequently left gazing by itself in the middle of a park, is a defect. Sheltered and even close walks in so very uncertain a climate as ours, are comforts ill-exchanged for the few picturesque days that we enjoy: and whenever a family can purloin a warm or even something of an old-fashioned garden from the landscape designed for them by the undertaker of fashion, without interfering with the picture, they will find satisfactions on those days that do not invite strangers to come and see their improvements.'

Repton's answer was to introduce or re-introduce the balustraded terrace, the *parterre*, the conservatory or the trellis-covered walk – any of which afforded not only a visual link between house and lawn but somewhere relatively dry underfoot. That both considerations weighed with him is certain. Aesthetically, he thought it 'proper to provide a nice gradation from the wilder scenery of the park to the more finished and dressed appearance of the gardens'.[11] He also believed in consulting 'the comfort and convenience' of the proprietor of the place.

His practical approach was very much in accord with Jane Austen's own. 'Nothing can be so ill-calculated for the purposes of habitation as a house on the summit of a hill', he wrote, while Donwell Abbey, and Mr Parker's former residence at Sanditon, are just two of the homes *she* praises for their snugness, obtained though that quality is at the expense of noble views.

Colour had been banished from the great parks by 'Capability' Brown, but in the last quarter of the eighteenth century interest in flowers revived, stimulated by the exotic new varieties brought back by voyagers from all parts of the globe. By 1789 there were over five thousand species under cultivation at Kew. The flower garden newly created for Fanny Dashwood when she becomes mistress of Norland, Lady Bertram's flower garden at Mansfield and Elizabeth Elliot's 'own sweet flower garden' at Kellynch are three examples from the novels of Jane Austen of this new source of genteel female pleasure, which Repton did much to promote. (Of course, cottagers and middling people, like the Austens themselves, had gone on cultivating flowers, amidst their vegetables, fruit and herbs, all through the century – it is the great parks with pretensions to fashion which we are considering here.)

In this, as in so much else, the greatest novelist and the greatest landscape gardener of their generation are in sympathy – notwithstanding her unenthusiastic reference to him in *Mansfield Park*, which will be examined in a later chapter. Take Repton's description of his transform-ation of Cobham, for Lord Darnley, for example:

'The house is no longer a huge pile standing naked on a vast grazing ground. Its walls are enriched with roses and jasmines; its apartments are perfumed with odours from flowers surrounding it on every side; and the animals which enliven the landscape are not admitted as an annoyance. All around is neatness, elegance, and comfort; while the views of the park are improved by the rich foreground, over which they are seen from the terraces in the garden, or the elevated situation of the apartments.'

Neatness, elegance, comfort – these are the qualities which Jane Austen also extolled.

It is a curious quirk of the English spirit, that when society achieved the ability to render its world neat and comfortable, a fascination for the dark, the wild and the terrifying should begin to take hold of its collective imagination. Thus began the fashion for all things Gothic, gathering momentum from about the middle of the eighteenth century, and mani-festing itself both in literature – the 'horrid' novels of nightmare happen-ings which Jane Austen delighted to burlesque – and in architecture, where it resulted in a rich crop of mock ruins amid the gardens of England.

A nation that can afford to build ruins has both money and creative energy to spare. From their elegant and comfortable mansions the Georgians experienced a delicious thrill looking at their fake castles and abbeys and dwelling on the melancholy thoughts they inspired. As Lord Kames, in his *Elements of Criticism* published in 1762, debated, 'whether should a ruin be in the Gothic or Grecian form? In the former, I think, because it exhibits the triumph of time over strength; a melancholy but not unpleasing thought; a Grecian ruin suggests rather the triumph of barbarity over taste, a gloomy and discouraging thought.'

Ten years later William Gilpin laid it down that 'it is not every man who can build a house that can execute a ruin. To give the stone its mouldering appearance – to make the widening chink run naturally through all the joints – to mutilate the ornaments – to peel the facing from the internal structure – to show how correspondent parts have once united, though now the chasm runs wide between them – and to scatter heaps of ruin around with negligence and ease, are great efforts of art; much too delicate for the hand of a common workman; and what we very rarely see performed. Besides, after all that art can bestow, you must put your ruin at last into the hands of nature to adorn and perfect it. If the mosses and lichens grow unkindly on your walls – if the streaming weather stains have produced no variety of tints – if the ivy refuses to mantle over your buttress, or to creep among the ornaments of your Gothic window – if the ash cannot be brought to hang from the cleft, or long, spiry grass to wave over the shattered battlement – your ruin will be still incomplete – you may as well write over the gate, "Built in the year 1772".'[12]

They were most to be envied, of course, who happened to have genuine medieval remains on their property, remains which could either be left as adornment to the landscape, or incorporated into the fabric of the house itself. Hence Catherine Morland's incomprehension at the Tilneys' seeming 'so little elated by the possession of such a home' as Northanger Abbey. Gilpin, whose standards were high, as we have seen, felt that a man should not attempt to build a ruin unless he had £30,000 to spend.[13] Blaise Castle, however, cost only a tenth of that sum to build in 1766[14] – which was still ten times the cost of building a model cottage for a labourer.[15]

The Gothic taste spread from ruins to the houses themselves. Decorative rather than structural, it was at first applied as detail – the pointed windows, the castellated parapet – to perfectly symmetrical façades. From using Gothic to thrill and terrify and induce melancholy contemplation, the Georgians turned to using it as a delightful variation of style after decades of fastidious Palladianism. By the turn of the century, architects such as Nash were even venturing upon asymmetrical designs. In Terence Davis's felicitous phrase, this was 'the pretty, provocative, evocative toy version' of its medieval and high-Victorian counterparts.[16] Perhaps because it was acknowledged to be playful, it was used more often by the great landowners for their estate cottages and lodges than for their own homes – and it was nowhere seen to more advantage than by the sea.

No visual detail was too small to escape the attention of the arbiters of taste. Edmund Bartell, in his *Hints for Picturesque Improvements in Ornamental Cottages* of 1804 advised, 'suffer the tendrils of ivy to mantle luxuriantly over the windows . . . they may sometimes be allowed to aspire even to the chimney, where their delicate tendrils flaunting in the breeze are seen to advantage; but if carried further than this the very profusion destroys the effect, and produces a heaviness that is disagreeable'.

Some landlords attempted to rebuild whole villages in the picturesque style, sweeping away everything they found offensive to the eye and replacing it with model cottages. If the newly married Rushworths had been content to stay at Sotherton, and carry out their improvements,

Luscombe Castle (1815) One of the earliest examples of an irregular Gothic house, Luscombe Castle was built in 1800–1801 by John Nash for the banker Charles Hoare at the seaside resort of Dawlish, which Jane Austen visited in the summer of 1802

perhaps their next step would have been to rebuild the village at their gates, for Maria found the existing cottages 'a disgrace'. An early and famous example of wholesale rebuilding was Nuneham Courtney in Oxfordshire, built by Lord Harcourt. Later attempts, such as Blaise Hamlet in Gloucestershire, designed by John Nash, were to be much more successful, consciously irregular and picturesque; but having seen only the tidy rows of Nuneham, Gilpin wrote: 'Indeed I question whether it were possible for a single hand to build a picturesque village. Nothing contributes more to it, than the various styles in building, which result from the different ideas of different people. When all these little habitations happen to unite harmoniously; and to be connected with the proper appendages of a village – a winding road – a number of spreading trees – a rivulet with a bridge – and a spire, to bring the whole to an apex – the village is complete.'[17]

Such was the charm of most of the villages Jane knew. The small provincial towns, too, had grown up in piecemeal fashion, acquiring their eighteenth-century façades in the normal course of expansion, infill and refurbishment. The result was the characteristic English street, in which houses of all shapes and sizes grew comfortably attached to one another, unified by the use of local building materials.

A reasonably sized village might contain a variety of rural craftsmen – blacksmith, miller, carpenter – and perhaps a general shop selling such commodities as the cottagers could not produce for themselves: tobacco, tea, sugar. A small town, on the other hand, though it might have only a couple of thousand inhabitants, and consist of only a few streets surrounded by green fields, was very different in function and flavour from even the largest villages. Trade was its *raison d'être*. Its working people were engaged in trades or occupations not directly connected with the land, and were dependent for their food on shops and markets, though vegetables were grown in town gardens. Towns had their inns and their schools, their merchants and their small manufacturers, their professional men such as doctors and lawyers, and perhaps a sprinkling of retired gentlefolk who wanted to live near the amenities it could offer. Working people of all levels of prosperity lived above and behind their business premises, and there was as yet little segregation of the classes, no evacuation of the towns once the working day was over.

Towns could afford a spirit of independence denied to the villages, for they neither enjoyed the protection nor suffered the domination of the local magnate. An interesting comparison is afforded in *Pride and Prejudice* between Darcy's relationship to Lambton: 'they had nothing to accuse him of but pride; pride he probably had, and if not, it would certainly be imputed by the inhabitants of a small market town, where the family did not visit. It was acknowledged, however, that he was a liberal man, and did much good among the poor,' and Lady Catherine's to Hunsford: 'Whenever any of the cottagers were disposed to be quarrelsome, discontented or too poor, she sallied forth into the village to settle their differences, silence their complaints, and scold them into harmony and plenty'.

Royal Crescent, Bath (1804) Unsurpassed as urban architecture, the Royal Crescent was completed in the year of Jane Austen's birth. It was one of the customs of Bath to walk here on a Sunday; the characters in *Northanger Abbey*, and Jane Austen herself, did so

Each town at that period possessed its own distinctive character; and of course there were all sorts of towns, cathedral towns, market towns, coaching towns, ports. Yet another category was added in the eighteenth century, with the emergence of a wholly new type of town: the fashionable resort of leisure.

Bath was the first and most splendid example. Its planned, mathematically precise streets of uniform houses designed to look not so much like a row of individual dwellings as the single, imposing front of a great mansion were an innovation. Virtually all medieval Bath was swept scornfully away, and a golden ashlar classical city erected in its place – truly a manifestation in stone of all the eighteenth century stood for. The circus and the crescent were invented to delight the eye and demonstrate the superiority of the Age of Reason. The streets were paved and swept, sedan chairs provided to carry people of quality up and down the hills, assembly rooms built for socializing at night, a routine laid down for following by day. Everything animate and inanimate, was ordered, rational, civilized, correct. Bath's influence on the manners of the early Georgian age was immense, smoothing away the boorishness of the aristocracy and the provincialism of the country gentry, regularizing conduct, cultivating the social graces, spreading the new ideas; while its influence on the townscapes of England was of almost equal importance.

But though Bath soon had its imitators – some of which were preferred by Jane Austen – it was not eclipsed until the Romantic movement at the turn of the century helped to foster a new interest in the English coastline, hitherto disregarded. By then the lighter, more graceful Regency style of architecture had evolved, perfectly suited, with its bow windows, wrought-iron balconies or Gothic ornament, to the summery, rather frivolous atmosphere of the little fishing villages puffed up suddenly into resorts of fashion.

The Georgians invented the holiday away from home. Never before had quantities of people travelled for travel's sake, to pursue pleasure and to gratify curiosity. As a consequence many improvements came to be made, and the period in which Jane Austen lived was the golden age of coaching. By raising money through the introduction of turnpikes, roads which had been rutted tracks, dusty in summer, muddy or frozen hard in winter, were kept in a reasonable state of repair. Carriages were better sprung and padded, horses bred especially for roadwork, coaching inns brought up to the standards of comfort and cleanliness their ever more fastidious patrons demanded. New atlases were published in a lighter format, suitable for use on a journey rather than in a library.

There were two methods of travel: in the public stagecoach, which one might board or alight from at any point, or in a private vehicle, one's own or hired for the journey, stopping every few miles to change horses at inns along the route. This was 'going post', and was of course much more genteel: 'I assure you we came post,' boasts Lucy Steele, of their journey from Exeter to London. Such a journey took three days, and despite all the improvements human ingenuity could devise, travellers must often have felt cramped, confined, jolted, too hot or too cold, and possibly frightened, as carriage accidents could and did occur.

But the appetite for travel was insatiable. Nobody had done more to stimulate it than William Gilpin, schoolmaster, clergyman and amateur artist, who during Jane's childhood inaugurated a new kind of travel literature, the illustrated picturesque tour. He journeyed through various regions of Britain assessing the scenery according to his theories of what was and was not picturesque and he opened many people's eyes to natural beauty. His tours were made in the 1770s, circulated in manuscript and published some fifteen or twenty years later. By the 1790s, when Jane was writing her first three novels, the word 'picturesque' was on everybody's lips, and writers were quarrelling in print as to its definition. Gilpin himself said merely 'we precisely mean by it that kind of beauty that would look well in a picture'.

Though first his school, and then his vicarage, kept Gilpin in the south of England all his working life, he was a north country man, and to him no scenery excelled that of the Lake District. What distinguished the picturesque from the merely beautiful was in his opinion roughness, wildness, ruggedness and intricacy. In his *Western Tour* he found all of the interior of Devon 'an uninteresting scene'. Even more amusing was his wholesale rejection of the Isle of Wight 'which in every part has been disfigured by the spade, the coulter and the harrow . . . of all species of cultivation, cornlands are the most unpicturesque. The regularity of cornfields disgusts; and the colour of corn, especially near harvest, is out of tune with everything else.' Gilpin deplored, for his purposes, just those scenes of agricultural prosperity which Jane Austen was to praise in *Emma*, and through Edward Ferrars to defend in *Sense and Sensibility*.

Why, then, was Jane Austen 'early enamoured of Gilpin on the Picturesque'[18] and did she name him, in one of her juvenile scraps, as one of 'the first of men'? His didactic and sometimes absurd views provided her with a great deal of fun, but it was more than that. He awakened her to the great variety of natural beauty contained within the British Isles, and introduced her to parts of her country which she visited only later, or not at all. He helped her to appreciate the delights of English scenery, and he confirmed her patriotic view that it was the loveliest in the world. His love of England, indeed, was enough to win her favour. She paid him the supreme compliment of responding to him in all of her early novels.

Gilpin prefaced his *Lakes Tour*, published in 1786, with a general survey of the topography of England, and an investigation into the special qualities of the English landscape. As a passage which Jane Austen enjoyed and which influenced her youthful feelings, and as a contemporary view of the country into which she was born, Gilpin's words round off the present chapter:

> From whatever cause it proceeds, certain, I believe, it is, that this country exceeds most countries in the *variety* of its picturesque beauties. I should not wish to speak merely as an Englishman: the suffrages of many travellers, and foreigners, of taste, I doubt not, might be adduced.
>
> In some or other of the particular species of landscape, it may probably be excelled. Switzerland may perhaps exceed it in the beauty of its wooded valleys; Germany, in its river views; and Italy, in its lake scenes. But if it is to yield to some of these countries in *particular* beauties I should suppose that on the *whole* it transcends them all. It exhibits perhaps more variety of hill, and dale, and level ground, than is anywhere to be seen in so small a compass. Its rivers assume every character, diffusive, winding and rapid. Its estuaries and coast views are varied, of course, from the form and rockiness of its shores. Its mountains and lakes, though they cannot perhaps rival, as I have just

Derwentwater (1802) 'A Lake in Cumberland' was one of the pictures in Fanny Price's East Room. Many of Jane Austen's contemporaries travelled to view the rugged scenery of the English Lakes after reading William Gilpin

observed, some of the choice lakes of Italy . . . are yet in variety, I presume, equal to the lake scenery of any country.

But besides the variety of its beauties, in some or other of which it may be rivalled, it possesses some beauties which are peculiar to itself.

One of these peculiar features arises from the intermixture of wood and cultivation, which is found oftener in the English landscape than in the landscape of other countries. In France, in Italy, in Spain and in most other places, cultivation and wood have their separate limits. Trees grow in detached woods; and cultivation occupies vast, un-bounded common fields. But in England, the custom of dividing property by hedges, and of planting hedgerows, so universally prevails, that almost wherever you have cultivation, there also you have wood.

Now although this regular intermixture produces deformity on the nearer grounds, yet, at a distance, it is a source of great beauty. On the spot, no doubt, and even in the first distances, the marks of the spade, and the plough; the hedge and the ditch; together with all the formalities of hedgerow trees, and square divisions of property, are disgusting in a high degree. But when all these regular forms are softened by distance – when hedgerow trees begin to unite, and lengthen into streaks along the horizon – when farmhouses and ordinary buildings lose all their vulgarity of shape, and are scattered about, in formless spots, through the several parts of a distance – it is inconceivable what richness, and beauty, this mass of deformity, when melted together, adds to landscape. One vast tract of wild uncultivated country, unless either varied by large parts, or under some peculiar circumstances of light, cannot produce the effect. Nor is it produced by unbounded tracts of cultivation; which, without the intermixture of wood, cannot give richness to distance. Thus English landscape affords a species of *rich distance*, which is rarely to be found in any other country. You have likewise from this intermixture of wood and cultivation, the advantage of being sure to find a tree or two, on the foreground, to adorn any beautiful view you may meet with in the distance.

Another peculiar feature in the landscape of this country arises from the great quantity of English oak with which it abounds. The oak of no country has equal beauty: not does any tree answer all the purposes of scenery so well. The oak is the noblest ornament of a foreground: spreading, from side to side, its tortuous branches, and foliage, rich with some autumnal tint. In a distance also it appears with equal advantage, forming itself into beautiful clumps, varied more in shape, and perhaps more in colour, than the clumps of any other tree. The pine of Italy has its beauty, hanging over the broken pediment of some ruined temple. The chestnut of Calabria is consecrated by adorning the foregrounds of Salvator. The elm, the ash, and the beech, have all their respective beauties: but no tree in the forest is adapted to all the purposes of landscape, like the English oak.

Among the peculiar features of English landscape, may be added the embellished garden, and park scene. In other countries, the environs of great houses are yet under the direction of formality. The wonder-working hand of art, with its regular cascades, spouting fountains, flights of terraces, and other achievements, have still possession of the gardens of kings, and princes. In England alone the model of nature is adopted.

This is a mode of scenery entirely of the sylvan kind. As we seek among the wild works of nature for the sublime, we seek here for the beautiful: and where there is a variety of lawn, wood and water, and these naturally combined, and not too much decorated with buildings, nor disgraced by fantastic ornaments, we find a species of landscape, which no country, but England, can display in such perfection: not only because this just species of taste prevails nowhere else, but also because nowhere else are found such proper materials. The want of English oak, as we have just observed, can never be made up, in this kind of landscape especially. Nor do we anywhere find so close and rich a verdure. An easy swell may, everywhere, be given to the ground: but it cannot everywhere be covered with a velvet turf, which constitutes the beauty of an embellished lawn.

The moisture, and vapoury heaviness of our atmosphere, which produces the rich verdure of our lawns, gives birth to another peculiar feature of the English landscape – that obscurity, which is often thrown over distance. In warmer climates especially, the air is purer. Those mists and vapours which steam from the ground at night, are dispersed with the morning sun. Under Italian skies very remote objects are seen with great distinctness. And this mode of vision, no doubt, has its beauty; as have all the works, and all the operations of nature – but at best, this is only one mode of vision. Our grosser atmosphere (which likewise hath its seasons of purity) exhibits various modes, some of which are in themselves more beautiful, than the most distinct vision.

Haziness just adds that light, grey tint – that thin, dubous veil, which is often beautifully spread over the landscape. It hides nothing. It only sweetens the hues of nature – it gives a consequence to every common object, by giving it a more indistinct form – it corrects the glares of colours – it softens the harshness of lines; and above all, it throws over the face of landscape that harmonizing tint, which blends the whole into unity, and repose. *Mist* goes farther. It spreads still more obscurity over the face of nature. Even the *fog*, which is the highest degree of a gross atmosphere, is not without its beauty in landscape, especially in mountain scenes.

To these natural features, which are, in a great degree, peculiar to the landscape of England, we may lastly add another, of the artificial kind – the ruin of abbeys; which, being naturalized to the soil, might indeed, without much impropriety, be classed among its natural beauties.

Ruins are commonly divided into two kinds: castles and abbeys. Of the former few countries perhaps can produce so many, as this island; for which various causes may be assigned. The feudal system, which lasted long in England, and was carried high, produced a number of castles in every part. King Stephen's reign contributed greatly to multiply them. And in the northern counties, the continued wars with Scotland had the same effect. Many of these buildings, now fallen into decay, remain objects of great beauty.

In the ruins of castles, however, other countries may compare with ours. But in the remains of abbeys no country certainly can. Where popery prevails, the abbey is still entire and inhabited; and of course less adapted to landscape.

Abbeys formerly abounded so much in England, that a delicious valley could scarce be found, in which one of them was not stationed. The very sites of many of these ancient edifices are now obliterated by the plough, yet still so many elegant ruins of this kind are left, that they may be called, not only one of the peculiar features of the English landscape, but may be ranked among its most picturesque beauties.

2

Steventon:
A Young Lady in her own Village

Scenes must be beautiful, which, daily view'd,
Please daily, and whose novelty survives
Long knowledge and the scrutiny of years.
William Cowper, The Task, 1784

Involvement in a small rural community was always what suited Jane Austen best, both as a person and as a writer. 'You are collecting your people delightfully; three or four families in a country village is the very thing to work on', she wrote to an aspiring novelist niece – though her own practice was varied occasionally and to good effect by the introduction of scenes from London, Bath and so forth. She was humorously aware that 'if adventures will not befall a young lady in her own village, she must seek them abroad', but though her own journeys were increasingly profitable to her art, as I hope to show, return to the country village was essential to both her contentment and her creativity.

The place to which she was attached from her earliest years was Steventon, in north Hampshire. Her youthful impressions were formed in this quiet agricultural village, which was to be her home for the first twenty-five years – the greater part of her life. Here, scenery which was pleasant but unspectacular found its way to her heart – and, as a consequence, rendered her suspicious, for a long time, of the claims made on behalf of wilder and grander landscapes to excite emotions of sublimity. Fertile pastures, tidy fields of crops, sheltering trees and hedgerows, pretty cottage gardens in which familiar flowers mingled with well-tended produce – these were the scenes to which she was early accustomed, and which satisfied her as being equally 'sweet to the eye and to the mind'.

Born in the Rectory on 16 December 1775, she was the seventh of eight children of the Reverend George Austen, who, as a farmer as well as a clergyman, was doubly involved in the life of his parish. Writing the next day to announce Jane's birth to relations in Kent, he very typically reveals the practical interest in his glebe farm which, together with his scholarly appreciation of landscape theory, was to contribute so much to his daughter's love and understanding of nature:

'Last night the time came, and without a great deal of warning, everything was soon happily over. We have now another girl, a present plaything for her sister Cassy and a future companion. . . . Your sister thank God is pure well after it, and sends her love to you and my brother. . . . Let my brother know his friend Mr Evelyn is going to treat us with a ploughing match in this neighbourhood on next Tuesday, if the present frost does not continue and prevent it, Kent against Hants for a rump of beef; he sends his own ploughman from St Clair. Does my brother know a Mr Collis, he says he is very well acquainted with him, he visited me to buy some oats for Evelyn's hunters.'[1]

Jane's birthplace was an unpretentious but aesthetically satisfying building, with a pair of sash windows either side of a central front door, which was protected by a little trellised porch, five windows to correspond on the upper storey, and three dormers jutting from the roof. It had been rebuilt for the Austens' occupation in the 1760s and, without much money to lavish on it, was plain but homely. The back of the house, perhaps retained from the earlier building, was less Georgian in appearance, with two projecting wings, in one of which Mr Austen had his study. Here he taught not only his own sons – James and Henry until they went to university, Edward until he came to be adopted by rich relations in Kent, and Frank and Charles until they joined the naval academy at the tender age of twelve – but paying pupils, two or three at a time, who lived with the family. To these inhabitants must be added a fair quota of servants, and it is not surprising that the Rectory could accommodate further guests only in the Christmas or midsummer holidays when the pupils had gone home. The only two girls of the family, Cassandra and Jane, shared a bedroom, and continued to do so all their lives, even when the gradual departure of their brothers into the world made more space. They did however then appropriate another upstairs room for their own daytime use, where they kept their books and piano, where they sat to talk and sew, and where Jane's first three novels were written.

She grew up then in the midst of a large, affectionate family, notable for their sunny natures and their loyalty, their love of books and sense of fun, their sharp intelligence and lively interest in the world about them. By the end of the century Mr Austen's library contained some five hundred volumes, including, almost certainly, much of the contemporary poetry, major and minor, inspired by the English landscape, and perhaps the prose not only of Gilpin, but of the other writers who in the 1790s contributed to the discussion (amounting in some cases to argument) on the concept of the picturesque: Richard Payne Knight, Uvedale Price and Humphry Repton.

These were subjects which intrigued the whole family, but particularly the two classical scholars, James and Henry, whose interest was so durable that both, in middle age, were to follow Gilpin's tours in search of picturesque beauty. It is known that James, eleven years older than Jane, influenced her early reading, rather as Edmund Bertram did Fanny's. Like Edmund, James was solemn, conscientious and ardent, fell in love too easily, and became a clergyman. His literary ambition and deep feelings found outlet in the lifelong habit of writing poetry. Heartfelt but undistinguished, much of it celebrates the beauties of the English countryside.

James Austen was uncomfortably aware that Gilpin had seen nothing to praise in the scenery between Winchester and Basingstoke, where Steventon was located. In the very year of Jane's birth Gilpin travelled that road and wrote that it 'passes through a country, with little picturesque beauty on either hand. It becomes by degrees flat and unpleasant, and soon degenerates into common-field land, which, with its striped divisions, is of all kinds of country generally the most unpleasant'.[2] This is interesting because it tells us that enclosure had not yet transformed the face of the countryside in these parts; it also explains why Jane's mother found the scenery 'unattractive' when transplanted here on her marriage.[3] During Jane's childhood enclosure wrought its gentle magic on the landscape about Steventon – but still it was not picturesque. Nevertheless, James and Jane could not help loving the 'simple scenes' they knew so intimately. Jane's response to this paradox was to derive a great deal of fun from the absurdities of picturesque stipulation; James' was to write defensive poetry:

> True taste is not fastidious, nor rejects,
> Because they may not come within the rule
> Of composition pure and picturesque,
> Unnumbered simple scenes which fill the leaves
> Of Nature's sketch book[4]

The village of Steventon is not on any through-route but nestles unobtrusively within the elongated V-shape formed by two roads radiating from the town of Basingstoke – west to Andover and south-west to Winchester – and is connected to both by a network of narrow lanes, mere cart-tracks in the last quarter of the eighteenth century. They must often have been impossibly muddy, or baked or frozen into hard, jolting ruts. The Austens kept a carriage, but it could not always negotiate these lanes, and in any case the horses, like Mr Bennet's, were usually required about the farm. Jane and Cassandra were accustomed to and fond of walking, when necessary wearing pattens (wooden clogs with metal rings on the sole to prevent slipping) as protection against the mud. There is no reference to the girls ever riding on horseback, though their brothers all did so, and even hunted, on any mount they could appropriate for the chase.

An inhabitant of the Rectory from the next generation described Steventon as 'a small village of cottages, each well provided with a garden, scattered about prettily on either side of the road'.[5] At the southern end of the village street stood first the glebe farm buildings and then the Rectory itself; beyond that a very minor lane led to the grey Tudor manor house and the 700-year-old church, standing together aloof from the workaday village, sheltered by sycamores, elms, and a yew tree as old as the church itself. About the place where Jane Austen learnt to worship there was a sense of English rectitude, simplicity and peace truly immemorial. The violets at the foot of the church walls had grown there for centuries undisturbed.

From her home, then, Jane Austen could walk in one direction to find herself in scenes of activity and seasonal occupation, or in the other to refresh the spirit in an area of great tranquillity and repose.

The lane running north from Steventon for a mile meets the Andover road at Deane, where Mr Austen held a second living (the combined population of the two parishes was only 300) and where the twice daily London stage-coach halted. South of Steventon the network of tracks meets that stretch of the Winchester road known as 'Popham Lane' and it was here, at the Wheatsheaf Inn, that the Austens collected and paid for their letters. These then were their two primary points of contact with the outside world.

The lane to Deane was a particularly frequent walk of Jane and Cassandra's, for the unwanted parsonage house there was let by their father for several years to the widow of a clergyman, Mrs Lloyd, and her three daughters, Martha, Eliza and Mary, who became lifelong friends of the Austens. When James Austen married and became his father's curate he moved into Deane with his bride, and the Lloyds obligingly found another house to rent. Their doing so introduced Jane to another part of her native county, eighteen miles to the north-west, where Hampshire meets Berkshire and Wiltshire, for during the 1790s she was often invited to stay with the Lloyds at Ibthorpe House.

Here she found herself in surroundings, both natural and manmade, more consciously charming than anything she was used to at Steventon. The Lloyds' new home was the perfect early Georgian small house, of rosy chequered brickwork, with a hipped roof, dainty dentil frieze, perfectly proportioned sash-windows and a scrolled canopy over the central front door. Standing in its snug walled garden, Ibthorpe House is 'neatness, elegance and comfort' on a modest scale, just right for an establishment of ladies. As at Steventon Rectory, the back of the building was older, dating back to the Tudor period; if Jane ventured to the kitchen and 'offices' she would have seen low beamed ceilings and diamond-paned windows. And venture she probably did, since the Lloyds were not rich and kept few servants.

The flinty hamlet of Ibthorpe belongs to the parish of Hurstbourne Tarrant, where an ancient church, a stream, and a group of thatched, half-timbered cottages in flower-filled gardens combined to create one of the loveliest, most quintessentially English villages imaginable: 'a sight worth going many miles to see', was William Cobbett's verdict in the 1820s. Jane walked there often to church, and to pay social calls on the rector's family. But for such 'desperate walkers' as herself and her friend Martha Lloyd, the rolling chalk downs and richly timbered valley sides of this upland area of Hampshire, with its sweeping views, were even more tempting (and recall the type of country that tempted the Dashwoods to take air and exercise at Barton).

James Austen, too, found room in his heart for Ibthorpe. His first wife having died, he came courting Mary Lloyd, and married her on a crisp snowy January day in 1797, in the Norman church of Hurstbourne Tarrant. Fifteen years later, on their anniversary, he recalled the scene:

Cold was the morn and all around
Whitened with new fall'n snow the ground;
Yet still the sun, with cheering beam,
Played on the hill and vale and stream;
And almost gave to Winter's face
Spring's pleasing cheerfulness and grace. . . .[6]

Another north Hampshire house where Jane often stayed overnight with a family of sisters was Manydown Park, home of Alethea, Catherine and Elizabeth Bigg. This was a much grander place than Ibthorpe House, with a sweeping staircase of delicate ironwork ascending to a noble first-floor reception room lit by a large bay window. The grounds of Manydown were equally impressive, with some fine oak trees, a specimen cedar, and a fashionable ha-ha. Of this splendid place Jane Austen might have been mistress, for her friends' only brother proposed to her in 1802; but after some hesitation, she chose not to marry him.

Manydown Park was near Basingstoke, and Jane often used to sleep there after attending the Basingstoke assembly, held monthly through the winter, rather than hazard the unlit lanes to Steventon. The 'Assembly Room' at Basingstoke was only the upper storey of a coaching inn, such a

Manydown Park (1831) Jane Austen often stayed overnight here after attending the Basingstoke assembly. Had she accepted the proposal of Harris Bigg-Wither in 1802, she would have been mistress of this house

room as the Crown at Highbury afforded.[7] Jane sometimes danced in much more noble surroundings. The Hampshire aristocracy would occasionally hold a private ball to which the neighbouring gentry were condescendingly invited. Thus Jane had the opportunity to see in all their night-time glory the great country seats of the neighbourhood: Hurstbourne House, Hackwood Park and Kempshott Park.

Steventon Manor was part of the extensive possessions of Thomas Knight, who had bestowed the living on his kinsman, George Austen. As the local representative of the landowning family – the Knights themselves resided in Kent – Mr Austen was accepted on equal terms by the landed gentry of the area; Mrs Austen's aristocratic lineage also helped. So although they were only a clergyman's family, and not at all rich, the Austens paid morning visits to and dined at all the gentlemen's residences in the neighbourhood: Laverstoke, Freefolk Priors, Oakley Hall, Dummer House, Deane House, Ashe Park and Steventon Manor (which was let to tenants). And then there was Ashe House, really a rectory, on the main Andover road, to which Jane would often walk to visit the rector's wife, one of her dearest friends, Mrs Lefroy. Ashe House is an exquisitely pretty small Georgian confection, with a segmental fanlight over the door.

But though Jane's eyes were accustomed to the elegance and perfect proportions of graceful Georgian buildings small and large, it must not be forgotten that she was also familiar with the humbler tenements of the poor. Her letters often refer to charitable visits in the two parishes of which her father had charge. And she herself had spent the first year of her life in a labourer's cottage. Like all her siblings, she had been farmed out for her infancy to 'a good woman at Deane'.

One of the constant themes of discussion at Steventon Rectory was 'improvements'. Much had been done even before Jane's birth, but throughout her twenty-five years' residence there her parents were enthusiastically planting and landscaping their modest grounds.

They had begun by planting a screen of chestnuts and spruce fir to shut out the view of the farm buildings, and then they had cut an imposing carriage 'sweep' through the turf to the front door. Alongside the public lane leading to the church, but on their own property, they created a broad hedgerow of mixed timber and shrub, carpeted by wild flowers and wide enough to contain within it a winding footpath for the greater shelter and privacy of the family in their frequent walks to the church: indeed it was known by them as the 'Church Walk'. A similar hedgerow called the 'Elm Walk' skirted their meadows and enclosed the occasional rustic seat where weary strollers could rest. All this was growing to maturity with Jane herself.

But like so many of their generation, the Austens were incorrigible improvers, and right up to the moment when they suddenly decided to retire from Steventon, they were planting and altering on a grand scale. In October 1800 Jane wrote to Cassandra, then staying with their brother Edward in Kent, 'Our improvements have advanced very well; the bank along the Elm Walk is sloped down for the reception of thorns and lilacs; and it is settled that the other side of the path is to continue turfed and be planted with beech, ash and larch'. A month later she reported, 'Hacker has been here today, putting in the fruit trees – a new plan has been suggested concerning the plantation of the new enclosure on the right-hand side of the Elm Walk – the doubt is whether it would be better to make a little orchard of it, by planting apples, pears and cherries, or whether it should be larch, mountain-ash and acacia.'

The Rectory grounds, as planned by the Austens, bear a remarkable resemblance to Cleveland, in Jane's first completed novel, which 'had its open shrubbery, and closer wood walk, a road of smooth gravel winding round a plantation led to the front, the lawn was dotted over with timber, the house itself was under the guardianship of the fir, the mountain-ash and the acacia, and a thick screen of them altogether, interspersed with tall Lombardy poplars, shut out the offices'. The Austens' pretensions, however, ran to neither a greenhouse nor a Grecian temple.

In fact the garden at Steventon Rectory was a happy compromise between fashionable ideas and down-to-earth utility – typical of the balanced Austen approach to life. Part of the ground 'was occupied by one of those old-fashioned gardens in which vegetables and flowers are combined, flanked and protected on the east by a thatched mud wall'.[8] All the fruit, vegetables, and herbs consumed by the family were raised here. The Austens' strawberry beds were famous, and Mrs Austen was one of the first people in the neighbourhood to grow potatoes. (She had great difficulty in persuading the cottagers to cultivate this alien crop.)[9]

Her responsibilities also included the poultry-yard and the dairy. She supervised making all the butter and cheese, baking all the bread and brewing all the beer and wine required by a large household. With the exception of such commodities as tea, coffee, chocolate and sugar, the Austens were virtually self-sufficient in food. On his glebe lands Mr Austen grew oats, barley and wheat, and reared cattle, pigs and sheep, able not only to feed his family, but to sell the surplus. His loyal baliff, John Bond, always delighted with his master's success, perhaps suggested William Larkins and his relationship to Mr Knightley. As Jane once wrote of her father 'He and John Bond are now very happy together, for I have just heard the heavy step of the latter along the passage'.

Her letters of November and December 1798, written to Cassandra in

Kent, where their brother Edward had recently become the owner of Godmersham Park and a gentleman farmer, are full of farming talk:

'You must tell Edward that my father gives 25 shillings a piece to Seward for his last lot of sheep, and, in return for this news, my father wishes to receive some of Edward's pigs.' 'We are to kill a pig soon. . . . I am likewise to tell you that one of the Leicestershire sheep, sold to the butcher last week, weighed 27 lb and ¼ per quarter.' 'Mr Lyford gratified us very much yesterday by his praises of my father's mutton, which they all think the finest that was ever ate.' 'My father is glad to hear so good an account of Edward's pigs, and desires he may be told, as encouragement to his taste for them, that Lord Bolton is particularly curious in *his* pigs, has had pigstyes of a most elegant construction built for them, and visits them every morning as soon as he rises.' 'My mother wants to know whether Edward has ever made the hen-house which they planned together.'

These then were among the daily concerns of the family in which Jane grew up. As Cassandra was to say many years later, 'there is so much amusement and so many comforts attending a farm in the country that those who have once felt the advantages cannot easily forget them'.[10] The easy transition from the intellectual to the practical, which seemed so natural in that family and in those circumstances, shaped Jane's outlook and made her into a writer whose created worlds, however sparing in detail, are securely anchored in the turn of the seasons and in the sense of the countryside as a source of nourishment both physical and spiritual.

3

Oxfordshire and Berkshire:
Early Influences

Lorn is the landscape since the blissful prime,
When on the daisy-darting sod I played,
Caught the quick radiance quiv'ring through the lime,
Breathed the fresh odours of its evening shade,
And, where my school-companions crossed the glade,
Lo! other sweet memorials. . . .

Richard Polwhele,
The Influence of Local Attachment, 1798

Jane's earliest visits from home were made in these two counties, in each of which she went briefly to school, and in which many of her family connections had their homes. Later, in both her life and her novels, these two very central counties of England figured chiefly as places to be passed through in journeys from one part of the country to another, journeys which were broken in towns such as Oxford, Banbury, Newbury or Reading.

The city of Oxford played an important part in the lives of several of the Austen family, and there is a sense in which it brought Jane into existence, for it was there, almost certainly, that her parents met in the late 1750s or early 1760s.

George Austen had been connected with the university since 1747, when, at the age of sixteen, he was awarded the Tonbridge Fellowship at St John's.[1] In 1753 he was ordained deacon there, having obtained his Master's degree. For the next five years he resided at St John's only during the summer holidays, spending the chief part of the year teaching at his old school, Tonbridge in Kent. But at the beginning of 1758 he returned to live full time at Oxford, becoming first assistant chaplain and then proctor of his college – 'the handsome proctor', as he was called. Although he accepted the living of Steventon in November 1761 he continued to live at Oxford, only moving to Hampshire on his marriage in April 1764. The removal ended a seventeen-year connection with St John's, a connection which was to be renewed in the next generation.

As for Jane's mother, she spent the first twenty years of her life in Oxfordshire, and her family's links with the university were extensive. Her father, Thomas Leigh, was a Fellow of All Souls and held the college living of Harpsden, near Henley-on-Thames, where Cassandra was born in 1739. Even when, in the early 1760s, Thomas Leigh retired to Bath with his wife and two daughters, there were still two uncles for Cassandra to visit in Oxford: her mother's brother, William Walker, Principal of New Inn Hall, and her father's brother, Theophilus Leigh, Master of Balliol. It was probably in the home of Theophilus (whose two daughters were close in age to Cassandra) that Jane's parents did their courting, though the marriage itself took place in Bath.

That Jane knew Harpsden, the scene of her mother's childhood, is highly probable, for her cousin Edward Cooper became curate there in 1793. He was the only son of Cassandra's elder sister Jane, and had just married Caroline Lybbe Powys, whose mother recorded in her diary for May of that year, 'Edward and Caroline went to Harpsden to live, a very pretty place near Henley'.[2] Mrs Austen had grown up amid such prettiness and on first seeing Steventon had found it tame in comparison – but there is no hint that her daughter, equally attached to *her* native place, shared that view. Writing in the summer of 1799 of a proposed visit to Harpsden, she is wholly without enthusiasm; certainly her lifelong antipathy to her pompous cousin must have had a lot to do with her attitude, but had she never been there before she would surely have expressed curiosity, at the least. Certainly her brother Henry stayed with the Coopers in January 1796, when Jane wrote to her sister Cassandra

Henley-on-Thames (1813) At nearby Harpsden Jane Austen's mother grew up and later Jane herself may have visited her cousin Edward Cooper at the rectory there

(spelling the name the way it was then pronounced), 'Henry goes to Harden today in his way to his Master's degree'.

It was through the Coopers that Jane came to be sent to school at Oxford, when she was only seven. Jane Cooper, Edward's sister, was going to a school recently established by her paternal aunt, Mrs Ann Cawley, widow of a former Principal of Brasenose. The Austens decided to send their daughters too. After the three cousins had been there a few months, however, Mrs Cawley moved the school to Southampton, and not long after that, an outbreak of 'putrid fever' brought them home. Jane's residence in Oxford was therefore very brief, but has a certain importance from being her first experience of life away from home. The bustle of a university city must have made a great contrast to the rural quiet of Steventon on her alert and impressionable mind.

Not only was Cassandra with her, but their eldest brother James was at that time a resident of Oxford, on hand to help counteract any unbearable homesickness. James was even younger than his father when he matriculated – just fourteen – and he was invited to dine with his formidable great-uncle, Theophilus Leigh, still Master of Balliol after fifty years. James himself remained at Oxford for eleven years, from 1779 to 1790. In 1788 he was joined there by his brother Henry, and while their time overlapped, they collaborated to found, edit and largely write a weekly paper called *The Loiterer*. Both James and Henry were able to claim one of the six founder's kin fellowships to their father's old college, St John's, by proving their descent, through their mother and *her* mother, from the sister of the founder of the college, Sir Thomas White.

We get a delightful glimpse of the brothers during their time at Oxford together from a letter written by their cousin Eliza, Comtesse de Feuillide (who, after being widowed in the aftermath of the French Revolution, was many years later to become Henry's wife); and it is pleasant to think of the seven-year-old Jane, on her arrival in Oxford, being met by her grown up brother James and being taken on a similar tour. Eliza wrote:

I am but just returned from an excursion into Berkshire, during which we made some little stay in Oxford. My cousin James met us there, and as well as his brother was so good as to take the trouble of showing us the lions. We visited several of the colleges, the museum etc., and were very elegantly entertained by our gallant relations at St John's, where I was mightily taken with the garden and longed to be a fellow that I might walk in it every day, besides I was delighted with the black gown and thought the square cap mighty becoming. I do not think you would know Henry with his hair powdered and dressed in a very *tonish* style, besides he is at present taller than his father. . . .[3]

When James left Oxford it was to become a thorough-going Hampshire man, confining his life's work to a cluster of neighbouring parishes; but Henry preserved connections with Oxfordshire well into middle age, and Jane often mentioned his visiting there, on business as well as pleasure. Having decided against the Church as a career, and in favour of soldiering, it was the militia of the county of Oxfordshire which he joined, later being promoted to captain and adjutant. To become an officer in the militia it was necessary to furnish proof of land-holdings in the county concerned, and impoverished young men like Henry had to find a friend to vouch for them. Presumably Henry's friends were from Oxfordshire rather than Hampshire. 'I suppose you have heard from Henry himself that his affairs are happily settled', wrote Jane to Cassandra in November 1798. 'We do not know who furnishes the qualification. Mr Mowell would have readily given it, had not all his Oxfordshire property been engaged for a similar purpose to the Colonel. Amusing enough!'

After enjoying the military life for some years and marrying Eliza, Henry left the army to set up as a banker in London, where the couple enjoyed a highly sociable, civilized and prosperous way of life. Keeping up with his influential friends in Oxfordshire led to Henry's being appointed Deputy Receiver of Taxes in that county, a position which entailed frequent visits. In April 1811, he was staying at The Blue Boar, in Cornmarket, Oxford and in February 1813 he broke his journey in the Oxfordshire town of Wheatfield. Shortly after this he was promoted to Receiver-General, 'a promotion which he thoroughly enjoys', wrote Jane. Henry suffered a severe illness during the last two months of 1815, but he had no sooner recovered than 'he thinks of going to Oxford for a few days', reported Jane, who was in London to nurse him. And when, the following March, through no fault of his own his firm went bankrupt, Henry's thoughts immediately turned to his old university. Within a fortnight he had decided to become a clergyman: 'Now the old learning was to be looked up, and he went to Oxford, to see about taking the necessary degree.'[4]

Though the university had done so well by her father and brothers – and they by it – Jane seems to have had no very good opinion of the education offered there. Edmund Bertram's recollection, 'At Oxford I have been a good deal used to have a man lean on me for the length of a street', brings an echo of the picture painted by the boor John Thorpe:

Oxford! There is no drinking at Oxford now, I assure you. Nobody drinks there. You would hardly meet with a man who goes beyond his four pints at the utmost. Now, for instance, it was reckoned a remarkable thing at the last party in my rooms, that upon an average we cleared about five pints a head. It was looked upon as something out of the

Oxford (1813) Jane Austen's family had many links with the University, and she herself went briefly to school in the city

common way. *Mine* is famous good stuff to be sure. You would not often meet with anything like it in Oxford – and that may account for it. But this will just give you a notion of the general rate of drinking there.

And Edward Ferrars, bewailing his lack of purpose in life, explains, 'A young man of eighteen is not in general so earnestly bent on being busy as to resist the solicitations of his friends to do nothing. I was therefore entered at Oxford and have been properly idle ever since.' However, when circumstances oblige him to earn a living, he goes to Oxford to be ordained. Henry Tilney is another Oxford student who becomes a clergyman.

Fanny Price gets a hasty glimpse of her cousin Edmund's college when she passes through the city with William on their journey from Mansfield to Portsmouth. When Henry Crawford leaves Mansfield and Maria Bertram for Bath, it is the Oxfordshire town of Banbury, famous then as now for its cross, which he hopes to reach by the first night.

Frank Churchill passes through Oxford on his journey from Yorkshire to Surrey, while both Oxford and Blenheim feature in the route which Elizabeth and the Gardiners take from Hertfordshire to Derbyshire.

Unlike the other journeys mentioned, this latter is undertaken solely for the pleasure of sightseeing, rather than to visit relatives, and the two places, described at length in Gilpin's *Lake Tour*, are named as worthy of such attention, not just stages to be passed through. That they stopped and looked around the magnificent home of the Dukes of Marlborough seems implied, for by the time they reach Derbyshire Elizabeth professes herself 'tired of great houses; after going over so many, she really had no pleasure in fine carpets or satin curtains'.

Jane Austen's second and more significant experience of school was in Berkshire: more significant in that she was that much older when she went, was there a full two years – as Mr Austen's bank accounts show, from the midsummer of 1785 to that of 1787 at least[5] – and most of all that the surroundings into which she found herself transplanted were wholly different from anything she had known hitherto.

The establishment of the kindly Mrs La Tournelle was located in the gatehouse of the abbey at Reading, a romantic and picturesque building dating from the twelfth century. A pupil who was there three years after Jane described it as 'an antique gateway with rooms above its arch, and with vast staircases on either side, whose balustrades had originally been gilt'.[6] To provide more accommodation Mrs La Tournelle also rented a large adjoining house, 'encompassed by a beautiful old-fashioned garden, where the children played under tall trees in hot summer evenings.' From the top of an embankment which partially enclosed the garden, the girls could look down upon the 'magnificent ruins' of the abbey itself. Consecrated by Becket in 1125, this abode of the Benedictine monks had once been 'the third in size and wealth of all English abbeys'. It must surely have been in Jane Austen's fifteen-year-old mind when she wrote of Henry VIII in her humorous *History of England*, 'nothing can be said in his vindication, but that his abolishing Religious Houses and leaving them to the ruinous depredations of time has been of infinite use to the landscape of England in general'.

In the other direction the gatehouse afforded an almost equally interesting view. Immediately before it lay an open green belonging to the town and known as the Forbury. Beyond that 'rose the tower of the fine old church of Saint Nicholas', 'the jutting corner of Friar Street' and the 'old irregular shops of the market-place'. Quaint town, old-fashioned garden, ancient ruins – these were the scenes which enriched Jane Austen's imagination from her tenth to her twelfth year, extended her visual experience of England and introduced her to some of its historic remains.

Other early visits were doubtless paid in Berkshire, though no records

Abbey Gatehouse, Reading (1801) Jane Austen's second experience of school was in this historic and picturesque building

of them exist, for her Cooper uncle and aunt lived at Sonning in that county, while her other uncle and aunt on the maternal side, the Leigh Perrots, possessed a splendid mansion called Scarlets, six miles from Maidenhead on the Reading road. James Leigh, brother of Mrs Austen and Mrs Cooper, had at an early age inherited the estate of Northleigh in Oxfordshire from his great-uncle Thomas Perrot, on condition he adopt that surname. On attaining his majority, James demolished the house at Northleigh, sold the land to the Duke of Marlborough, and built Scarlets, to which he and his wife became devotedly attached. It is inconceivable that the Austens never visited them there: Mrs Austen was very close to her brother and young James Austen was generally regarded as the childless Leigh Perrots' heir. Scarlets, a grand house run by a proud and unbending mistress, must have struck the young Jane Austen with its contrast to the informality and bustle of Steventon Rectory and the happy, homely atmosphere of the Abbey School.

There was one home in Berkshire which more closely resembled in tone and status Steventon Rectory, and which Jane visited periodically from her youth to the last year of her life. This was Kintbury Rectory, home of the Reverend Thomas Fowle and his wife Jane, who was sister to Mrs Lloyd of Ibthorpe. Situated half-way between Newbury and

Hungerford, Kintbury is another of the 'remarkably pretty' villages known to Jane Austen. The Kennet and Avon canal, which was eventually to reach Bath, passed through the village from 1797, bringing occasional liveliness to this otherwise green and tranquil spot. The Rectory itself had its own source of liveliness in its four clever sons.

The two elder Fowle boys, Fulwar and Tom, both intended for clergymen, were among George Austen's pupils at Steventon, where they forged a firm friendship with James Austen, who came midway between them in age. In turn he was invited to be a visitor at Kintbury. Fulwar eventually married his cousin Eliza Lloyd, while Tom became engaged to Cassandra Austen. Fulwar was offered the living of Elkestone in Gloucestershire, where he and Eliza began their married life, but Tom had to wait for another living in the gift of their rich kinsman, Lord Craven, to fall vacant.

Meanwhile, to earn and save some money, Tom accepted the offer of Lord Craven to accompany his regiment as chaplain to the West Indies. To be with him during his final days in England, Cassandra was invited to stay at Kintbury Rectory. Perhaps the Austen sisters had never been separated before; anyway, Jane's earliest preserved letters to Cassandra were sent to her at Kintbury.

Tom sailed from Falmouth on 8 January 1796; in February 1797 he died of yellow fever, and in May of that year the news at last reached Hampshire, whereupon Cassandra put on full widow's weeds, and never seems to have contemplated matrimony thereafter.

Many years later James wrote a long poem in celebration of the happy and carefree times he had spent at Kintbury. Addressing the memory of Tom Fowle, 'Friend of my soul, and Brother of my heart!' he wrote:

> For I had many a scene of pleasure planned
> When safe returned to thy dear native land.
> Thy wanderings passed should a long tale afford
> To friends assembled round the social board.
> Much did I hope (it was a vision fair
> And pity it should melt into thin air)
> Our friendship soon had known a dearer tie
> Than friendship's self could ever yet supply,
> And I had lived with confidence to join
> A much loved sister's trembling hand in thine.[7]

Thereafter, as has been noted, both Jane and Cassandra were regular visitors at Kintbury, which was enlivened by the return of Fulwar, Eliza and their growing family to live with the older generation, and crowded even, one would think, by the addition of no fewer than three impoverished female relations of the Fowles – two single ladies, and the widowed mother of one of them.[8] The earlier part of the poem by James Austen already quoted, 'Lines Written at Kintbury, May 1812', is worth giving for the description it affords of a place known and loved by Jane Austen, as well as for its genuine feeling for nature which he surely helped foster in her and which he shared with her:

> In this gay season, when midst genial showers
> And sun's soft gleaming, spring the vernal flowers,
> When each succeeding morn a brighter green
> Discloses, spreading o'er the woodland scene;
> Midst scenes, whose varied landscape ever new
> Presents fresh beauties to the unsated view,
> Where sloping uplands catch the sun's first beam,
> Where winding through the meadow, Kennet's stream
> Reflects an outline true, but tint less bright,
> The gray Church tower, tall tree, and mansion white.
> Why, as each well known object strikes my sight
> Must pensive sorrow mix with gay delight?
> Can sorrow entrance find midst scenes like these,
> Can Nature's beam this season cease to please?
> Less softly blows the breeze, or flows the stream
> Than when entranced in Youth's delightful dream
> I roamed along its banks, nor marked the time,
> How rapidly it passed, till distant chime
> Of village clock and slow retiring light
> Proclaimed the near approach of sober night?
> Oh! no, with equal freshness blows the breeze,
> And hues as vernal tint the budding trees,
> Light airs as sweetly cool the rippling stream,
> And softly fades the day's departing gleam;
> Unchanged the scene on which so oft I've gazed,
> Nor have I lost the taste (kind heaven be praised)
> To prize them as I ought; they still excite
> Joys undescribed and undefined delight.
> It is not that I feel their beauties less,
> Because I scarcely can the sigh repress;
> Rises that sigh because each object here,
> Brings back the thought of many a former year
> And faithful memory recalls the scenes
> (O'er leaping the long space which intervenes)
> When warm with youth, and spirits light as air,
> And little of Life's future ills aware

The present I enjoyed, and nought could see
In the perspective of futurity,
But hours of health and pleasure, ease and mirth,
A vision never realized on Earth.
And though Life's scenes with various sorrows fraught
Have since those days a soberer lesson taught,
I cannot yet, (and if there live a man
I would not choose him for my friend, who can)
With stoic apathy and bosom cold
The scenes of youthful joys unmoved behold.
And hence the mixed sensations which I feel
Of joy and sorrow, o'er my bosom steal;
Hence, while intent upon the stream I gaze
My mind reverts to scenes of other days,
And as I trace the green and willowed shore
I think on joys that can return no more.

The Reverend Thomas Fowle also held the nearby living of Hamstead Marshall, which on his death in 1806 was offered to James Austen, who declined on grounds of conscience,[9] Kintbury itself passing to the next generation, Fulwar Craven and Eliza. (See *Jane Austen's Family*, pp. 145–6). Between them and the Austens there seems to have been much mutual help with provisioning; writing from Southampton in February 1807 Jane lamented, 'It vexed me that I could not get any fish for Kintbury while their family was large; but so it was, and till last Tuesday I could procure none. I then sent them four pair of small soles . . . they cost six shillings, and they travelled in a basket which came from Kintbury a few days before with poultry, etc.' In October 1808 the message was, 'Tell Henry that a hamper of apples is gone to him from Kintbury.' How reminiscent of *Emma*!

Through the Fowles Jane knew something of the Dundas family of Barton Court – in effect the squires of Kintbury – as well as of Lord Craven of Ashdown Park, a few miles away. 'Eliza has seen Lord Craven at Barton, and probably by this time at Kintbury, where he was expected for one day this week', reported Jane in January 1801. 'She found his manners very pleasing indeed. The little flaw of having a mistress now living with him at Ashdown Park, seems to be the only unpleasing circumstance about him.'

Newbury was a centre of social activity – Jane mentions the races and the assembly there in several letters – while Windsor enjoyed the superiority bestowed on it by royal residence. In 1798 Jane remarked on the wealth and happiness of the Windsor neighbourhood and seventeen years later wrote: 'We are to go to Windsor in our way to Henley, which will be a great delight.' It is to Windsor, 'to the house of a very old friend in Windsor', that Mr Churchill and Frank go from Richmond after the death of Mrs Churchill and 'the departure of the funeral for Yorkshire'. From Windsor Frank is easily able to ride to Highbury, in Surrey; ' "Yes, Frank came over this morning, just to ask us how we did" '.

When Cassandra was planning a journey home from Cheltenham, 'If there were but a coach from Hungerford to Chawton!' lamented Jane. From London in 1813 she wrote, 'I should not wonder if we got no farther than Reading on Thursday evening – and so, reach Steventon only to a reasonable dinner hour the next day.' This is echoed in *Sense and Sensibility* when Mrs Jennings and Mrs Palmer, having travelled with the Dashwood sisters from London to Cleveland in Somerset, 'talked of the friends they had left behind [to follow them] and wondered whether Mr Palmer and Colonel Brandon would get farther than Reading that night.' And on the journey already mentioned of Fanny and William from Mansfield to Portsmouth, they 'made no stop anywhere, till they reached Newbury, where a comfortable meal, uniting dinner and supper, wound up the enjoyments and fatigues of the day.' Fanny and William are travelling north to south, Colonel Brandon east to west, but both pass through Berkshire.

Jane's last visit to the county was made in the spring of 1816, when she stayed at Kintbury once again. Fulwar and Eliza 'thought that her health

Windsor (1801) 'We are to go to Windsor in our way to Henley, which will be a great delight,' wrote Jane in 1815

was somewhat impaired, and observed that she went about her old haunts, and recalled old recollections connected with them in a particular manner, as if she did not expect ever to see them again.'[10] This recollection surely proves that she had a deep affection for the place – and that her thoughts, four years after the composition of James' poem, were remarkably in tune with his.

4

Kent:
Country House Life

> . . . and not a tattered roof
> Or mouldering stone affords one single touch
> Of *picturesque*; but *happy man* dwells here,
> With peace and competence and sweet repose,
> And bliss domestic; these the mental eye
> Suffice to charm, and all *it* sees is good.
> John Aikin, *Picturesque; A Fragment,* 1791

After Hampshire, the county best known and best loved by Jane Austen was Kent. It was the home of all her paternal forebears, and of some of the wealthiest of her relations. 'Kent is the only place for happiness: everybody is rich there', she once humorously wrote, and over a period of twenty-five years, from a series of comfortable country houses and great parks, each with 'its beauties and its prospects', she received a vision of England that was gracious, mellow, affluent, well-ordered, and very lovely.

Her first known visit to Kent took place when she was twelve and a half, in the summer of 1788. With her parents and sister she stayed in the home of her father's uncle Francis Austen, who had amassed a considerable fortune from the law and by marrying two wealthy wives. The second of these, namesake and godmother to Jane, had died six years before, and Francis Austen, aged ninety, lived alone at the Red House, Sevenoaks, which he had purchased in 1743. His way of life was hospitable but formal: he attached great importance to doing everything correctly.

At the time of Jane's visit the redbrick, symmetrical, imposing house, nine windows wide and four storeys high, and occupying an important position in the town, was just over a hundred years old, and represented the late seventeenth century ideal, with its confident big-hipped roof supported by richly carved brackets. The property possessed its own stables, and originally, as an old engraving shows, a large, formal, *parterre*-style garden which adjoined the estate of Knole. (The Duke of Dorset had been a client of Francis Austen, who had named one of his own sons Sackville.) By 1788 the garden could hardly have escaped

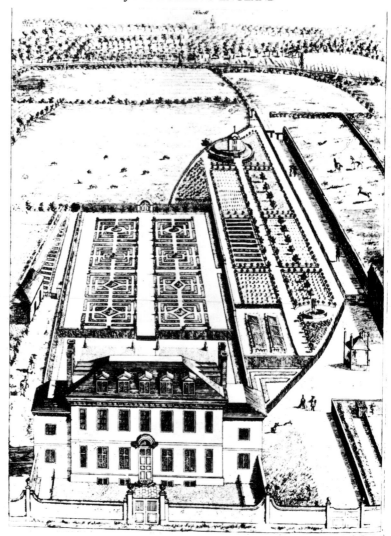

The Red House, Sevenoaks (1719) Jane Austen visited this house, home of
her great-uncle Francis, when she was twelve. This view gives a good
idea of what English gardens looked like before Georgian 'improvements'

'improvement', unless in gardening as in dress Francis Austen stuck as
rigidly to the fashions of his youth: 'he wore a wig like a bishop' and his suit
'retained a perfect identity of colour, texture and make to his life's end'.[1]

The writer of these words, Jane's brother Henry, added, 'It is a sort of
privilege to have seen and conversed with such a model of a hundred years

since'. To Jane too it was a privilege to experience briefly a style of living from another age – a privilege perhaps not fully appreciated at the time, for it must have been rather daunting to a child to be the guest of this formidable great-uncle. None of her grandparents had survived into her lifetime, and Francis Austen was the only relation of that generation whom she met.

She knew that her father owed a great deal to his uncle's generosity and sense of family solidarity. The Austens of Kent had, over the course of many centuries, made their fortunes from the wool trade, until they were able to live like gentlemen in two substantial houses, Broadford and Grovehurst. As younger sons, however, Francis, William (Jane's grandfather) and several other brothers, all of whom had been born to affluence at Broadford, had been apprenticed to trades and professions. William became a surgeon in Tonbridge, but died when Jane's father was six. Francis Austen not only paid for his clever nephew to be educated at Tonbridge Grammar School, but later presented him with the second living of Deane which made such a vital contribution to his income. The visit of 1788 kept the Steventon family fresh in the old man's memory; when he died three years later Francis left George £500, despite having more than a dozen descendants of his own.

The area around Tonbridge and Sevenoaks was full of Austen cousins. The most notable included the senior branch of the family, at Broadford; George's boyhood friend, the Reverend Henry Austen, who had preceded him as (absentee) rector of Steventon, had held the comfortable Kent livings of Chiddingstone and West Wickham, but was now retired and living at Tonbridge; and Francis' own eldest son, Motley, independently wealthy through Francis' wise choice of his mother and godmother, and his own wise choice of a wife. Motley had been a pupil of George Austen at Tonbridge School. At the time of the Austens' visit he was living at Lamberhurst, but when his father died he sold The Red House, which was too much in the centre of town to suit the present taste, and bought the splendid country estate of Kippington outside Sevenoaks. Motley had a large family which included a Jane Austen only four months younger than her 'Hampshire-born' namesake – whose head must have whirled if she was introduced to half these new relations.

And then there was George's half-brother, the child of his mother's first marriage, William Walter. With their daughter Philadelphia the Walters were invited to dine at The Red House on the second evening of the Austens' visit. In a letter which Philadelphia wrote to her brother James we have an outsider's impression of Jane, 'very like her brother Henry, not at all pretty and very prim, unlike a girl of twelve,' and of the family generally, 'all in high spirits and disposed to be pleased with each other.'[2]

The following day the Austens spent at Seal, where the Walters rented a house. 'The more I see of Cassandra the more I admire', continued Philadelphia. 'Jane is whimsical and affected.'

That evening Jane gained some impression of her great-uncle's importance in the town when the bells of Sevenoaks Church were rung to celebrate the return of his second son, John, a soldier, from the East Indies. Twenty-four hours later the Austens left Sevenoaks, but whether to make any visits elsewhere in the county is not known. To travel so far for four days seems improbable, in view of their usual practice and of their many connections in Kent – but anything beyond Sevenoaks and Seal must remain supposition. It is surely not unlikely however, whether or not the family actually stayed with Henry Austen in Tonbridge, that the girls were taken there to see the school where their father had been successively pupil and master, and the parish church where both his parents lay buried.

All that is known for certain, after their leaving Sevenoaks on 24 July, is that they dined with George's sister Mrs Hancock and her daughter Eliza in London on their way back into Hampshire, one evening before 22 August, when Eliza wrote to Philadelphia Walter, 'I am sure the meeting with our Steventon friends gave you great pleasure, they talked much of the satisfaction their visit into Kent had afforded them.'[3]

Among those satisfactions for Jane was surely an insight into her own family history and origins. This visit laid the foundations of her knowledge of Kent, which was henceforth to be concentrated in the eastern part of the county.

Indeed, it is not improbable that the 1788 visit concluded there, at Godmersham near Canterbury, home of Thomas and Catherine Knight – and of Jane's brother Edward, then aged twenty. The Knights, wealthy and childless, had adopted the fortunate Edward as heir to their three estates of Godmersham in Kent, and Steventon and Chawton in Hampshire. (It was Mr Knight's father, another Thomas, who had presented the living of Steventon to his distant cousin, George Austen.) During his teens Edward came to spend more and more of his time at Godmersham, until he was living there permanently, and it is unlikely that the Austens would be in the same county as their son and his benefactors without going on to visit them, especially as Edward was about to embark on a lengthy absence from England.

In the spring of 1791, shortly after returning from a Grand Tour of Europe, Edward became engaged to Elizabeth, daughter of Sir Brook Bridges, of Goodnestone Park, a rich neighbour of the Knights. Her father died during the course of that year and her brother inherited the Great House and the title, while her mother and unmarried sisters moved into Goodnestone Farm, in which, while grander than it sounded,

Godmersham Park (1785) Jane frequently visited this beautiful country estate after it became the property of her brother Edward in 1798

'everything seems for use and comfort', wrote Jane approvingly when she stayed there several years later.

In the summer of 1791 Edward accompanied the Knights and a party of Mrs Knight's relations – twelve people altogether – on a tour to the English Lakes, then just beginning to be admired, largely thanks to the publication of Gilpin's *Lakes Tour* five years previously. Jane had the opportunity to hear Edward's impressions when she was with him in 1794 and 1796, and she took up the idea of a northern tour in *Pride and Prejudice*, which belongs to this period.

Edward and Elizabeth were married in December 1791, and moved into a smaller manor house named Rowling in a hamlet a mile from Goodnestone, where Jane stayed with them in 1794 and 1796. On the first visit she was accompanied by Cassandra and her parents and they had 'a long hot journey into Kent'. The second visit was made with her brother Frank, and her letters home to Cassandra give us many little details of life at Rowling.

There was much socializing between the three Goodnestone households. One evening, 'We dined at Goodnestone and in the evening danced two country dances and the *boulangeries*. . . . We supped there, and walked home at night under the shade of two umbrellas'. Another evening they dined at Nackington, ten miles away, travelling in two carriages, and returning by moonlight. There was one evening walk to Crixhall Ruff, a fine oak wood, which Jane had evidently admired on her first visit, and by which Frank was now 'much edified'. In the daytime the brothers went shooting: 'Delightful sport! They are just come home; Edward with his two brace, Frank with his two and a half. What amiable young men!' Some venison was sent to them from Godmersham, which the two brothers visited, presumably on horseback, in the rain.

In the year of this visit, 1796, Jane was writing the first version of *Pride and Prejudice*, then called *First Impressions*, several chapters of which were set in Kent. ' "Are you pleased with Kent?" ' Darcy asks Elizabeth. 'A short dialogue on the subject of the country ensued, on either side calm and concise.' In fact there is little in the novel specific to Kent, beyond a couple of place names: Mr Collins' letter is dated Hunsford, 'near Westerham', and Lady Catherine, attempting to direct Elizabeth's journey back to London, cries, ' "Where shall you change horses? Oh, Bromley, of course – if you mention my name at the Bell, you will be attended to." ' Kent seems to have been chosen so that the characters may travel via London rather than for any other reason. Although attempts have been made by some commentators to associate Hunsford Parsonage and Rosings with real locations, in my view they are wholly creations of their author's mind, as is every other country house and village of which she wrote. What Kent did contribute to her imaginative world, I believe, was firstly the experience of living among the landed and leisured classes as one of themselves, which gives reality to such scenes as those at Rosings, and secondly the vision of a park-like landscape in which nature and civilization are perfectly balanced.

In Kent 'Elizabeth had often great enjoyment out of doors. Her favourite walk . . . was along the open grove which edged that side of the park, where there was a nice sheltered path, which no one seemed to value but herself.' Observation of nature, quiet enjoyment of the seasons, are essential qualities in Jane Austen's approved characters; Fanny Price is to possess them at their most highly developed, but they distinguish Elizabeth too, even when her mind is occupied by Mr Darcy's proposal:

> Totally indisposed for employment, she resolved soon after breakfast to indulge herself in air and exercise. She was proceeding directly to her favourite walk, when the recollection of Mr Darcy's sometimes coming there stopped her, and instead of entering the park, she turned up the lane, which led her farther from the turnpike road. The park paling was still the boundary on one side, and she soon passed one of the gates into

the ground. After walking two or three times along that part of the lane, she was tempted, by the pleasantness of the morning, to stop at the gates and look into the park. The five weeks which she had now passed in Kent, had made a great difference in the country, and every day was adding to the verdure of the early trees.

Jane's fondness for the similar walks around Rowling and Goodnestone is apparent from a letter of August 1805, when she was the guest, for a few days, of Lady Bridges at Goodnestone Farm. It was seven years since Edward had left Rowling, nine, perhaps, since Jane had last seen it. 'We have walked to Rowling on each of the two last days after dinner, and very great was my pleasure in going over the house and grounds. We have also found time to visit all the principal walks of this place, except the walk round the top of the park, which we shall probably accomplish today.'

In 1794 Thomas Knight died, leaving Godmersham to his widow for life, thereafter to Edward, but four years later Mrs Knight decided that the mansion was too large for her sole occupancy, and that Edward and his growing family should take her place, while she retired to a house in Canterbury called White Friars. In arriving at her decision she hoped to benefit not only Edward, Elizabeth and their children, but the tenants and servants of the estate, which she felt would be better managed by a man. The Edward Austens took possession in the summer of 1798, and in August his parents and sisters began a two month visit there.

It was a splendid house, the most splendid in which Jane Austen was ever made to feel at home. It had been built for the elder Mr Knight in 1732, of red brick with ashlar dressings, seven bays wide, and lower two-storeyed wings were added in 1781. Three *oeil-de-boeuf* windows at mezzanine level give peculiar charm to a dignified façade, which has pedimented ground floor windows, an imposing doorcase with Tuscan columns and a hipped roof from which five dormers look out above a low parapet. The rosy brick contrasts agreeably with the lush green of its surroundings. The house sits comfortably in the valley of the Stour, in grounds notable for their fine timber. The Godmersham plantations were for profit as well as beauty.

Edward's woods were so numerous as to merit individual names: there was Bentigh, and Canty Hill, and the Temple Plantation – this last enclosing a Doric temple which perhaps suggested the Grecian temple at Cleveland, in *Sense and Sensibility*. There was a wilderness, a narrow avenue of tall lime trees, and between them all spread the smooth lawns of the deer park.

Jane Austen was at Godmersham again in 1805, 1808, 1809 and 1813. (If any visits were paid between 1798 and 1805 – which seems likely – they were in company with Cassandra, and no letters survive to record them.)

Her appreciation of Kent deepened and found expression as she grew older. 'The country is very beautiful. I saw as much as ever to admire in my yesterday's journey,' she wrote on arrival at Godmersham in June 1808. This visit was made with her brother James and his wife Mary, while Cassandra stayed at home. Jane reported, 'Yesterday passed quite à la Godmersham: the gentlemen rode about Edward's farm, and returned in time to saunter along Bentigh with us; and after dinner we visited the Temple plantations. . . . James and Mary are much struck by the beauty of the place. Today the spirit of the thing is kept up by the two brothers being gone to Canterbury in the chair.' She was fully alive to the changes that took place in the intervals between her visits: 'How Bentigh has grown! And the Canty Hill plantation!' she observed in September 1813.

It was not only at Godmersham, but at several neighbouring properties where the Edward Austens visited, that Jane saw the English country house and garden at the height of their glory. Lancelot Brown was the genius who had done more than any other man to realize the 'capabilities' of the latter, and in Kent Jane was personally familiar with what a recent authority has termed 'one of the most perfect picturesque garden landscapes in the whole body of his work'.[4] This was at Chilham Castle, the grounds of which actually adjoined those of Godmersham. Here a Jacobean house (built, in front of an old Norman keep, on five sides of a hexagon, with nearly enclosed courtyard, gabled porch and corner turrets – quite different from the classical mansions with which Jane was chiefly familiar in Kent) stood at the top of a steep bank cut into four terraces, which Brown retained, together with an old Judas tree and some splendid yews. Thus far, the steepness of the site probably left him little option; but the grounds had been enlarged to 350 acres, and there was much else for him to do. He created a lake to fill the bottom of the valley, and a series of beautifully contrived vistas down its length, while his planting was on a grand scale. Both visually and historically it was and is a romantic spot, to which the greatest of English landscape gardeners did justice. No danger here of his sometimes 'vapid sheets of lawn': at Chilham Brown respected and responded fully to 'the genius of the place'.

The village of Chilham formed a worthy overture to the castle, the gates of which opened off one side of the village square, lined with Tudor and Jacobean cottages, flower-clad, timber-framed and many-gabled. The plan of the village harks back to the Middle Ages, with the workforce clustered at the great lord's gates. The village stands on a plateau, with little streets descending from each corner of the square.

There was frequent visiting between Godmersham and Chilham, in which the Miss Austens, when staying with their brother, were naturally included. We know that Cassandra was at a ball there in 1801, and that Jane dined there in 1813, when she remarked, directing her humour at

Chilham Castle (1808) Immediately adjoining the grounds of Godmersham, this unusual Jacobean house set in a park landscaped by Brown was well known to Jane Austen

herself, 'By the bye, as I must leave off being young, I find many *douceurs* in being a sort of chaperon, for I am put on the sofa near the fire and can drink as much wine as I like'. A few days previously they had paid a morning visit to Chilham, but found nobody in. However, there were fourteen people at the dinner, and 'We had music in the evening, Fanny and Miss Wildman played, and Mr James Wildman sat close by and listened, or pretended to listen'. James Wildman, the son of the house, was for several years an admirer of Jane's niece Fanny. 'I like Chilham Castle for you', Jane wrote to her, hardly surprisingly, when Fanny was undecided how to receive his attentions in 1817.

The match, however, came to nothing, and it was a further eight years before Fanny was to marry and become mistress of another fine Kentish house, Mersham-le-Hatch. This was the seat of the Knatchbull family – Fanny became Lady Knatchbull – to which Mrs Knight had belonged before her marriage. The daughter of a younger son, she had been brought up at Chilham Rectory.[5] Jane writes of 'going to each house at Chilham and to Mystole' on their morning visits. The latter place, which she found 'so pretty' was the home of their acquaintance Lady Fagg and her five daughters.

In Kent too, Jane became familiar with the work of a contemporary architect whose name she introduced, in a somewhat unfavourable context, into one of her early novels. Robert Ferrars, that most foolish of characters, pontificates:

'I advise anybody who is going to build, to build a cottage. My friend Lord Courtland came to me the other day on purpose to seek my advice, and laid before me three different plans of Bonomi's. I was to decide on the best of them. "My dear Courtland," said I, immediately throwing them all into the fire, "do not adopt either of them, but by all means build a cottage." And that, I fancy, will be the end of it.'

Joseph Bonomi, 1739–1808, had been born and trained as an architect in Rome, and came to England in 1767 at the invitation of the Adam brothers. He was employed to design a new house for the Finch-Hatton family at Eastwell Park, close to Godmersham, between 1793 and 1799, a period coinciding with three visits into east Kent by Jane Austen. She must often have heard its architecture discussed – even criticized. Though a classical house, Eastwell was endowed with 'deliberate impropriety': the immense portico consisted of five columns rather than the correct four or six, emphasizing that it was to be entered laterally; the entablature was lacking the frieze, and the Ionic columns supported 'a coarse Michelangelesque cap'.[6] These are the remarks of one of our most eminent architectural historians, who sums up Bonomi: 'there is a marked insensibility about [his] designs – or is it merely the strangeness of an Italian hand meddling with the English tradition?' Jane Austen's contempt of foreigners was not likely to be lessened by such flaunting of the rules.

That she was familiar with the household at Eastwell from an early date is evident from her mentioning the name of the music teacher employed there in a letter of 1799. In August 1805 she told Cassandra, 'Our visit to Eastwell was very agreeable. They were very civil to me, as they always are. . . . It was considerably past eleven before we were at home.'

Another house built at the very end of the eighteenth century with which Jane was well acquainted, staying overnight there on two occasions, in September 1805 and again eight years later, was Sandling, near Hythe, the home of William Deedes and his wife Sophia, who was one of Elizabeth Austen's many sisters. Sandling too had its architectural talking-point. Before she had seen the place for herself, Jane wrote to Cassandra in October 1800:

In talking of Mr Deedes's new house, Mrs Bramston told us one circumstance, which, that we should be ignorant of it before must make Edward's conscience fly into his face; she told us that one of the sitting-rooms at Sandling, an oval room with a Bow at one end, has the very remarkable and singular feature of a fireplace with a window, the centre window of the Bow, exactly over the mantlepiece.

When in 1808 Jane was staying at Godmersham with her brother James, she told Cassandra, 'James and Edward are gone to Sandling today; a nice scheme for James, as it will show him a new and fine country. Edward certainly excels in doing the honours to his visitors, and providing for their amusement.' The following day she added, 'My brothers returned last night at ten, having spent a very agreeable day. . . . James admires the place very much.'

As a landholder involved to a certain extent in the administration of his county – he was High Sheriff in 1801 – Edward introduced Jane to a glimpse of life beyond the round of country house visiting.[7] On 2 November 1813 she wrote, 'Edward and I set off in the chair to Canterbury. . . . He went to inspect the Gaol, as a visiting magistrate, and took me with him. I was gratified, and went through all the feelings which people must go through I think in visiting such a building.' The prison was then new, built from red brick between 1806 and 1810 – just one indication of the prosperity of Canterbury.

Another was the Dane John, the defensive mound transformed in 1790 by Alderman James Simmons, at the cost of £1,500, into a pleasure garden complete with noble avenue of limes – like the ones at both Godmersham and Donwell. The cathedral city of Canterbury, rich alike in medieval remains and fine Georgian architecture, was well known to Jane Austen. She went there frequently from Godmersham, to shop, to pay morning calls, perhaps even to dance – there is reference in her letters to the subscription balls held monthly through the winter at Delmar's Assembly Rooms.

In June 1808 she stayed overnight at White Friars, the house in Canterbury which Mrs Knight had purchased ten years before. 'It was a very agreeable visit. There was everything to make it so; kindness, conversation and variety, without care or cost.' Cassandra had paid a similar visit to Mrs Knight the previous year, when Jane had feared that they might become so attached that they would have to make their home in Canterbury, 'which I should not like so well as Southampton.' A year later the widowed Mrs Austen and her daughters almost did move to Kent, to 'a house at Wye'; but in the end they remained in Hampshire, which, Jane wrote, probably with something more than her usual complacence on such matters, 'will be best'. Besides a natural prepossession in favour of her native county, she may have felt that living in Kent would put them in the awkward position of poor relations – with a wide circle of acquaintance made through Edward whom they would not have the means to visit or to

Canterbury (1808) In this county town Jane Austen shopped, visited friends, and, on one occasion, accompanied her brother in his inspection of the gaol

entertain. The 'happy indifference of east Kent wealth' was theirs only as visitors, not as residents.

In her many journeys into Kent, Jane became very familiar with the London to Canterbury road, and particularly with those towns where horses were changed and meals were taken: Dartford, Rochester, Sittingbourne and Ospringe. In October 1798, returning with her parents to Steventon from Godmersham, where Cassandra had been left to help Elizabeth through a confinement, Jane wrote from the Bull and George at Dartford:

> You have already heard from Daniel [The Godmersham coachman], I conclude, in what excellent time we reached and quitted Sittingbourne. . . . It wanted five minutes of twelve when we left Sittingbourne, from whence we had a famous pair of horses, which took us to Rochester in an hour and a quarter; the postboy seemed determined to show my mother that Kentish drivers were not always tedious. . . . Our next stage was not quite so expeditiously performed; the road was heavy and the horses indifferent. However . . . we were very little more than two hours

and a half coming hither, and it was scarcely past four when we stopped at the inn. My mother took some of her bitters at Ospringe, and some more at Rochester, and she ate some bread several times. . . . My day's journey has been pleasanter in every respect that I expected. I have been very little crowded and by no means unhappy. . . . We had one heavy shower on leaving Sittingbourne, but afterwards the clouds cleared away, and we had a very bright *crystal* afternoon.

At Dartford the Austens evidently visited the library between arriving and dining at the Bull and George. There was also a 'little adventure' when, a quarter of an hour after their arrival, 'it was discovered that my writing and dressing boxes had been by accident put into a chaise which was just packing off as we came in, and were driven away towards Gravesend in their way to the West Indies . . . Mr Nottley immediately despatched a man and horse after the chaise . . . they were got about two or three miles off.' As for the comforts of the inn, 'We have got apartments up two pair of stairs, as we could not be otherwise accommodated with a sitting-room and bed-chamber on the same floor, which we wished to be. . . . We sat down to dinner a little after five, and had some beef-steaks and a boiled fowl, but no oyster sauce. . . . My father is now reading the *Midnight Bell* which he has got from the library, and mother is sitting by the fire.'

Ten years later Jane described a journey along the same route but in the other direction, from London to Godmersham:

Our first eight miles were hot; Deptford Hill brought to my mind our hot journey into Kent fourteen years ago; but after Blackheath we suffered nothing, and as the day advanced it grew quite cool. At Dartford, which we reached within the two hours and three-quarters, we went to the Bull, the same inn at which we breakfasted in that said journey, and on the present occasion had about the same bad butter. At half-past ten we were again off, and, travelling on without any adventure reached Sittingbourne by three. Daniel was watching for us at the door of the George, and I was acknowledged very kindly by Mr and Mrs Marshall, to the latter of whom I devoted my conversation, while Mary went out to buy some gloves. A few minutes, of course, did for Sittingbourne; and so off we drove, drove, drove, and by six o'clock were at Godmersham.

A total of ten and a half hours.

David Waldron Smithers points out that the 'Bull' and the 'Bull and George', both mentioned by Jane Austen, were two quite separate establishments at Dartford.[8] The former, erected in 1703 on the site of a much older inn, was built around four sides of a coaching yard, with balconies all round at first-floor level. Both inns took their names from the seal given by a priory to a lodging place for pilgrims.

In *Sense and Sensibility*, Dartford is the location of Lady Elliot's 'cottage' which includes a dining parlour, a drawing-room and a saloon!

Ramsgate is another town in Kent which it seems Jane Austen visited. The writer Egerton Brydges, brother of the Austens' neighbour Mrs Lefroy of Ashe Parsonage, knew Jane slightly as a child at Steventon, and recorded in his autobiography, 'the last time I think I saw her was at Ramsgate in 1803.'[9] No letters from Jane survive from 1803, but as her brother Frank was stationed at Ramsgate that year a visit to the town by the Austens is not improbable. On the renewal of war after the Peace of Amiens, Frank Austen was appointed to raise and organize a corps of 'Sea Fencibles' to defend the stretch of the Kent coast between North Foreland and Sandown. His headquarters were at Ramsgate, where he was remarked upon as being '*the* officer who knelt in church' and where he met his future wife, Mary Gibson, a resident of the town.

Jane Austen's references to Ramsgate, in both letters and novels, are consistent with a personal knowledge of the place, which she evidently disliked. She wrote of an acquaintance, 'Edward Hussey is warned out of Pett, and talks of fixing at Ramsgate. Bad taste! He is very fond of the sea however; some taste in that – and some judgement too in fixing on Ramsgate, as being near the sea.' And from Godmersham in 1813, 'This morning we had Edward Bridges unexpectedly to breakfast with us, in his way from Ramsgate where is his wife, to Lenham where is his church – and tomorrow he dines and sleeps here on his return. They have been all the summer at Ramsgate, for *her* health, she is a poor honey – the sort of woman who gives me the idea of being determined never to well.'

In *Pride and Prejudice*, Ramsgate is where Georgiana Darcy passes the summer, and where Wickham almost succeeds in persuading her to elope with him. Tom Bertram of *Mansfield Park* idles away a week at Ramsgate with some fashionable friends, and calls upon the Sneyd family, who have lodgings at Albion Place. He tells Mary Crawford, ' "When we reached Albion Place they were out; we went after them, and found them on the pier." ' In a few brief references the flavour of Ramsgate as a smart and heartless place is established, and the older, inland resort of Tunbridge Wells fares no better: both Mary Crawford and William Walter Elliot are in the habit of staying there.

A little down the coast from Ramsgate was the much less fashionable Deal, where lodgings were cheap enough for naval families, attracted here by the Downs, the safe anchorage offshore protected by three castles built by Henry VIII. The Crofts of *Persuasion*, early in their married life, had lodgings at Deal, which the admiral recalls as 'snug', though his wife

Ramsgate (1808) A favourite place with Tom Bertram and his friends, Ramsgate may have been visited by Jane Austen herself in 1803. One of her sisters-in-law came from here

was not happy to be left there alone while he was on the North Sea. Similarly Frank Austen's wife Mary took lodgings at Deal while he was away in the Baltic, commanding HMS *Elephant*. Jane wrote to Frank from Godmersham in 1813, 'I shall be sorry to be in Kent so long without seeing Mary, but I am afraid it must be so. She has very kindly invited me to Deal, but is aware of the great improbability of my being able to get there'.

This is just one of the many remarks in Jane Austen's letters which illustrate her dependence, regarding travel, on first her father and then her brothers. In June 1808 she was explicit: 'I shall be sorry to pass the door at Seal without calling, but it must be so . . . and till I have a travelling purse of my own, I must submit to such things.' (There is no record of her visiting her Walter relations at Seal after 1788, though this remark twenty years later implies that there had been intermediate visits.) She was occasionally irked by her lack of independence, but knowing that the kindness of her brothers would have led them to alter their plans had they known of any opposing wish of her own, she was scrupulous to conceal all such preferences. Her phraseology shows how completely she left the decisions to them.

In 1806 Elizabeth Austen's youngest sister, Harriot Bridges, of whom Jane was very fond, married the Reverend George Moore, Rector of Wrotham and son of an Archbishop of Canterbury. Wrotham lies just off the Maidstone to Guildford road – on the way back to London in fact – and in 1808, when Edward was to escort Jane home at the end of her visit to Godmersham, 'Harriot is very earnest with Edward to make Wrotham in his journey, but we shall be in too great a hurry to get nearer to it than Wrotham Gate.'

At the conclusion of Jane's last visit to Godmersham however, in November 1813, she and Harriot had their wish. 'It seems now quite settled that we go to Wrotham on Saturday, the 13th, spend Sunday there, and proceed to London on Monday, as before intended. I like the plan. I shall be glad to see Wrotham.' A few days later she enlarged on their plans, 'We are to be off on Saturday before the post comes in, as Edward takes his own horses all the way. He talks of nine o'clock. We shall bait at Lenham.'

The last night Jane ever spent on Kentish soil, therefore, was passed in the Rectory at Wrotham. George Moore had demolished the old Rectory shortly after his arrival in the parish, and had commissioned Samuel Wyatt to build its replacement in 1801–2. A classical front, and three bays in a segmental bow, topped by a shallow lead dome, made this one of the grandest rectories of Jane's acquaintance – hardly surprising as the archbishop was patron of the living, and the remains of a former episcopal palace lay just east of the church. It was fitting that Jane's last hours in Kent, where she had experienced so much pleasant hospitality, should be passed in such an elegant home.

But delightful though it all was, with her impeccable sense of the priorities of life she kept her Kentish experiences in perspective. Towards the close of her 1808 visit she wrote to Cassandra,

In another week I shall be home – and then, my having been at Godmersham will seem like a dream, as my visit to Brompton does already. The orange wine will want our care soon. But in the meantime for elegance and easy and luxury; the Hattons and Milles dine here today – and I shall eat ice and drink French wine, and be above vulgar economy. Luckily the pleasures of friendship, of unreserved conversation, of similarity of taste and opinions, will make good amends for orange wine.

5

Bath:
Legacy in Stone

Paid bells and musicians,
Drugs, nurse and physicians,
Balls, raffles, subscriptions and chairs;
Wigs, gowns, skins and trimming,
Good books for the women,
Plays, concerts, tea, negus and prayers.
Christopher Anstey,
The New Bath Guide, 1776

Jane Austen was an unwilling inhabitant of Bath for five years of her life. Before that she had been a frequent visitor to the city. It was part of her heritage in both its cultural and its physical manifestations. Perhaps no place has ever so completely embodied the one within the other.

Let our first glimpse of Bath be through the eyes of a foreigner, Louis Simond, who arrived there in 1810, midway between the period of Jane's residence and her use of the city in *Persuasion*. Bath, Simond wrote,

> is certainly very beautiful. It is built of freestone, of a fine cream-colour, and contains several public edifices, in a good taste. We remarked a circular place called the Crescent, another called the Circus; all the streets straight and regular. This town looks as if it had been cast in a mould all at once; so new, so fresh, so regular. The building where the medical water is drank, and where the baths are, exhibits very different objects; human nature, old, infirm or in ruins, or weary and ennuyé. Bath is a sort of great monastery, inhabited by single people, particularly superannuated females. No trade, no manufactures, no occupations of any sort, except that of killing time, the most laborious of all. Half of the inhabitants do nothing, the other half supply them with nothings: multitude of splendid shops, full of all that wealth and luxury can desire, arranged with all the arts of seduction.[1]

On a personal level Jane Austen might find much to dislike, but on an artistic level there was much to respond to here. Of her novels only *Pride and Prejudice* contains no reference to Bath, while two full length studies are offered in *Northanger Abbey* and *Persuasion*. Separated in their composition by some fifteen years, these two portraits of the same face reveal the subject at different ages and in different moods.

The same distinctions apply equally to the artist. The Bath of the pleasurable short visit in *Northanger Abbey* reflects Jane's own experience in the 1790s, while the Bath of perpetual confinement portrayed in *Persuasion* was reality to her in the first years of the new century.

The significance of Bath, both as a product and as a promulgator of Georgian ideas and aspirations, can hardly be exaggerated. The city played a unique part in facilitating the new eighteenth century pursuits – of pleasure, of polished manners, of social contacts, of correct taste. Provided they had a certain amount of education, leisure and money to spend, people from all levels of society could mingle and learn from each other, enjoy civilized pleasures, and feel free to improve themselves – in many senses of the word. It was this sense of freedom, this provision of the conditions required for a (relatively) socially mobile population that Bath contributed to the national good. The existence of Bath prevented a build-up of such social unrest as a repressed and frustrated emergent class are likely to generate. As Smollett wrote, 'Even the wives and daughters of low tradesmen . . . insist upon being conveyed to Bath where they may hobble country dances and cotillions among lordlings, squires, counsellors and clergy'.[2]

The increasing pressure from below, however, eventually (in the second half of the century) had two effects. Firstly it drove off the top layer to establish new fashions elsewhere; and secondly it induced in those who took their place at the top, the gentry, a desire for greater privacy and exclusivity. No longer content to 'hobble' with anyone who could afford the subscription to the assemblies, these people began to prefer private parties and prided themselves on avoiding 'the showy, *tonish* people who are only to be seen by going to the Rooms, which we never do', as Fanny Burney wrote in 1780.

Beneath this fastidious layer, which included such snobs as Sir Walter Elliot and Lady Dalrymple, came the 'clergymen may be, or lawyers from town, or half pay officers, or widows with only a jointure', enumerated in another context by Lady Denham. Since these classes were more numerous than the aristocracy who had first patronized Bath, the city appeared more popular than ever, and the demand for houses steadily grew. A thousand were built in the 1790s alone, proving that Bath was very far from being in decline when Jane Austen first knew it.

Bath's architectural glory, indeed, considerably postdated its social glory. Only the Parades, Queen Square and the Circus had been built when dukes and duchesses flocked to Bath. No change of taste occurred with their departure, however, and the city expanded northwards with beautiful homogeneity in terraces, squares and crescents of Palladian

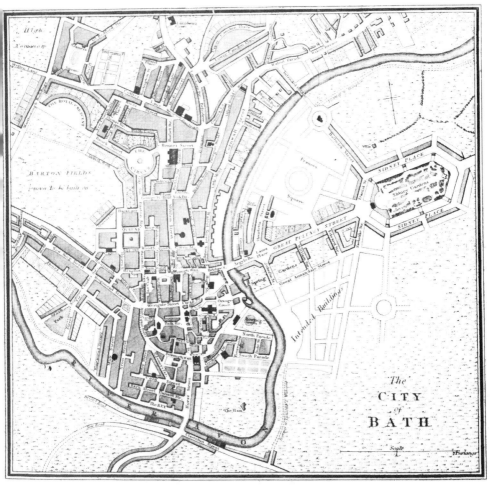

Bath in 1805

houses in golden stone. The Royal Crescent, the most glorious creation in a glorious city, was completed in the very year of Jane's birth.

The expansion northwards resulted in the erection of the New or Upper Rooms so that people in the new lodgings did not have to descend to the town at night. The city spread as far as it could northwards up the very steep hills, crescent after crescent rising above one another, affording magnificent views but steep walking home. Sir Walter Elliot is very proud of the 'lofty, dignified situation' of his house in Camden Place (an unfinished crescent: unstable land at one end prevented completion) but poor Anne often has to 'toil' up the hill to return.

To the south and east the city was checked by the river Avon curving round; the low-lying area by the river was developed, but with few pretensions to fashion. Beyond the river to the south a hill as steep as any in Bath prevented building: Beechen Cliff, 'that noble hill whose beautiful verdure and hanging coppice render it so striking an object from almost any opening in Bath'. Indeed, the greenery of Bath's many surrounding hills is never out of view, adding immeasurably to the charm of the city. As Fanny Burney wrote, Bath 'is . . . the only town for us, since here, all the year round, there is always the town at command and always the country for prospect, exercise and delight'.

To open up a whole new area for development, Pulteney Bridge was built across the river due east of the town. Execution of this beautiful design by Robert Adam, this three arched bridge lined both sides with shops, with a Venetian window in the centre, and domed pavilions both ends, was contemporaneous with the building of the Royal Crescent. The new building area was level and many fine new streets were made, including Great Pulteney Street.

The high density living that all this implied suited the society-orientated people of the greater part of the eighteenth century. They possessed lawns and woods in the country; when they passed a season in town, they wanted to feel that they were in a town, revelling in the dry, clean pavements, and experiencing no need for individual gardens. The walled plots behind the town houses were extensions of the servants' territory – for washing or stabling or keeping the coal. The family lived on the first floor, and when they left the house it was invariably through the front door. Indeed, the Georgians appeared to care nothing for the backs of their houses, which in Bath show an astonishing want of proportion and pattern in the fenestration, so perfect in front.

Bath however was rich in public parks, where the favourite pursuits of seeing and being seen could take place. Chief amongst these were the lawns in front of the Royal Crescent, where it was fashionable to walk on a Sunday; Jane Austen, and her characters in *Northanger Abbey*, all did so. In the new town east of the river, at the end of Great Pulteney Street, a large new park was set out and named Sydney Gardens. Here were provided such entertainments as music, fireworks and public breakfasts. A 'moveable orchestra', two bowling greens and a labyrinth are shown on a map of Sydney Gardens of 1803.

The Upper Rooms have already been mentioned; the Lower Rooms and the theatre were both in the central, older part of the town. Only the narrow street pattern betrayed the pre-Georgian origins of this area; few of the old gabled houses were allowed to stand as rebuilding swept them away. In this area were the various bathing establishments, the Pump Room and the abbey.

Queen Square (1804) Jane Austen stayed here in 1799 and admired its 'cheerful situation' – but by 1814 the Musgrove girls could call the square old-fashioned

The heart of the city has always been the abbey churchyard, called the pump-yard in *Northanger Abbey*. A spacious paved area where the sedan-chairs, and their blue-coated attendants, waited for customers, the churchyard is pleasantly enclosed by the west front of the abbey on the east; the Pump Room, with its inscription 'Water is Best' in Greek on the south; the Colonnade on the west; and a row of shops on the north, between two of which is the archway which Catherine Morland and Isabella Thorpe passed through to Cheap Street.

These then were the main features of the city which Jane Austen knew so well and described so accurately. It is not known when she first visited Bath; there may have been many visits while she was growing up. Her uncle and aunt, Mr and Mrs Leigh Perrot, owned a house at No 1, The Paragon, where the Austens were always made welcome. We do know that Jane certainly stayed there in the last two months of 1797.

In May 1799 there was a change of perspective when she lodged in Queen Square with her mother, brother Edward, his wife and two eldest children, aged five and six. Jane found the situation of Queen Square much more pleasant than that of the Paragon – which, forming a narrow funnel at the end of the main London road into the city, and with the houses on the opposite side of the street towering above by virtue of their hillside position, certainly is rather oppressive. 'We all unite in a dislike of that part of the town', wrote Jane on one occasion.

Queen Square, on the other hand, was 'spacious, open and airy . . . wholesome and agreeable', according to Smollett.[3] He wrote when the square was relatively new; by 1814 it was considered old-fashioned enough for the Miss Musgroves to insist, ' "We must be in a good situation – none of your Queen Squares for us!" ' In 1799, however, Jane asserted stoutly, 'I like our situation very much; it is far more cheerful than the Paragon, and the prospect from the drawing-room window, at which I now write, is rather picturesque, as it commands a perspective view of the left side of Brock Street, broken by three Lombardy poplars in the garden of the last house in Queen's Parade.'

Any trees were welcome to Jane Austen in a town; and she was sufficiently well versed in the rules of the picturesque to know that three was an aesthetically pleasing number. As she made Elizabeth Bennet say to Darcy, who had a Bingley sister hanging on each arm, ' "No, no, stay where you are – you are charmingly grouped, and appear to uncommon advantage. The picturesque would be spoilt by admitting a fourth." '

Bath is the setting for another joke at the expense of the picturesque, when Catherine Morland accompanies Henry and Eleanor Tilney on a walk to Beechen Cliff. The Tilneys call for her at the Allens' lodgings in Great Pulteney Street, from where they descend the steps just before Pulteney Bridge to reach the river, and follow the riverside footpath all the way round the city to the south. Here the view of Beechen Cliff reminds Catherine of the south of France – that is, what she has read about it in novels. The Tilneys, however, have a more educated response to the landscape.

> They were viewing the country with the eyes of persons accustomed to drawing, and decided on its capability of being formed into pictures, with all the eagerness of real taste. Here Catherine was quite lost. She knew nothing of drawing – nothing of taste: and she listened to them with an attention which brought her little profit, for they talked in phrases which conveyed scarcely any idea to her. The little which she could understand however appeared to contradict the very few notions she had entertained on the matter before. It seemed as if a good view were no longer to be taken from the top of an high hill, and that a clear blue sky was no longer proof of a fine day. . . .
>
> She confessed and lamented her want of knowledge; declared that she would give anything in the world to be able to draw; and a lecture on the picturesque immediately followed, in which [Henry's] instructions were so clear that she soon began to see beauty in everything admired by him, and her attention was so earnest, that he became perfectly

satisfied of her having a great deal of natural taste. He talked of fore-grounds, distances and second distances – side screens and perspectives – lights and shades; – and Catherine was so hopeful a scholar, that when they gained the top of Beechen Cliff, she voluntarily rejected the whole city of Bath, as unworthy to make part of a landscape.

These are paragraphs rooted in the eighteenth century. Here is no heartfelt, spontaneous delight in nature such as was to diffuse the later novels of Jane Austen; but an endorsement of the importance of taste, despite the counterbalancing irony. Henry's subsequent 'easy transition from a piece of rocky fragment and the withered oak which he had placed near its summit' shows him in the characteristically eighteenth century act of re-arranging the scenery to improve the picture – possibly even introducing elements which were not there. The view from Beechen Cliff is very lovely, and Catherine's rejection is meant to be amusing; it is also a little dig at Uvedale Price, who in 1798 argued that Bath was not picturesque.

Although Catherine leaves Bath without regret when she, and the narrative, move on to Northanger Abbey, she has experienced no sense of confinement during her sojourn in the city, has indulged in no hankering for the country. There is a fresh and simple enjoyment of the pleasures of Bath in this novel, expressed by Catherine when Henry warns her that it is *de rigeur* to become tired of Bath after six weeks:

'Well, other people must judge for themselves, and those who go to London may think nothing of Bath. But I, who live in a small retired village in the country, can never find greater sameness in such a place as this, than in my own home; for here are a variety of amusements, a variety of things to be seen and done all day long. . . . I really believe I shall always be talking of Bath, when I am at home again – I *do* like it so very much. . . . Oh! who can ever be tired of Bath?'

What Henry Tilney calls Catherine's 'honest relish of balls and plays and everyday sights' recurs no more in Jane Austen's fiction. In *Sense and Sensibility* Bath is where Eliza Williams is allowed to 'range over the town' and falls prey to Willoughby. In *Mansfield Park* Henry Crawford goes there to avoid justifying those expectations which his attentions to Maria Bertram have aroused. In *Emma* Mr Elton and Miss Hawkins, both on the

View of Bath (1794) This was how the city looked when Jane Austen came to know it in the 1790s. A thousand houses were built here in this decade alone, but the surrounding country remained unspoiled

lookout for a good match, meet and become engaged in Bath. And in *Persuasion* the 'littlenesses of a town' are fully exposed.

By this time Bath had become more a place of residence, less a resort. People went there to be 'important at comparatively little expense'. Its character was increasingly one of 'elegant stupidity'. And Jane Austen herself had suffered from being an enforced resident of the town.

In November 1800 Mr and Mrs Austen made the sudden decision to retire from their duties at Steventon and to settle in Bath. That the decision *was* sudden is unquestionable. Earlier that very month they had been making extensive improvements to their garden and buying new furniture for the Rectory. With the exception of one cherished, comfortable bed, all their furniture had to be sold on their removal, the cost of transportation being prohibitive. Books, pictures, piano – everything had to be disposed of, everything amid which Jane had grown up. But it was place, rather than property, which it was such a wrench to her to leave.

She was twenty-five and Cassandra twenty-eight, but they had no choice but to accompany their parents wherever they chose to live. The sisters had made the mistake of both being away from Steventon at once, leaving their parents the privacy to discuss and settle the momentous idea. No wonder that when Jane returned from a visit to Ibthorpe to be greeted airily by her mother with the news, she is said to have fainted away.

It was not only the greatest change that her life had ever known, but a change which was unwelcome in its nature. To exchange the rambling rectory with its gardens and glebe lands, its opportunities for solitude, liberty, the observation of the seasons and the delight of growing things, for a town house without a garden; to exchange the sense of belonging and being useful to a community for the showy, class-ridden, trivial daily round of a town – these were what she deplored. All her letters of the next few weeks to Cassandra at Godmersham were subsequently destroyed. Presumably they contained too much anguish and complaint. By January Jane had managed to reconcile herself to the idea. It is therefore to *Persuasion* that we must look for her true feelings, repressed for the sake of family harmony. Anne Elliot 'disliked Bath, and did not think it agreed with her,' dreaded 'the possible heats of September in all the white glare of Bath' and 'persisted in a very determined, though very silent, disinclination for Bath'.

One of the many things about Bath which Jane Austen did not like was the climate. Low in its bowl of hills, it can be airless and stifling – a 'stewpot', Hester Thrale Piozzi (one-time neighbour of the Austens in Gay Street) called the city. That is when it is not wet. In Jane Austen's letters and novels there are many references to the rain in Bath.

On her arrival in Bath in May 1799 she had written, 'Poor Elizabeth has had a dismal ride of it from Devizes, for it has rained almost all the way, and our first view of Bath has been just as gloomy as it was last November twelvemonth'. Now, on entering the city in May 1801 as a resident, she wrote with some perversity, 'the first view of Bath in fine weather does not answer my expectations; I think I see more distinctly through rain. The sun was got behind everything, and the appearance of the place from the top of Kingsdown was all vapour, shadow, smoke and confusion.'

There is a crossness about the letters written at this period as, from their base at the Paragon, the guest of an aunt she disliked, Jane and her mother looked for a house to rent. (Mr Austen and Cassandra, visiting in Kent, were to join up with them later.) 'Another stupid party last night; perhaps if larger they might be less intolerable, but here there were only just enough to make one card table, with six people to look on, and talk nonsense to each other.' Jane must have felt her time was being dreadfully wasted, and her politeness stretched to breaking-point. 'I cannot anyhow continue to find people agreeable,' she added.

Escaping into the country walks with which the environs of Bath abounded, afforded a certain measure of relief. During the 1799 visit she had made two such walks 'across some fields to the village of Charlcombe, which is sweetly situated in a little green valley, as a village with such a name ought to be', and to Weston, another village, inhabited, apparently, chiefly by laundresses.[4] Now, two years later, the same route was followed:

Our grand walk to Weston was again fixed for yesterday, and was accomplished in a very striking manner; every one of the party declined it under some pretence or other except our two selves, and we had therefore a *tête a tête*; but *that* we should equally have had after the first two yards, had half the inhabitants of Bath set off with us. It would have amused you to see our progress; we went up by Sion Hill, and returned across the fields; in climbing a hill Mrs Chamberlayne is very capital, I could with difficulty keep pace with her – yet would not flinch for the world. On plain ground I was quite her equal – and so we posted away under a fine hot sun, *she* without any parasol or shade to her hat, stopping for nothing; and crossing the churchyard at Weston with as much expedition as if we were afraid of being buried alive. After seeing what she is equal to, I cannot help feeling a regard for her. As to agreeableness, she is much like other people.

Five days later she had a second expedition to report:

I walked yesterday morning with Mrs Chamberlayne to Lyncombe and

Widcombe. . . . Mrs Chamberlayne's pace was not quite so magnificent on this second trial as in the first; it was nothing more than I could keep up with, without effort; and for many, many yards together on a raised narrow footpath I led the way. The walk was very beautiful as my companion agreed, whenever I made the observation. And so ends our friendship, for the Chamberlaynes leave Bath in a day or two.

Lyncombe and Widcombe lie south of the city, in a valley east of Beechen Cliff, and indeed are very beautiful. Here Ralph Allen, one of the creators of Georgian Bath, had built his splendid country house, Prior Park, to display the capabilities of Bath stone, which came from quarries in his possession. Prior Park, where both Alexander Pope and Henry Fielding were visitors, commands a magnificent view down the valley to the city of Bath in the distance.

All the houses which Jane and her mother examined proved to have something wrong with them: they were too small, too damp, or faced the wrong way. Nothing had been found by the time of Cassandra's arrival in the city, after which there are no more letters from Bath. The Austens evidently decided it would be worth paying more and obtaining a house superior to those they had been regarding as within their reach, for they eventually settled at 4, Sydney Place. This was a very desirable situation, in a terrace facing Sydney Gardens and approached from the city via Great Pulteney Street.

This charming town house, on level ground and with a leafy view from its front windows, was Jane's home for three years. Eventually it had to be given up, presumably proving too expensive, and the family moved to Green Park Buildings, in the unfashionable southern part of the city near the river, and which they had formerly rejected as being too damp. Here, in January 1805, Mr Austen died, and was buried in the same church in which he had been married forty years earlier, St Swithins, Walcot Street.

Mrs Austen and her daughters now found their income even more reduced – indeed, it was only through the generosity of all the brothers in making them an annual allowance that they were able to maintain a home at all – and they moved to a series of ever cheaper lodgings – first in Gay Street, and then Trim Street. This insecurity and change of home every six months must have given to Jane's feeling for Bath what the discovery of damp in Green Park Buildings had once given to their views of settling there: the 'coup de grace'.

When she came to write *Persuasion*, therefore, some nine or ten years after leaving the city, her mood was more sombre and her portrayal more critical than in *Northanger Abbey*. Both passages are set in January and February but while that in *Northanger Abbey* has clarity and freshness, that in *Persuasion* is heavy and oppressive with grey skies and rain. Partly this is the result of Jane's greater attention to the seasons which all three late novels evince, partly it is a question of seeing with the heroine's eyes. On 'entering Bath on a wet afternoon', Anne 'caught the first dim view of the extensive buildings, smoking in rain, without any wish of seeing them better. . . .'

Unlike Catherine Morland or Jane Austen herself, Anne has no opportunity to ramble beyond the city. It really is physical as well as social constriction to her. Anne enters her father's house 'with a sinking heart, anticipating an imprisonment of many months, and anxiously saying to herself, "Oh! when shall I leave you again?" '

There is in the Bath scenes of *Persuasion* the constant feeling of being surrounded and hemmed in by crowds of people, and not only in the formal social gatherings. When Anne enters Bath her ears are assailed by 'the bawlings of newsmen, muffin-men and milkmen, and the ceaseless clink of pattens'. On one occasion, as Sir Walter 'stood in a shop in Bond Street, he had counted eighty-seven women go by, one after another, without there being a tolerable face among them . . . There certainly were a dreadful multitude of ugly women in Bath; and as for the men! they were infinitely worse. Such scarecrows as the streets were full of!' In Molland's, the pastry-cooks in Milsom Street, where Anne shelters from the rain, there is a 'little crowd'. When she spots Captain Wentworth in Great Pulteney Street 'there were many other men about him, many groups walking the same way'. It culminates in that memorable scene in which the newly-reconciled lovers, walking from Union Street to the Gravel walk, 'slowly paced the gradual ascent, heedless of every group around them, seeing neither sauntering politicians, bustling housekeepers, flirting girls, nor nursery-maids and children. . . .'

The Gravel Walk runs behind the houses on the south side of Brock Street, connecting the Circus with the Royal Crescent. On the other side of the Royal Crescent, running downhill at right angles to it, is Marlborough Buildings, where the Wallises have their lodgings. This is one of the pleasantest locations in Bath, looking east over the lawns of the Royal Crescent from the front windows and west across undeveloped countryside from the back. Too good for the Wallises! Lady Dalrymple's lodgings are in Laura Place, the diamond-shaped 'square' out of which issues Great Pulteney Street. The White Hart Inn, at which the Musgrove party stays and where Captain Wentworth writes his letter to Anne, is directly opposite the Colonnade and Pump Room. Mary, stationed at her window, can watch the comings and goings at the Pump Room, and sees Mr Elliot meeting Mrs Clay beneath the Colonnade.

Although some further expansion had taken place at the edges, very little had changed in the central part of Bath between the writing of *Northanger Abbey* and *Persuasion*. Laid out and built up with Georgian

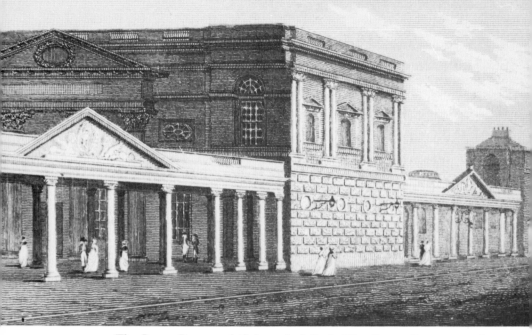

The Pump Room and Colonnade (1803) The Pump Room was the favourite meeting place of Catherine Morland and Isabella Thorpe; while under the Colonnade, Mr Elliot and Mrs Clay were observed in their clandestine assignation

standards of town planning and architecture, a memorial in stone to the ideas of those who created it, there was little scope for improvement. But one change was made, and it can be traced in the two novels. For many decades the Bear Inn and its yards stood between the Baths and Pump Room and the new streets of the upper town. Matthew Bramble, in *Humphrey Clinker*, complained that from Queen Square 'communication with the Baths is through the yard of an inn, where the poor trembling valetudinarian is carried in a chair, betwixt the heels of a double row of horses, wincing under the curry-combs of grooms and postillions, over and above the hazard of being obstructed, or overturned, by the carriages which are continually making their exit or entrance'. The alternative access was through the pedestrian-only Union Passage, termed in *Northanger Abbey* 'that interesting alley'. In 1806 the Bear Inn was demolished, and Union Street cut through, parallel to Union Passage. The last remnant of inconvenient old Bath had been tidied away. Appropriately, in *Persuasion*, it is in Union Street that the lovers are united, with 'smiles reined in and spirits dancing in private rapture' as Charles Musgrove leaves them together, to visit a gunsmith in the Market Place.

Mary Musgrove speaks of the 'nice pavements' of Bath, but when Anne is indulging in 'musings of high-wrought love and constancy' in her walk from Camden Place to Westgate buildings, 'it was almost enough to spread purification and perfume all the way'. Presumably Jane Austen felt the streets of Bath would have benefited from such.

In Westgate Buildings Anne visits her old school friend, now in distressed circumstances. Mrs Smith, 'a poor infirm, helpless widow' has come to Bath for the sake of the bathing 'and was now in lodgings near the hot-baths, living in a very humble way, unable even to afford herself the comfort of a servant, and of course almost excluded from society'.

This lodging in Westgate Buildings is the most miserable 'home' which Jane Austen portrayed: 'her accommodations were limited to a noisy parlour, and a dark bedroom behind'. Sir Walter is suitably 'severe' when he discovers where Anne has been.

'Westgate Buildings!' said he; 'and who is Miss Anne Elliot to be visiting in Westgate Buildings? A Mrs Smith. . . . And what is her attraction? That she is old and sickly. Upon my word, Miss Anne Elliot, you have the most extraordinary taste! Everything that revolts other people, low company, paltry rooms, foul air, disgusting associations are inviting to you. . . . Westgate Buildings must have been rather surprised by the appearance of a carriage drawn up near its pavement!'

The Austens had considered Westgate Buildings themselves. In 1801, before leaving Steventon, Jane had written, 'Westgate Buildings, though quite in the lower part of the town are not badly situated themselves; the street is broad and has rather a good appearance.'

Perhaps in *Persuasion* she was exploring how low the unsupported woman, without the security of a private fortune, could sink. 'Single women have a dreadful propensity for being poor', she admitted in 1817, just six months after completing *Persuasion*. Her own maintenance depended on her brothers' generosity; the security and stability of the Steventon days was over.

6

Devon and Dorset:
The Romance of the West Country

There is a pleasure in the pathless woods.
There is a rapture on the lonely shore,
There is society, where none intrudes,
By the deep Sea, and music in its roar:
I love not Man the less, but Nature more,
From these our interviews . . .
    Lord Byron, *Childe Harold*, 1812

When, in the closing months of the eighteenth century, Mr and Mrs Austen made their decision to retire to Bath, an intrinsic part of the plan was that they should escape from the heat of the city every summer by taking a seaside holiday. It was, indeed, this element that consoled Jane for all the rest. 'The prospect of spending future summers by the sea or in Wales is very delightful', she wrote in anticipation. The family never did venture into Wales, but for the next few years, until they were living on the coast themselves at Southampton, they spent several weeks every summer in one of the newly fashionable West Country resorts.

As a concept, the annual seaside holiday was still quite new, and it was rather enterprising of Jane's parents, in their old age, to adopt the novel habit. For the greater part of the eighteenth century the places to go, when one wanted a change from home, had been the inland spas – Bath and its imitators. Then the idea of a holiday was to meet and mix with other people: to exercise good manners: to see and be seen. But the highly civilized, highly sociable lifestyle was losing its appeal. An expansion in the population, and particularly in the leisured, affluent part of the population, was putting pressure on the cities, weakening their exclusivity, and throwing a wholly new charm over the notions of solitude and escape. People whose parents and grandparents had marvelled over the clean pavements, the good shops, the highly organized assemblies of Bath, now were beginning to seek out natural beauty, wildness and seclusion. We have been endeavouring to get away from each other ever since.

In this sense Jane Austen stands exactly balanced between the eighteenth century way of thinking and the nineteenth. Her preference for the country, her scorn of the empty civilities of town life, find unequivocal expression in both her letters and her novels; yet she could never be so lost to nature as to forget, even for a moment, the claims of society upon her. Indeed, village life was preferred by her precisely (though not exclusively) because it enabled people to fulfil their social duties more meaningfully; and her suspicion of some of the excesses of enthusiasm for nature expressed in her time, was a shrinking from putting the self, the individual's response, before anything else. From Marianne and her useless passion for dead leaves, to the farmer in *Persuasion* 'meaning to have spring again', all her novels tend to this view; nevertheless there was a discernible shift, and her experiences in Devon and Dorset can be seen to have done much to create it.

> And all, impatient of dry land, agree
> With one consent to rush into the sea,

wrote Cowper, one of Jane's favourite poets, of the new trend. In 1789 George III put the royal stamp of approval on the idea when he recuperated his health at Weymouth – which place, some sixty years earlier, Defoe had only been able grudgingly to describe as 'a clean agreeable town, considering its low situation so near the sea'. Now Weymouth attracted rich visitors, and a host of other places expanded themselves in competition. 'Since George III introduced the fashion of regularly going to the southern coast for health, doctors have been advising it in all consumptive cases. The particular spot designated for this purpose,' wrote Dr Granville, 'has extended west and south, farther and farther every eight or ten years; from Weymouth to Sidmouth, from Sidmouth to Exmouth, and so on to Dawlish and Teignmouth. . . .'[1] The Austens were to visit most of these resorts in the early years of the nineteenth century.

As had been the case with the inland spas, the quest for health was the ostensible motive for visiting them, though the quest for pleasure and fresh experience was not far behind. Sea-bathing was considered to be particularly efficacious if undertaken in cold weather and early in the morning, when the pores were supposed to be closed. Accordingly, the first seaside holidays were often taken at unseasonable times of the year. Fanny Burney described such a visit to Brighton in November 1782: 'We rose at six o'clock in the morn and by the pale blink o' the moon went to the seaside where we had bespoken the bathing-woman to be ready for us, and into the ocean we plunged. It was cold but pleasant. I have bathed so often as to lose my dread of the operation.'[2]

Even more horrific was the case of Jane's own cousin, Eliza, who spent January and February 1791 at Margate for the sake of her sickly little son. A doctor had assured her that 'one month's bathing at this time of year was more efficacious than six at any other. . . . The sea has strengthened him wonderfully and I think has likewise been of great service to myself. I still continue bathing notwithstanding the severity of the weather and frost and snow, which is I think somewhat courageous.'[3]

The medical profession liked to keep the direction of sea-bathing under their own control; Dr Russell, one of its earliest advocates, advised that though 'sea-water is embued with many and great virtues, the unskilful may make a very bad use'.[4] Such cautions influenced even such an experienced bather as Fanny Burney. At Sidmouth, in 1792, in the favourable month of August, with the sea 'calm and gentle as the Thames', she longed to bathe, but 'having no advice at hand, I ran no risk.'

In *Persuasion* Mary Musgrove – no stoic – enjoys bathing in the latter half of November. But the resort of Lyme is portrayed as 'deserted and melancholy' then, the assembly rooms shut up, 'the lodgers almost all gone': evidently, by 1814, the season had shifted somewhat. September and October seem to have been the Austens' own favourite holiday months, though one year at least they were still at the coast as late as the first week in November.

Perhaps, like Anne Elliot, the Austens 'dreaded the possible heats of September in all the white glare of Bath', and perhaps it was during these four consecutive autumns spent in the genial climate of the west that Jane came especially to love 'the influence so sweet and so sad of the autumnal months in the country'. The sharp mornings melting into mild days, the often very blue skies and seas showing to advantage the changing tints of the foliage, make these very lovely months indeed along the coast of Devon and Dorset.

A hankering for the sea in fact slightly pre-dated the Austens' decision to retire to Bath, for 'the Dawlish scheme' as Jane termed it was under discussion in November 1800, while the improvements in the garden at Steventon which we have noted were in progress. 'I have had a most affectionate letter from Buller', Jane wrote to Cassandra that month: Richard Buller being a former pupil of George Austen, son of a Bishop of Exeter, recently married and appointed Vicar of Colyton, in East Devon. 'He is very pressing in his invitation to us all to come and see him at Colyton, and my father is very much inclined to go there next summer – it is a circumstance that may considerably assist the Dawlish scheme.' (And a tribute, surely, to George Austen's pleasantness as a teacher.)

Perhaps Dawlish was the first place the Austens thought of for a holiday – its fame was such that Jane Austen could poke fun at Robert Ferrars' littleness of mind by saying, 'it seemed rather surprising to him that anybody could live in Devonshire, without living near Dawlish'. However, it was soon obvious that it would be a great deal more convenient to combine Colyton (a lovely village of mainly Tudor architecture, parts of the vicarage dating back to 1529) with Sidmouth, on the same side of the Exe estuary. 'Sidmouth is now talked of as our summer abode,' reported

*Sidmouth (c.*1810) Jane Austen's first holiday in Devon was spent here in 1801. Note the rail for tethering horses, and the bathing machines

Jane in January, by which time plans for the removal to Bath were well advanced. As we have seen, the Austens spent the early part of the summer house-hunting in Bath; having taken a lease from Michaelmas, they set off for their first holiday by the sea. This is confirmed in a letter written by Eliza on 29 October 1801. 'I conclude that you know of our uncle and aunt Austen and their daughters having spent the summer in Devonshire. They are now returned to Bath where they are superintending the fitting up of their new house. Their eldest son James,' she adds, incidentally, 'is now in possession of Steventon, where he has made such alterations and embellishments that it is almost a pretty place – not however that I have seen it.'[5] Odd how nobody but Jane ever seemed satisfied with the Rectory – which continued to be tinkered with for another twenty-five years, until it was considered by Edward, its then owner, and about to install his own son as rector, as 'unworthy of being the Rectory house of a family living, and ... it was pulled down for the purpose of erecting a new house in a far better situation.'[6]

An anonymous *Guide to All the Watering and Sea-Bathing Places* published in 1810, though a little later than the date of Jane's West Country visits, is invaluable for helping us to recapture the distinctive character of the various resorts which she was to come to know. Of Sidmouth it says,

As a watering-place it is now much frequented, the company every season generally amounting to three hundred. With respect to accommodation, Sidmouth has to boast of an elegant ball-room; and on the beach a commodious tea-room and shed frequented by ladies as well as gentlemen. Neither should be overlooked the livery stables, nearly opposite the London Inn, a neat circular building, with a fountain in the centre.

The inhabitants are remarkable for their healthy appearance, and for their longevity. Such, indeed, might be naturally expected, from the suitability of the air, the fine dry soil, and a situation the most delicious, open to the ocean, yet not subject to fogs, and screened from all but the southern winds. The rides and walks about Sidmouth are very pleasant, and at every turn present a variety of romantic and beautiful views.

The Austens liked Devon enough to return the following year, and this time they did stay at Dawlish, and perhaps Teignmouth too, on the stretch of coastline notable for its red cliffs. Teignmouth lay on the mouth of a river, busy with fishing vessels; an early (1773) visitor to the resort had been Fanny Burney, who had marvelled at the sight of the village women, bare-legged, drawing in the nets – a sight still popular with visitors in 1810. The topography of its neighbour Dawlish was more intimate if less lively, with a narrow stream meandering between grassy banks down the length of the village to the sea. Both places were beginning to acquire, in addition to their native thatch and cob cottages, a sprinkling of new terraces, and villas fit for visitors of quality.

According to the *Guide* of 1810:

Dawlish is delightfully situate in a valley, on all sides surrounded by high grounds, except towards the east, which opens towards the cerulean expanse; fronting which, on the strand, are some good lodging-houses. Further up the vale a range of neat buildings present themselves; among which are two inns, with tolerable accommodations.

Dawlish (*c*.1830) The natural beauties of Dawlish are apparent from this view, but there were fewer buildings when Jane passed the summer of 1802 here

Opposite is an overshoot water-mill, which has a very romantic effect; higher up, where the valley contracts, are several genteel lodging-houses, facing the sea; and each possessing a small plat before it, neatly railed in.

From hence to the church is a continuation of straggling cottages on each side of the road for a space of half a mile. Here we come to a bridge, contiguous to which is another mill, and two pleasant dwelling houses. The manor house, with its bell cupola, and high poplars, increases the beauty of the picture; while the church, a handsome Gothic pile, with its surrounding elm-rows, gives a kind of finish to the scene.

The bathing machines are numerous, and well-conducted. The beach in front of the lodging-houses has a gentle descent to the sea, which is generally pure and clear. The promenade is kept in excellent repair, and extends in a straight line across the strand. It may be lengthened at pleasure by a ramble under the cliffs which are here bold, precipitous and of a tremendous height.

At first it was resorted to by those who wished for more retirement than they could enjoy at well-frequented places; but by degrees, its pure salubrious air, the conveniences it afforded for bathing, and its natural beauties, pointed it out as an eligible summer retreat.

The new buildings, such as they were in 1802, were in the pretty, playful style of architecture so appropriate at a seaside place. A house on a larger scale at Dawlish, and in the height of fashion architecturally, was Luscombe Castle, designed by John Nash, and built during 1800–1801. Since this was the summer home of Charles Hoare, a member of the London banking family patronized by the Austens, it is possible that Jane visited Luscombe. Standing in a deeply wooded valley at the back of the town, it is an early essay in the picturesque, unusual because it is asymmetrical, with castellations, short square tower, and large windows divided by stone tracery. Nash was to build many such 'castle' houses; this was one of his earliest. The grounds were landscaped by Humphry Repton, who was in partnership with Nash for a short period.

Among the amenities which a resort had to offer if it hoped to attract visitors was a library. The existence or otherwise of a library is mentioned again and again in the 1810 *Guide*. At Dawlish 'the library was particularly pitiful and wretched twelve years ago', recalled Jane in August 1814. She has been asked to read the opening chapters of a novel written by her niece Anna, set in Dawlish, to which Anna had never been. 'I am not sensible of any blunders about Dawlish,' Jane assured her, but she did correct her on one or two points. 'Lyme is towards forty miles distant from Dawlish and would not be talked of there – I have put Starcross instead. If you prefer

Exeter, that must always be safe. . . . They must be *two* days going from Dawlish to Bath; they are nearly one hundred miles apart.'

In 1803 the Austens chose to stay at Lyme, in Dorset, and they were still there on 5 November to witness a great fire that broke out of control. Writing five years later of a fire at Southampton, Jane said, 'the flames were considerable, they seemed about as near to us as those at Lyme, and to reach higher.'

Again the 1810 *Guide* sets the scene for us:

Lyme is built on the declivity of a craggy hill, at the head of an inlet of the sea, and contains many respectable looking houses, with pleasant gardens, particularly in the upper part of the town; but the streets are steep, rugged and unpleasant. In the lower part the houses are mean, and the streets so intricate, that a stranger, it has been wittily remarked, will sometimes find himself bewildered, as if he were entangled in a forest, or the labyrinth of a fox-den. Here the lower order of the inhabitants in general reside, having that position which nature and fortune assigned to them. To be a person of consideration at Lyme, it is necessary to toil up hill, and to fix one's abode where it is in danger of being assailed by every wind that blows.

Altogether, however, Lyme is not an unpleasant place for company in the bathing season, for whose use and accommodation several machines are erected on the beach, which is pebbly, and consequently uncomfortable for walking. Lyme has a small Assembly Room, Card-Room and Billiard table, conveniently arranged under one roof; and had the library been joined to it, all the amusement which the place can furnish would have been comprised in one building. The situation for this edifice is happily chosen, as it commands a charming marine view as far as the Isle of Portland, eight leagues off, and the interior is compact and well arranged.

The Golden Lion and the Three Cups are respectable Inns, and lodgings may generally be procured on easy terms. Lodgings and boarding at Lyme are not merely reasonable, they are even cheap; the dissipations for the healthy, and the suitable accommodation for the sick, are within the reach of ordinary resources. It is frequented principally by persons in the middle class of life. . . . The resources for intellectual improvement or gratification are here pretty much what they are in places of a similar nature: the libraries are neither copious nor select; although principally composed of novels, many of the best even in that class of books are wanting.

This is an unusually jaundiced tone for the *Guide* to take, and it found no echo in Jane Austen. Her affectionate and durable feelings for Lyme were to find expression, some thirteen years later, in the pages of *Persuasion*, and particularly in the passage in which she allows herself, uncharacteristically, to stray away from her characters:

> ... as there is nothing to admire in the buildings themselves, the remarkable situation of the town, the principal street almost hurrying into the water, the walk to the Cobb, skirting round the pleasant little bay, which in the season is animated with bathing machines and company, the Cobb itself, its old wonders and new improvements, with the very beautiful line of cliffs stretching out to the east of the town, are what the stranger's eye will seek; and a very strange stranger it must be, who does not see charms in the immediate environs of Lyme, to make him wish to know it better. The scenes in its neighbourhood, Charmouth, with its high grounds and extensive sweeps of country, and still more its sweet retired bay, backed by dark cliffs, where fragments of low rock among the sands make it the happiest spot for watching the flow of the tide, for sitting in unwearied contemplation; the woody varieties of the cheerful village of Up Lyme, and above all, Pinny, with its green chasms between romantic rocks, where the scattered forest trees and orchards of luxuriant growth declare that many a generation must have passed away since the first partial falling of the cliff prepared the ground for such a state, where a scene so wonderful and so lovely is exhibited, as may more than equal any of the resembling scenes of the far-famed Isle of Wight: these places must be visited, and visited again, to make the worth of Lyme understood.'

There is nothing else like this in the whole of Jane Austen's writing: nothing so indulgent, so irrelevant to the characters, so free of irony or reservation, so detailed and descriptive – so didactic, even. It is proof of the remarkable effect which Lyme in particular, and the sea in general, wrought upon her. She permits herself a little further intrusion in the next paragraph, when her characters linger on the shore 'as all must linger and gaze on a first return to the sea, who ever deserve to look at it at all'.

It was evidently the 'romantic' and 'wonderful' stretches of the untamed coastline that appealed to her; once a fishing village had become so fashionable, crowded and built-up that it was just another social centre she regarded it with as much distaste as she did Bath. Weymouth, a few miles from Lyme, came into this category; as we have seen, it had been one of the first resorts to become popular, and it was still patronized by royalty in Jane Austen's time. Charlotte Jennings visited her uncle at Weymouth; Tom Bertram idled six weeks there; and part of Mr Knightley's condemnation of Frank Churchill, before he has even met him, is, 'we hear of him for ever at some watering-place or other. A little while ago, he was at Weymouth', where, of course, he formed the illicit engagement to Jane Fairfax which is productive of so much unhappiness.

On the principal that Lyme 'must be visited, and visited again', the Austens returned in 1804, in company with Henry and Eliza. It would seem that the choice of destination had at one time been between Weymouth and Lyme; that all six were together at Lyme, and that Jane and her parents remained there while the other three spent a few days at Weymouth.

'Your account of Weymouth contains nothing which strikes me so forcibly as there being no ice in the town',

Jane wrote to Cassandra from Lyme on 14 September.

For every other vexation I was in some measure prepared, and particularly for your disappointment in not seeing the Royal Family go on board on Tuesday, having already heard from Mr Crawford that he had seen you in the very act of being too late, but for there being no ice what could prepare me? Weymouth is altogether a shocking place, I perceive, without recommendation of any kind, and worthy only of being frequented by the inhabitants of Gloucester. I am really very glad that we did not go there, and that Henry and Eliza saw nothing in it to make them feel differently.

Certainly Weymouth at this time would not have suited Jane at all. *The Western Flying Post* for 10 September 1804 gives this account (and explains Jane's joke about Gloucester):

Weymouth, September 8th. Arrived here this town's original patron, his Royal Highness the Duke of Gloucester, on a visit to the Royal Family, all of whom, we are happy to observe, enjoy good health and spirits. The king rises very early and visits the camps before breakfast, then embarks with the family for a cruise in the Royal Sovereign yacht, attended by the two others, the frigates, and a fleet of yachts of every description, returns to an evening parade and lastly visits the theatre. This is making the most of his time. The town was never known to be fuller of company than this season, since the Royal Family has been here.

The mention of camps and parades reminds us that this was the height of the Napoleonic invasion scare – that a flotilla of troop-carrying barges was believed to be assembled in a French port – and that Jane's own brother Captain Francis Austen had been employed until May of that year

Weymouth (1810) One of the most fashionable and frequented of seaside resorts in the Regency period, Weymouth was the scene of Frank Churchill's secret engagement to Jane Fairfax

in organizing a corps of 'sea fencibles' to defend the coast around Ramsgate, and was now commanding a ship blockading Boulogne. The Georgians certainly did not allow this serious threat to their national security to interfere with their carefree enjoyment of life; indeed, one gains the impression that the military presence added a pleasantly patriotic spice to the other pleasures of the coastline for some people.

Jane's letter of 14 September, already quoted from, is the only one to survive from any of their seaside lodgings, and it is valuable for the glimpses it gives of the quiet tenor of the Austens' daily life on holiday. It would seem that following the departure of half their party to Weymouth, the remainder had moved into smaller lodgings, with their servants James, Jenny and Molly:

We are quite settled in our lodgings by this time as you may suppose, and everything goes on in the usual order. The servants behave very well, and make no difficulties, though nothing certainly can exceed the inconvenience of the offices, except the general dirtiness of the house and furniture and all its inhabitants. Hitherto the weather has been just what we could wish – the continuance of the dry season is very necessary to our comfort. I endeavour as far as I can to supply your place and be useful, and keep things in order. . . .

The Ball last night was pleasant, but not full for Thursday. My father stayed very contentedly till half past nine (we went a little after eight), and then walked home with James and a lanthorn, though I believe the lanthorn was not lit, as the moon was up; but this lanthorn may sometimes be a great convenience to him. My mother and I stayed about an hour later. . . . I called yesterday on Miss Armstrong. . . . We afterwards walked together for an hour on the Cobb. . . .

The bathing was so delightful this morning and Molly so pressing with me to enjoy myself that I believe I stayed in rather too long, as since the middle of the day I have felt unreasonably tired. I shall be more careful another time, and shall not bathe tomorrow as I had before intended. Jenny and James are walked to Charmouth this afternoon. I am very glad to have such an amusement for him, as I am very anxious for his being at once quiet and happy. He can read, and I must get him some books.

The picture of George Austen, walking home in the moonlight with the protection – probably the arm to lean on – of a servant, is the last we have of him; he died the following January in Bath. Mrs Austen's sons, with the exception of Charles, who was serving abroad and was still very poor, all offered to contribute an annual sum towards the maintenance of their mother and sisters. Henry, sounding horribly like John Dashwood, though surely possessing very different feelings, calculated that Mrs Austen 'will be in receipt of a clear 450 pounds per annum – she will be very comfortable, and as a smaller establishment will be as agreeable to them, as it cannot but be feasible, I really think that my mother and sisters will be full as rich as ever. They will not only suffer no personal deprivation but will be able to pay occasional visits of health and pleasure to their friends.'[7]

Happily this was the case, and thanks to her brothers' generosity Jane was able to continue to improve her knowledge of England. The summer following her father's death, so that they need not lack their annual escape from Bath, Edward proposed to escort them on holiday. That April Jane received a letter from Henry in which 'he offers to meet us on the sea-coast if the plan, of which Edward gave him some hint, takes place. Will not this be making the execution of such a plan, more desirable and delightful than ever. He talks of the rambles we took together last summer with pleasing affection.' Worthing, not too great a distance from Edward's home in Kent, and Henry's in London, was chosen for the holiday of 1805: Jane visited Devon and Dorset no more, but the memory of their natural beauty remained vividly within her, as we have seen from the passage in *Persuasion*.

One of the reasons that it did so may have been that, for a period that was all too brief, she saw the landscape of the West Country through the eyes of someone in love. On one of these four annual holidays she is believed to have met a young man who gained and returned her affection, and who was, even in Cassandra's fastidious opinion, worthy of exciting it. They arranged to meet again, but shortly afterwards he died. It is an insubstantial story, with no firm details, no documentary evidence, only a family tradition originating in a remark by Cassandra in her old age; there might be nothing in it at all; but most people who have studied and written about Jane Austen's life find it hard to resist the idea of her discovering romance amid scenes which she herself called romantic. The added depth which such an experience at such an age (about the same as Anne Elliot) would give to her response to nature may certainly be traced if we compare the Devonshire scenes of *Sense and Sensibility* with the Dorset ones of *Persuasion*.

Barton, in the earlier novel, is an intellectual landscape, not an emotional one. Its function is to explore ideas rather than to embody or illuminate the spiritual condition of the characters. Thus it is plainly set before us, admirably Devonshire in its character, certainly, but offered as a pretext for the discussions of the picturesque which are to follow.

The situation of the house was good. High hills rose immediately behind, and at no great distance on either side; some of which were open downs, the others cultivated and woody. The village of Barton was chiefly on one of these hills, and formed a pleasant view from the cottage windows. The prospect in front was more extensive; it commanded the whole of the valley, and reached into the country beyond. The hills which surrounded the cottage terminated the valley in that direction; under another name, and in another course, it branched out again between two of the steepest of them.

The subject of the picturesque was very topical when Jane Austen was writing *Sense and Sensibility* in the 1790s. Not only Gilpin, but many other even more didactic writers were engrossed by it. Uvedale Price's *Essay on the Picturesque* came out in 1794 and was filled with such elevated generalizations as 'Picturesqueness . . . appears to hold a station between beauty and sublimity. . . . It is the coquetry of nature; it makes beauty more amusing, more varied, more playful. . . .' Price's friend Richard Payne Knight published *The Landscape, a Didactic Poem* the same year, advocating roughness and intricacy at the expense of well-kept lawns and tidy homesteads. Jane Austen's description of the Dashwoods' Devonshire home, 'As a cottage it was defective, for the building was regular, the roof was tiled, the window shutters were not painted green, nor were the walls covered with honeysuckle', presumably owes something to Knight's lines:

Nor yet unenvy'd, to whose humbler lot
Falls the retired and antiquated cot;
Its roof with weeds and mosses cover'd o'er,
And honeysuckles climbing round the door;
While mantling vines along its walls are spread,
And clust'ring ivy decks the chimney's head.

Humphry Repton answered what he took to be personal criticism of his own taste by Price and Knight in these works with his *Sketches and Hints on Landscape Gardening* the following year; and John Aiken had published a poem critical of the picturesque didacticism in 1791. In *Picturesque; A Fragment* he wrote of 'the grave doctrines of the modern sage' and of 'Taste's great arbiter, too learned far to feel a vulgar joy'.

New follies spring; and now we must be taught
To judge of prospects by an artist's rules,
And Picturesque's the word.

Against this background then, and stimulated by these divergent and intensely-held views, Jane Austen wove the subject into *Sense and Sensibility*. She had an opinion of her own to offer, and made Edward Ferrars her mouthpiece. Here is Marianne attempting to instil into Edward some of her own ardour, and he sturdily resisting her:

'Now Edward', said she, calling his attention to the prospect, 'here is Barton valley. Look up it, and be tranquil if you can. Look at those hills! Did you ever see their equals? To the left is Barton Park, amongst those woods and plantations. You may see one end of the house. And there, beneath that farthest hill, which rises with such grandeur, is our cottage.'
    'It is a beautiful country,' he replied, 'but these bottoms must be dirty in winter.'
    'How can you think of dirt, with such objects before you?'
    'Because,' replied he, smiling, 'among the rest of the objects before me, I see a very dirty lane.'

Edward, teasing Marianne just as Jane Austen is teasing her readers, provoking them to re-examine the validity of their own responses, is not indifferent to natural beauty: that would indeed be reprehensible. (Fanny and John Dashwood, clearing away the old walnut trees and thorn bushes at Norland to erect a brash greenhouse that will be seen from all over the estate, are shown for the insensitive beings they are.) Edward, and Elinor by implication, admire the English landscape, but, to borrow a phrase from elsewhere in the novel, 'admire it no more than is proper': that is quietly, privately, without excessive enthusiasm, and *for the right reasons*. Rapture, irrational rapture, is regarded by their author with suspicion. It is perilously close to the profession of false sentiment. Edward's description of Barton, 'it exactly answers my idea of a fine country, because it unites beauty with utility', is surely endorsed by the youthful Jane Austen, at a time of her life when she had read and reasoned rather more than she had observed and felt. A solitary walk has revealed Edward's true appreciation of the scenery about Barton, though Marianne's eager enquiries immediately put him on the defensive:

> Edward returned to them with fresh admiration of the surrounding country; in his walk to the village, he had seen many parts of the valley to advantage; and the village itself, in a much higher situation than the cottage, afforded a general view of the whole, which had exceedingly pleased him. This was a subject which ensured Marianne's attention, and she was beginning to describe her own admiration of these scenes, and to question him more minutely on the objects that had particularly struck him, when Edward interrupted her by saying, 'You must not enquire too far, Marianne – remember I have no knowledge in the picturesque, and I shall offend you by my ignorance and want of taste if we come to particulars. I shall call hills steep, which ought to be bold; surfaces strange and uncouth, which ought to be irregular and rugged; and distant objects out of sight, which ought only to be indistinct through the soft medium of a hazy atmosphere. You must be satisfied with such admiration as I can honestly give. I call it a very fine country – the hills are steep, the woods seem full of fine timber, and the valley looks comfortable and snug – with rich meadows and several neat farm houses scattered here and there. It exactly answers my idea of a very fine country, because it unites beauty with utility – and I dare say it is a picturesque one too, because you admire it; I can easily believe it to be full of rocks and promontories, grey moss and brushwood, but these are all lost on me. I know nothing of the picturesque.'

Edward's own language proves that he is fully conversant with the terminology of the picturesque; however,

> 'I am afraid it is but too true,' said Marianne, 'but why should you boast of it?'
> 'I suspect,' said Elinor, 'that to avoid one kind of affectation, Edward here falls into another. Because he believes many people pretend to more admiration of the beauties of nature than they really feel, and is disgusted with such pretensions, he affects greater indifference and

less discrimination in viewing them himself than he possesses. He is fastidious and will have an affectation of his own.'

'It is very true,' said Marianne, 'that admiration of landscape scenery is become a mere jargon. Everybody pretends to feel and tries to describe with the taste and elegance of him who first defined what picturesque beauty was. I detest jargon of every kind, and sometimes I have kept my feelings to myself, because I could find no language to describe them but what was worn and hackneyed out of all sense and meaning.'

'I am convinced,' said Edward, 'that you really feel all the delight in a fine prospect which you profess to feel. But, in return, your sister must allow me to feel no more than I profess. I like a fine prospect, but not on picturesque principles. I do not like crooked, twisted, blasted trees. I admire them much more if they are tall, straight and flourishing. I do not like ruined, tattered cottages. I am not fond of nettles, or thistles, or heath blossoms. I have more pleasure in a snug farmhouse than a watch-tower – and a troop of tidy, happy villagers please me better than the finest banditti in the world.'

Edward certainly knew his Gilpin. 'The wild and rough parts of nature produce the strongest effects on the imagination; and we may add, they are the only objects in landscape, which please the picturesque eye. Everything trim, and smooth, and neat, affects it coolly', he wrote in *Remarks on Forest Scenery* of 1794; and his *Western Tour*, published four years later, laid it down that 'A distance must stretch away many leagues from the eye; it must consist of various intermediate parts; it must be enriched by numerous objects, which lose by degrees all form and distinctness; and finally perhaps terminate in faint purple mountains, or perhaps mix with the blue mists of ether, before it can pretend to the character of grandeur.'

But Edward's best joke was made at the expense of Gilpin's fondness for banditti. In an early work, his *Essay on Prints*, he had written of his favourite artist, Salvator,

His figures which he drew in exquisite taste are graceful and nobly expressive, beautifully grouped, and varied into the most agreeable attitudes. . . . We are told that he spent the early part of his life in a troop of banditti: and that the rocky and desolate scenes, in which he was accustomed to take refuge, furnished him with those romantic ideas of landskip, of which he is so exceedingly fond, and in the description of which he so greatly excels.

Salvator's scenes were Italian, but Gilpin advocated (and himself employed) banditti in English scenes too:

> 'milkmaids, ploughmen, reapers and all peasants engaged in their several professions we disallow. There are modes of landscape, to which they are adapted: but in the scenes we here characterize, they are valued for what in real life they are despised – loitering idly about, without employment. In wild and desert scenes, we are best pleased with banditti-soldiers, if not in regimentals, and such figures as coalesce in idea with the scenes in which we place them',

he wrote in *Instruction for Examining Landscape.*

Jane Austen was not the only person to find this ridiculous. Humphry Repton, in his *Sketches and Hints* of 1795, expressed the view that 'scenes of horror, well calculated for the residence of banditti' did not suit the needs of his patrons, and that such scenes would be 'absurd, incongruous and out of character . . . in the garden of a villa near the capital, or in the more tame, yet interesting pleasure grounds which I am frequently called upon to decorate'.

It is notable that in *Sense and Sensibility* there is no longing for the sea. Although Sir John Middleton is forever conducting parties of young people about the country on schemes of pleasure, not even Marianne expresses a desire to travel the very moderate distance which would have brought them to the coast. Barton 'four miles northwards of Exeter', can be only fourteen or fifteen miles from Dawlish – but that place is reserved, in the novel, for the honeymoon of vulgar Lucy Steele and foolish Robert Ferrars. The only use which is made of the sea is extremely utilitarian: the Dashwoods' furniture arrives from Sussex 'by water' – an interesting reflection on the state of the roads in the 1790s.

In contrast, none of the novels written after Jane Austen had seen the sea for herself is free from its powerful and pervading influence. It is the sea which makes Portsmouth at all bearable to Fanny; Emma feels deprived because she has never seen it; the characters in *Persuasion* are allowed to delight in it unreservedly, and *Sanditon*, drawing back somewhat from the romantic and unironic tone of *Persuasion*, yet takes a seaside resort as its very subject, as if under some impulse irresistible.

We have already seen how the description of Lyme, on its introduction into the novel, exceeds what is strictly necessary to the plot. The whole of the two-chapter passage at Lyme is possessed of a remarkable integration of feeling and place. 'The grandeur of the country, and the retirement of Lyme in the winter' are 'exactly adapted to' the mood of this novel, the most poetic, in two senses, of Jane Austen's work. Her own writing attains a poetic quality, and poetry is often the subject of her characters' thoughts.

In the country around Uppercross Anne repeats to herself lines of poetry, and at Lyme she finds herself discussing poetry, 'the richness of the present age', with Captain Benwick. On their last walk along the Cobb, 'Anne found Captain Benwick again drawing near her. Lord Byron's "dark blue seas" could not fail of being brought forward by their present view.'[8]

The association of the landscape, the season, the emotions and poetry which is dwelt on during the walk to Winthrop prepare the way for these scenes at Lyme.

> Anne's object was, not to be in the way of anybody. . . . Her *pleasure* in the walk must arise from the exercise and the day, from the view of the last smiles of the year upon the tawny leaves and withered hedges, and from repeating to herself some few of the thousand poetical descriptions extant of autumn, that season of peculiar and inexhaustible influence on the mind of taste and tenderness, that season which has drawn from every poet, worthy of being read, some attempt at description, or some lines of feeling. She occupied her mind as much as possible in such like musings and quotations

until she overhears a compliment paid by Captain Wentworth to Louisa Musgrove.

> Anne could not immediately fall into a quotation again. The sweet scenes of autumn were for a while put by – unless some tender sonnet, fraught with the apt analogy of the declining year, with declining happiness, and the images of youth and hope, and spring, all gone together, blessed her memory.

It is characteristic of Jane Austen that self-absorption should be immediately checked by 'another half-mile of gradual ascent through large enclosures, where the ploughs at work, and the fresh-made path spoke the farmer, counteracting the sweets of poetical despondence, and meaning to have spring again'. And so, as foreshadowed, when Anne reaches Lyme nature invigorates her, sea-breezes restore her bloom, and she begins the process of 'being blest by a second youth'. She is like Dr Shirley, who 'declares himself, that being by the sea, always makes him feel young again.'

There is great affection in Jane Austen's portrait of Lyme. Captain Harville's contrivances to make his 'small house, near the foot of an old pier of unknown date', comfortable and secure, and to 'defend the windows and doors against the winter storms to be expected', and above

Lyme Regis (1810) Jane Austen spent two happy holidays here, in 1803 and 1804, and made it the setting for a moving and memorable portion of *Persuasion*

all his hospitality 'from the heart' are offered for total approbation; and there is no irony in Anne and Henrietta's enjoyment of their pre-breakfast stroll:

'They went to the sands, to watch the flowing of the tide, which a fine south-easterly breeze was bringing in with all the grandeur which so flat a shore admitted. They praised the morning, gloried in the sea; sympathized in the delight of the fresh-feeling breeze. . . .' and Anne makes the occasion perfect, not by being carried away into useless raptures, but by readily 'entering into the feelings' of Henrietta, and saying 'all that was reasonable and proper on the business' of Dr Shirley's retirement, which would forward Henrietta's views of marriage. Anne represents the ideal balance between response to nature, and response to other people. 'I love not man the less, but nature more. . . .'

The accident on the Cobb at Lyme is the most dramatic incident in the whole of Jane Austen's writing outside her childhood burlesques. Suddenly to come upon Louisa being 'taken up lifeless' is a profound shock to any reader accustomed, hitherto, to the quiet *external* movement of a Jane Austen novel; and the response of one reader, Tennyson, is well known:

He was led on to Lyme by the description of the place in Miss Austen's *Persuasion*, walking thither the nine miles over the hills from Bridport. On his arrival he called on Palgrave, and refusing all refreshment, he said at once: 'Now take me to the Cobb, and show me the steps from which Louisa Musgrove fell'.[9]

Palgrave himself added, 'the persons she created in *Persuasion*, Tennyson remarked as we were returning, were more real and living to him than Monmouth and his followers, whose landing-place on the Western side of the Cobb we had just passed.'[10]

A few other references to places in Devon and Dorset remain to be noticed. Colonel Brandon, urgently summoned to London from Barton, goes on horseback as far as Honiton. 'I shall then go post.' Willoughby also makes Honiton his first stage on the same journey. Mr and Mrs Robert Ferrars, travelling from London to Dawlish, stop for fresh horses at the New London Inn, Exeter. A place for chance encounters, gossip, and the pursuit of 'beaux', Exeter is just fit to be the Miss Steeles' home: all Jane Austen's vulgar characters originate in cities. She had established its reputation in an early fragment, *Catharine*, written when she was just sixteen, in which she described the streets of Exeter 'infested' with officers and a company of strolling players. Though living only five miles away, Catharine could seldom prevail upon her cautious aunt to go shopping there.

The Steeles' uncle, Mr Pratt, has his educational establishment near Plymouth – into which port, in *Persuasion*, Captain Wentworth brings the *Asp*. Mr Elliot is travelling from Sidmouth to London when he stops at Lyme. We are not told where Anne and Frederick Wentworth make their home, though it could very likely be somewhere on the southern coast; but we do know that both Elinor and Marianne find their destiny at Delaford, that place of old-fashioned comfort and plenty – 'How Charlotte and I did stuff, the only time we were there!' – in Dorset.

In *Sense and Sensibility*, then, these two counties represent plenty and fertility, 'beauty and utility'; in *Persuasion*, their stirring sea-girt grandeur and power of rejuvenation set the tone. The first volume of *Persuasion* is Jane Austen's celebration of the romantic element in the English landscape: a celebration inspired and released by her own experiences in the West Country.

7

Bristol and Gloucestershire:
Gothic Interlude

Bless'd is the man, in whose sequester'd glade,
Some ancient abbey's walls diffuse their shade;
With mould'ring windows pierc'd, and turrets crown'd,
And pinnacles with clinging ivy bound.

Bless'd too is he, who, 'midst his tufted trees,
Some ruin'd castle's lofty towers sees;
Imbosom'd high upon the mountain's brow,
Or nodding o'er the stream that glides below.
Richard Payne Knight, The Landscape, 1794

'It is two years tomorrow since we left Bath for Clifton,' Jane reminded
Cassandra on 30 June 1808, 'with what happy feelings of escape!'

For five years she had lived obediently but reluctantly in Bath, trying
not to be discontented, but unable to write: the sense of release, still
remembered two years later, was immense, and Clifton came in for some
of its afterglow. When Mrs Austen and her daughters left Bath for ever in
July 1806, they had an entirely new home in view; but before settling
down, they planned to spend the summer travelling and visiting relations.
Their first stop was Clifton.

Now part of the city of Bristol, Clifton then lay just outside the ancient
city boundary, a Gloucestershire village rapidly growing into a salubrious
suburb and a fashionable resort to rival Bath. Why then should Jane have
preferred it so decidedly? Its attraction had a great deal to do with its airy
clifftop situation, its elevation by several hundred feet above the smelly,
workaday centre of the city, its proximity to the open green plateau of the
Downs. Clifton, moreover, was developed later than Bath, and designed
to satisfy the more fastidious tastes of a later generation.

Bristol had had its pretensions to be a spa fifty years before, but these
had centred on Hotwells, at the foot of the cliff, where a spring of

Clifton (1829) Perched on a cliff a little down river from the city of
Bristol, Clifton was visited by Jane Austen in 1806 and approved for its
airy, open situation

sulphurous water emerged at river level. Here the earliest lodging-houses, a pump room and a colonnade of shops had been built; here Fanny Burney brought her Evelina. The amenities of Hotwells were still patronized – Isabella Thorpe's party, it will be remembered, 'walked down to the Pump room, tasted the water, and laid out some shillings in purses and spars'. (That is, they were tempted to purchase some of the pretty trifles offered as souvenirs: spars were crystalline mineral fragments from the Avon Gorge, often fashioned into ornaments.) But when they chose their lodgings, most visitors preferred the elegant terraces, crescents and squares newly laid out on the slopes high above Hotwells. This area soon had its own amenities. In the very year of Jane's visit, 1806, the Clifton Assembly Rooms, in The Mall, were opened, comprising 'a noble reception saloon and tea-room, a ballroom highly furnished and decorated, a handsome cardroom, and a shop for pastry and confectionery with an adjoining room for soups, fruits and ices.'[1]

Jane Austen's partiality for Clifton was not suffered to diminish with the passage of time. In 1814 Martha Lloyd was planning to visit first her aunt Mrs Craven at Speen Hill and then her friends Captain Deans Dundas and his wife. Jane wrote to Cassandra that June, 'the middle of July is Martha's time, as far as she has any time. She has left it to Mrs Craven to fix the day. . . . Instead of Bath the Deans Dundases have taken a house at Clifton – Richmond Terrace – and she is as glad of the change as ever you or I should be, or almost. She will now be able to go on from Berks and visit them without any fears from heat.'

However, Martha's friends must have had a second change of mind, for at the beginning of September that year Jane wrote from London to Martha care of Captain Deans Dundas, RN, Pulteney Street, Bath: 'The weather can hardly have incommoded you by its heat. We have had many evenings here so cold, that I was sure there must be fires in the country. How many alterations you must perceive in Bath: and how many people and things gone by, must be recurring to you! I hope you will see Clifton.'

One is irresistibly reminded of Anne Elliot's 'dreading the possible heats of September in all the white glare of Bath': the very month of the very year when Jane was dreading them on Martha's account. But in 'I hope you will see Clifton' there seems to be a real affection independent of any comparisons with Bath.

In her fiction, from the very first, Bristol and Clifton are associated with health. Among the juvenilia *Lesley Castle* is unusual in having part of its action set in a real place. Eloisa Luttrell has been deranged by the sudden death of her lover; her pragmatic sister Charlotte writes, 'she is extremely ill, and her physicians are greatly afraid of her going into a decline. We are therefore preparing for Bristol, where we mean to be in the course of the next week.' A few days after their arrival she reports, 'Poor Eloisa is still so very indifferent both in health and spirits, and I very much fear, the air of the Bristol downs, healthy as it is, has been unable to drive poor Henry from her remembrance.'

The letters in this fragment are dated 1792, implying perhaps that Jane Austen had already visited the city by this date. Certainly she seems aware of its customs when she makes Charlotte write, in February, 'Eloisa's indisposition has brought us to Bristol in so unfashionable a season of the year, that we have actually seen but one genteel family since we came.' The Bristol directory for 1793 informed intending visitors that lodgings in Hotwells or Clifton would cost them ten shillings a week for each room between 25 March and 29 September, and only half that sum during the other six months of the year. In *Northanger Abbey* it is likewise February when Anne Thorpe claims, 'There is not a soul in Clifton at this time of year', yet how crowded Bath is exactly then! Catherine Morland has difficulty getting from one end of the Assembly Room to the other; the Allens, the Tilneys, and in *Persuasion*, Lady Russell, Viscountess Dalrymple, all chooose January and February for their visit to Bath – it 'belonged to the winter pleasures'. Jane Austen's exactitude on this point when she was only sixteen suggests that she was already acquainted with both resorts.

One of the characters in *Lesley Castle* is Mr Cleveland: 'a good-looking young man,' says Charlotte, 'I tell Eloisa to set her cap at him'. That phrase, so abhorrent to Marianne Dashwood, is one of several links with *Sense and Sensibility*, in which the name Cleveland is used again, this time for a house, Mr Palmer's residence, which 'was within a few miles of Bristol' on the Somerset side. Jane Austen shows a lively awareness of the place-names of the region: the little town of Clevedon is fourteen miles to the south-west of Bristol. In the grounds of Cleveland Marianne can think only of being in the same county as Willoughby's abode. 'Her eye, wandering over a wide tract of country to the south-east, could fondly rest on the farthest ridge of hills on the horizon, and fancy that from their summit, Combe Magna might be seen.' This is consistent with looking from Clevedon over the low-lying levels of north Somerset towards the Mendips; the villages in this area are rich in double-barrelled names, including Chew Magna, and many with the component Combe. Jane Austen's familiarity with Bristol and its environs during the 1790s when these early works were written is evident.

The association of Clifton with health-restoring properties is sustained in two of the later novels, *Persuasion* and *Emma*. Mr and Mrs Musgrove, who rarely stir from home without good reason, speak of having been to Clifton 'seven or eight years ago.' (Dating back from 1814, when the novel is set, this makes their visit coincide exactly with Jane Austen's own.) Since the Musgroves had then no daughters old enough to benefit from the social pleasures of the place, and since they are such a steady sort of people themselves, presumably they went there for their health. And Mrs Elton, hearing from Mr Weston that the ailing Mrs Churchill is coming south in search of a warmer climate, can hardly believe that she should choose London as her destination. "If she is really ill, why not go to Bath, Mr Weston? To Bath, or to Clifton?" '

Mrs Elton, of course, is the one true Bristolian of the novels – although her fiancé prefers her to be known as 'Miss Hawkins of Bath'. But Bristol was her home, 'the very heart of Bristol,' where she lives with an uncle, 'the drudge of some attorney'. Her father had been 'a Bristol merchant of course, he must be called,' although Emma suspects him of a lowly line of trade. The elder sister, Selina, has already escaped through marriage from that dreadful 'very heart of Bristol' and now lives in the much-vaunted 'Maple Grove', which is merely 'near Bristol'.

Jane Austen must have observed, in 1806, some years before she came to write *Emma*, the tendency of successful Bristol businessmen, great and small, to find that a town house in Clifton, elegant and elevated though it was, no longer satisfied their ambitions. To put an even greater distance between themselves and the city, to fulfil the desire for greater privacy, domesticity, and communion with nature, they were flocking to build villas in the Gloucestershire countryside beyond the Downs. It was merely a local expression of the nationwide movement, gathering momentum throughout Jane's lifetime, whereby a gregarious town-orientated society dissolved into a series of socially exclusive families, finding their own level, occupying their own plot of ground.

Child of her time, Jane herself showed these preferences and these aspirations: but she knew that many who professed to do so were motivated only by snobbery, anxiety to be in fashion, or false sentiment for nature. Maple Grove, with economy and deadly accuracy, pins the Sucklings in both social and geographical terms. This colonized corner of Gloucestershire is where Maple Grove must be located. We know that the house was near enough for Selina to go 'into Bristol' without a second thought; that although 'very retired' behind its shrubbery it was bothered by neighbours, those upstart Tupmans who had made their fortune in Birmingham (worse than Bristol!). We know that Mr Suckling had inhabited Maple Grove only eleven years, and that at best his father had purchased it just before he died, presumably at the end of a life spent in trade. And we most assuredly know that when the Sucklings twice went exploring in their *barouche-landeau*, the object of their drive was Kings-weston.

Built by Vanbrugh in the intervals when the Duchess of Marlborough's quarrelling had driven him from work at Blenheim, Kingsweston was the oldest, the grandest and the most remote of all the houses in this region, the one which all the others tried to imitate. 'Lord de Clifford has a fine seat at Kingsweston, enriched with plantations, and beautiful lawns and pasture grounds,' wrote a Gloucestershire historian in 1779.[2]

> It lies at a distance of about two miles from the Severn, which appears from thence like a large arm of the ocean with ships lying at anchor in Kingroad, either bound to or from the port of Bristol. From a little hill, not far from the house, the prospect is exquisitely beautiful, and uncommonly extensive, commanding the country on the Bristol Channel, from Pembrokeshire on one side, and Somersetshire on the other, almost up to the city of Gloucester, and the Welsh mountains, at a vast distance, for an evanescent ground. Turning southward, the view is less extensive, but not less agreeable, over a rich cultivated country, interspersed with villas, on the Gloucestershire side of the Avon, as far as the city of Bristol.

Herein lay the attraction of Kingsweston for such vulgar sightseers as the Sucklings and the Thorpes, for the rage for romantic views had, by the end of the eighteenth century, reached every level of the leisured society, even those who brought no discrimination or 'taste' to what they saw.

The grounds of Kingsweston adjoined those of the estate of Blaise, where we encounter the first of several Gothic associations which the county of Gloucestershire held for Jane Austen. John Thorpe, willing to tell any lie to tempt Catherine to Bristol, assures her that Blaise Castle is 'the oldest in the kingdom'. In fact it had been built a mere thirty years before, in 1766, and was a typical Georgian Gothic garden folly, unusual only in being semi-habitable.

Decorated on the exterior with all the paraphernalia of battlements, traceried windows and cruciform arrow slits, inside it was plastered, glazed and furnished like a miniature mansion. With a vestibule and dining-room below, and a sleeping chamber above, the castle was intended by its owner, Thomas Farr, to provide a retreat for meditation, as well as an object of picturesque beauty when viewed from the windows of his house below. Three narrow towers, one of them containing a spiral staircase, surrounded the central drum, whose flat roof serves as a belvedere from which to enjoy views almost identical with those from Kingsweston.

The architect was Robert Mylne, who was more accustomed to building elegant mansions, such as Goodnestone in Kent, well known to Jane Austen as the home of her sister-in-law Elizabeth Bridges. Compact, cosy and comfortable, Blaise is a far cry from the castle of Catherine Morland's imagination, which abounds in 'long galleries', 'broken arches', 'false hangings', 'trap-doors' and 'narrow, winding vaults'.

Blaise Castle (1796) Far from being 'the oldest in the kingdom', as John Thorpe assures Catherine Morland, Blaise Castle was just thirty years old when this engraving was made

Thomas Farr, a Bristol sugar merchant who became the city's Lord Mayor in the year of Jane Austen's birth, had purchased the Blaise estate in 1762. It consisted of an old gabled manor house and 400 acres of ground, mostly wooded and hilly, but including the remains of an old formal garden from which a triple avenue of elms marched straight to the top of a hill on which had once stood a medieval chapel dedicated to St Blaise. The last ruins of the chapel had been removed in the orderly first decade of the eighteenth century, to be replaced by a rather unsightly summer-house; and it was possibly regret for this act of insensibility which inspired Farr, at the height of the rage for ornamental antiquities, to spend £3,000 on his 'castle' while deferring the rebuilding of his low-lying and old-fashioned house.[3]

His bankruptcy in 1778, as a result of the effect of the American War of Independence on the transatlantic sugar trade, obliged him to sell the estate, which his castle had made as famous and well-visited as Kingsweston. Jane Austen surely expected her readers to laugh at Catherine's ignorance of Blaise. Among other visitors, John Wesley set out from Bristol at 6 a.m. one morning in 1788 expressly to see the castle, recording in his diary, 'Mr Farr, a person of exquisite taste, built it some years ago on the top of a hill which commands a prospect all four ways nothing in England excels'.

In 1789 the Blaise estate was sold for £11,000 to John Scandrett Harford, a Quaker banker, yet another Bristol businessman looking for a country seat.[4] In his passion for 'improvements', his adherence to the principles of the picturesque, and his indulgence in Gothic trifles, he exemplifies the three forces which motivated the eighteenth century landowners of England to fashion the landscape Jane Austen knew. (Incidentally his pious but non-Quaker son, of the same name, sat to Hannah More for her portrait of *Coelebs*, a novel of which Jane Austen wrote, 'My disinclination for it before was affected, but now it is real; I do not like the Evangelicals. Of course I shall be delighted, when I read it, like other people, but till I do I dislike it. . . . The only merit it could have, was in the name of Caleb, which has an honest, unpretending sound; but in Coelebs, there is pedantry and affectation. Is it written only to classical scholars?')

Having commissioned a design for an 'honest, unpretending' Palladian mansion to replace the old manor house, Harford turned his attention to the grounds, and called in the foremost landscape gardener of the time, Humphry Repton. The romantic nature of the scenery at Blaise, with its deep ravines, rocks and woods, meandering stream and glimpses of the greater river alive with shipping, made a worthy subject for Repton's art. 'The capricious taste of that sweeping improver Mr Repton has made this naturally beautiful place still more whimsically fantastical than it originally was' observed the *Guide* of 1810.

However, it is worth quoting at length from the book Repton himself produced containing his proposals, for in language and idea it brings us vividly into the world Jane Austen knew, and Repton's mixture of common sense and aesthetic sensibility would surely have earned her approval:[5]

The situation of the castle from whence this place takes its name . . . however sublime in itself as an occasional spot to be visited, must be wholly inapplicable to a family residence: it was therefore with much pleasure that I found the comfort of the house was not to be sacrificed to extensive prospect, but that several spots had been judiciously pro-posed, each partaking of the quiet and sequestered scenery in which this place so remarkably abounds. It is a most singular circumstance that within a short distance of the largest city in England except London, and even in the neighbourhood of the most frequented watering-place in the Kingdom, the woods and lawns and deep romantic glens belonging to Blaise Castle are perfectly secluded from the "busy hum of man".

Repton's major proposal was to make a new entrance, with a Gothic Lodge – Gothic to match the name of the estate, rather than Grecian to match the style of the house – and a long winding carriage drive approaching the house from the farthest point of the estate, and thus opening up the scenery for the enjoyment of carriage passengers.

When time has thrown its ivy and creeping plants over the rawness of new walls and fresh-hewn rocks, the approach will be in strict character with the wildness of the scenery, and excite admiration and surprise without any mixture of that terror which though it partakes of the sublime, is very apt to destroy the delights of romantic scenery. The gate being in character with the castle to which it is the prelude, introduces us to a wood with which it is in harmony, and I expect the stranger will be agreeably surprised to find that on quitting this wood, he is not going to a mouldering castle whose ruined turrets threaten destruction, and revive the horrors of feudel strife; but to a mansion of elegance, cheerfulness and hospitality where the comfort of neatness is blended with the rude features of nature, without committing great violence on the genius of the place. It may perhaps be urged that I have made a road where nature never intended the foot of man to tread, much less that he should be conveyed in the vehicles of modern luxury, but where man resides, nature must be conquered by art, and it is only the ostentation of her triumph, and not her victory, that ought ever to offend the correct eye of taste.

Of course the avenue had to go. Mr Rushton is right when he says in *Mansfield Park*, 'Repton would certainly have down the avenue'.

'This is the first instance in which I have been consulted where all improvement must depend on the axe, and though fully aware of the common objection to cutting down trees, yet it is only by a bold use of that instrument that the wonders of Blaise Castle can be properly displayed.'

As well as removing the remains of the avenue and breaking up the line where woods met lawn to give an irregular pattern, Repton made a clearing in the woods where

a cottage is proposed to be built. This cottage will give an air of cheerfulness and inhabitancy to the scene which would without it be too sombre, because the castle though perfectly in character with the solemn dignity of the surrounding woods, increases rather than relieves the apparent solitude. . . . A temple or pavilion in such a situation would receive the light and produce an object to contrast with the sameness of wood and lawn, but would not appear to be inhabited; while this, by its form will mark its intention, and the occasional smoke from the chimney will not only produce that cheerful and varying motion which painting cannot express, but it will frequently happen in a summer's evening that the smoke from this cottage will spread a thin veil along the glen, and produce that kind of vapoury repose over the opposite wood which painters often attempt to describe, and which in appearance so separates the two sides of the valley that the imagination will conceive it to be much wider and more extensive than it really is.

One of his sketches, says Repton, 'represents the first view of the castle after quitting the small lawn and entering the naked plain on which it is there discovered to be situated, although from any other point of view it appears as it ought to do, "embosom'd high in tufted trees"'. Here he shows his familiarity with Richard Payne Knight's poem *The Landscape*, written just two years earlier.[6]

Harford's later projects at Blaise were all carried out by the famous architect John Nash, who was to do so much for the townscape of London. At Blaise he built an orangery, a thatched dairy, and, in 1812, Blaise Hamlet: ten cottages *ornées*, each different, grouped informally about a village green. With their thatched or tiled roofs, low eaves, tall chimneys, diamond-paned windows, dove-lofts and rustic porches, they are a charming exercise in the village picturesque.

Catherine Morland never realizes her mistake about Blaise Castle, for that would be to anticipate the discoveries she must make, the disillusionment she must experience, at Northanger Abbey itself, that genuinely 'ancient edifice' in the county of Gloucestershire.

Her expectations of Northanger are based on passages such as this from Ann Radcliffe's *Romance of the Forest*:

He approached, and perceived the Gothic remains of an abbey; it stood on a kind of rude lawn, overshadowed by high and spreading trees, which seemed coeval with the building, and diffused a romantic gloom around. The greater part of the pile appeared to be sinking into ruins, and that which had withstood the ravages of time showed the remaining features of the fabric to be more awful in decay. The lofty battlements, thickly wreathed with ivy, were half demolished, and become the residence of birds of prey. . . .

From the distances and directions given, Northanger must lie within the triangle bounded by Tetbury, Cirencester and Stroud. (Petty France, where General Tilney stops two hours to bait the horses, is a roadside inn, so named, it is thought, because it seemed so remote from the rest of England.) Although it is genuinely old, Northanger disappoints all Catherine's expectations, having been made comfortable and modern.

An abbey! – Yes, it was delightful to be really in an abbey! – but she doubted, as she looked round the room, whether anything within her observation, would have given her the consciousness. The furniture was in all the profusion and elegance of modern taste. The fire-place, where she had expected the ample width and ponderous carving of former times, was contracted to a Rumford, with slabs of plain though handsome marble, and ornaments over it of the prettiest English china. The windows, to which she looked with particular dependence, from having heard the General talk of his preserving them in their Gothic form with reverential care, were yet less what her fancy had portrayed. To be sure, the pointed arch was preserved – the form of them was Gothic – they might be even casements – but every pane was so large, so clear, so light! To an imagination which had hoped for the smallest divisions, and the heaviest stonework, for painted glass, dirt and cobwebs, the difference was very distressing.

The exterior is more favourable to her wishes, though 'a smooth, level road of fine gravel' does not augur well.

She was struck, however, beyond her expectation, by the grandeur of the Abbey, as she saw it for the first time from the lawn. The whole building enclosed a large court; and two sides of the quadrangle, rich in Gothic ornaments, stood forward for admiration.

But further exploration produces further disappointment.

With the walls of the kitchen ended all the antiquity of the Abbey; the fourth side of the quadrangle having, on account of its decaying state, been removed by the General's father, and the present erected in its place. All that was venerable ceased here. The new building was not only new, but declared itself to be so; intended only for offices, and enclosed behind by stable-yards, no uniformity of architecture had been thought necessary. Catherine could have raved at the hand which had swept away what must have been beyond the value of all the rest, for the purposes of mere domestic economy.

The Abbey is an education – a finishing school of the mind – for Catherine Morland. Before the end of her visit, she was tired of the woods and the shrubberies – always so smooth and so dry; and the Abbey in itself was no more to her now than any other house. The painful remembrance of the folly it had helped to nourish and perfect, was the only emotion which could spring from a consideration of the building. What a revolution in her ideas! She, who had so longed to be in an Abbey! Now, there was nothing so charming to her imagination as the unpretending comfort of a well-connected Parsonage.

The modern structure posing as Gothic remains, the genuinely medieval building transformed into a home fit for civilized man: these are the two elements of her generation's pragmatic handling of their reverence for the past in which Jane found material for her comic genius to work on. A third manifestation was the new house built in the Gothic style, à la Strawberry Hill, of which there was an example well known to her within her own family: Adlestrop Park, on the northern extremity of Gloucestershire.

From Clifton, in July 1806, Jane Austen, her mother and sister proceeded to Adlestrop, where they stayed not at the Park but at the Rectory. This was unlikely to have been Jane's first visit. She had mentioned the possibility of visiting Adlestrop in 1799, and in 1801 met a woman in Bath who 'remembers us in Gloucestershire when we were very charming young women' which suggests an even earlier occasion (although this might refer to a visit to Fulwar and Eliza Fowle at Elkestone Rectory, near Cheltenham). Adlestrop Park was, so to speak, Mrs Austen's ancestral home. It had belonged to her branch of the Leigh family since the Reformation; her father had been born there, and during her lifetime it had passed successively to her uncle, her cousin, and her cousin's son.

This latter person, James Henry Leigh, was married to Julia, a daughter of Lord Saye and Sele; they were the occupants of the Park in 1806, while at the Rectory lived Mrs Austen's cousin, Thomas Leigh, and his unmarried sister, Elizabeth, who was godmother to Cassandra Elizabeth Austen, Jane's sister. Thomas Leigh had been married to yet another mutual first cousin, Mary, daughter of Theophilus Leigh of Balliol College, and sister of Mrs Cassandra Cooke. But Mary had died in 1797 so Thomas's sister had come to keep house for him; she was 'so wrapt up in him,' according to Jane, who had the highest regard for them both, describing Thomas as 'respectable, worthy, clever, agreeable,' and Elizabeth, 'your good Godmother', as 'excellent'. Jane Austen rarely praised the older generation of her relations; with such affection, the summer visit of 1806 must have been very agreeable.

In terms of their surroundings, there was everything to make it so. The

Cotswold countryside has a claim to be among the loveliest in England, its golden stone buildings most in harmony with nature. From the Rectory there is a superb view of the rolling landscape of 'Gloucestershire and Oxfordshire'.[7]

The Rectory had been built in 1670, at a cost of £1,500; altered and 'improved' over the years, it was an undistinguished property whose chief glory was to be found in the splendid cedar trees of its grounds. The village in 1779 consisted of about thirty-four houses and 200 inhabitants, whose dead lay in the churchyard given to the parish for that purpose by the Leighs in 1590. The church itself was twice rebuilt, in 1750 and 1765, 'owing to the unkindness of the workmen employed in the first rebuilding'.[8]

But it is the history of Adlestrop Park which is particularly interesting. Mrs Austen's great-grandfather, William Leigh, who died in 1690, converted a barn to make 'a large handsome seat near the church'; he also laid out extensive pleasure grounds 'ornamented with a canal, fountain and several alcoves, and expensive showy summer houses' in the formal old style of garden. Taste changed, and all was swept away, with the exception of one panelled room with a richly carved wooded fireplace and the staircase, which were incorporated into the new structure:

In 1750, and again between 1759 and 1762, much of the original house was pulled down and rebuilt on a larger scale by Sanderson Miller, who designed the exquisite south west front in his imaginative style of Gothic. It is symmetrical with a large central gable and smaller ones either side which have bays with fretted balustrades and crocketed pinnacles. The bays are panelled and decorated, and the windows have architraves with roll-mouldings and Gothic glazing. Polygonal ashlar buttresses, at the corners, crowned like medieval chimneys.

The gardens were laid out by Humphry Repton, and the large, square dovecote, with its four gables surmounted by a lantern, was perhaps built at the same time to replace an earlier one. In 1803 the park was further enlarged.[9]

'Among its picturesque features', announced a contemporary guide, 'may be ranked a small stream, which, in its progress down a hill, has its current checked by ledges of rocks, and at length falls into a lake at some distance from the house.'[10]

Adlestrop then offered for Jane's delectation a playful Gothic house, picturesque grounds, an old-fashioned parsonage, a rebuilt church, a small village (containing at least one thatched cottage ornée) and the scenic beauties of the Cotswold countryside.

To all this was added a house of extreme interest to the Austen family which Jane must have visited. Daylesford, less than two miles from

Adlestrop Park (1829) This Gothic mansion was owned by a cousin of Jane Austen, who stayed at the nearby Rectory, home of another member of the family, in 1806

Adlestrop, was the home of Warren Hastings, whose connections with the Austens were various and longstanding. Hastings was on good terms with his neighbour Thomas Leigh, and was at home in July 1806; it is inconceivable that the Austen ladies did not call on him and his wife.'[11]

Warren Hastings and George Austen, exact contemporaries, had probably known one another as youths in Kent, where Hastings' uncle had business interests. As a young widower in India, Hastings sent his only son, George, whose health was delicate, back to England, entrusting him to the care of George Austen, who was as yet unmarried. Little George Hastings accompanied Jane's parents on their honeymoon, and when, shortly afterwards, he died, Mrs Austen is said to have felt the loss as acutely as if it had been a child of her own.

In India, Warren Hastings looked for consolation and companionship in his widowhood to George Austen's sister, Philadelphia Hancock, whose husband was a surgeon in Bengal. It was rumoured there that she 'abandoned herself'[12] to him; she became pregnant after nine years of childless marriage, and Hastings not only stood godfather to the child, Eliza, but later settled £10,000 on her. In her turn Eliza gave the name of Hastings to the son of her first marriage.

Eliza's second husband was Jane's brother Henry, who, writing to congratulate Warren Hastings on his acquittal at the end of the long impeachment trial, revealed the Austens' attitude to their famous friend: 'Among the earliest lessons of my infancy I was taught by precept and example to love and venerate your name. I cannot remember the time when I did not associate with your character the idea of everything great, durable and good.'[13] Years later Jane was gratified by his admiration of her work. 'I long to have you hear Mr H.'s opinion of P. and P. His admiring my Elizabeth so much is particularly welcome to me.'

Eliza and Henry were regular visitors to Daylesford, but Eliza's first visit was made in August 1797, a few months before her second marriage. From Cheltenham she wrote,

> One of my principal inducements for coming here was the neighbour-hood of my old friends the Hastings's whom I am just returned from visiting. They have got a place called Daylesford, which is one of the most beautiful I ever saw. I will not wrong it by endeavouring to give a description of it, and it shall therefore suffice to say that the park and grounds are a little paradise, and that the house is fitted up with a degree of taste and magnificence seldom to be met with.[14]

Well might she say so. The house Hastings built and furnished at Daylesford was pure indulgence, intended to console himself for every past disappointment in his long and eventful life. Throughout his career in India, his ambition had been to buy back the property of his ancestors, Daylesford, which had passed out of his improvident family a few generations before. Having paid over the odds for a ramshackle house because it stood on the one plot of land which he desired above all other, he set about rebuilding.

> Nothing could be too good for Daylesford. Its stone was the finest Cotswold, from quarries beyond Burford at Windrush and Barrington. Its wrought ironwork came from the Soho works at Birmingham, and Wedgwood tiles from Etruria. Skilled London craftsmen lodged in the village a whole year, picking out cornices and shutters in pink and rose and two shades of green, varnishing mahogany sashes, gilding leaves, grain and honeysuckle. All the latest comforts were installed: a hot bath, plate-glass, a Bramah water-closet, and a muffin stove.[15]

The garden was laid out with walks, groves and a newly-created lake complete with islands, bridge and cascade. The planting included silver firs, spruce, Lombardy poplars, walnuts, hornbeam, almond, lilac, juniper, acacia, tamarisk, tulip trees, heliotrope, magnolias, peaches, apricots, nectarines and even a mango from Bengal. Hastings' daily walk round his pleasure grounds took '897 of my paces'.

Nothing could have been more English than the situation of Daylesford, set snugly in a fold of the hills looking south-west towards a distant view of the church of Stow-on-the-Wold high on the Fosse Way. But it was not wholly English in style, which would not have pleased the patriotic Jane Austen. The architect was Samuel Pepys Cockerell of the East India Company, who a few years later was to build an Indian extravaganza for his brother at Sezincote, in Gloucestershire, a remarkable house which the Prince Regent visited in 1807 and which helped to inspire the Brighton Pavilion. At Daylesford the Indian influence was confined to a great dome, which derived directly from Muslem architecture. Inside, however, the sumptuous decoration owed much to the East: ivory furniture, Indian silver, a sculptured marble fireplace depicting a Hindu sacrifice. Beneath the dome was Mrs Hastings' first-floor boudoir, with a circular ceiling painted to resemble the sky and lit by concealed windows.

Luxury and ostentation on this scale – and they left Hastings chronically in debt – were not to Jane Austen's taste. In 1805, the year before her visit, he paid assessed taxes on seven menservants, five garden labourers, two carriages, eight carriage horses, ten farm horses, three dogs, and hair-powder for four persons – there were seven untaxable female staff besides – all to service two childless old people. Like Catherine Morland, after seeing Daylesford she may well have felt 'there was nothing so charming to her imagination as the unpretending comfort of a well-connected Parsonage'.

After 1806, Jane Austen paid one more known visit into Gloucestershire. With Cassandra she spent three weeks in Cheltenham in May 1816. By then her health was beginning to fail and she may have been persuaded to try the spa waters by Mary Austen, with whom Cheltenham was a favourite place.

Cheltenham, which has grown and changed far more since Jane Austen knew it than either Bath or Clifton, was then just a simple summer resort, consisting of little more than a very long High Street, a grid of tree-lined walks and rides to the south of it, and a number of dispersed springs. Though the first of these had been discovered and proclaimed as early as 1716, poor road transport, and lack of water transport altogether, had hindered the conveyance of building materials, and postponed the town's growth until the post-Napoleonic era. Jane Austen was at Cheltenham therefore at a significant point in its history, just as it was celebrating a centenary, and on the eve of its emergence into a spacious and respectable nineteenth-century city, stately in architecture, decorous in tone. By

Cheltenham (1810) This spa was still largely undeveloped when Jane
Austen came here for her health in 1816

developing so late, Cheltenham never acquired the rakish reputation
which earlier resorts like Bath had painfully to shed. Jane Austen may well
have preferred it for that reason.

It would be interesting to know whether she was aware that the leafy
walks which gave the resort much of its pleasant character before the great
development, had been laid out, in the 1740s, by a Gloucestershire
landowner who had an ancestor in common with herself. He was
Norborne Berkeley, of Stoke Gifford near Bristol (another Georgian
Gothic mansion, built for him in the 1760s), later Lord Botetourt and a
Governor of Virginia. Like Jane he was descended from Sir Richard
Berkeley, whose daughter Catherine had married Rowland Leigh of
Adlestrop. The greatest of Norborne Berkeley's walks was a 900 yard
avenue of elms connecting the original well to the High Street. 'At its
northern end it did not reach the church, but the tower and spire, in the
manner so dear to these amateurs of the Gothic picturesque, were there to
close the vista down the newly embellished spa's leading feature; terraces
and squares were still lacking in so Arcadian a resort.'[16]

In 1780 Cheltenham's first Master of Ceremonies was appointed, two
years later the town was provided with a theatre, and in 1788 it was
honoured with a month's visit by George III. Accompanying the royal
party was Fanny Burney, who noticed with approval the 'long, clean and
well-paved street'. The King strolled informally along the walks, mingling
with his subjects in a new and delightful way.

As we have already seen, among the visitors of August 1797 was Jane's
cousin Eliza, who gives a vivid description.

The place is very full and I have met with many of my acquaintance amongst the rest some relations of my Aunt Austen, that is to say Mr and Mrs Leigh and Lord and Lady Saye and Sele. . . . There are plays three times a week which are exceedingly well attended, and Balls twice. . . . On Monday is the Master of Ceremonies' Ball. . . . I believe you have never been to this place, and therefore I think I am in duty bound to inform you that it consists of one very long and handsome street, and that the country about it is exceedingly pretty and offers a great variety of delightful walks.[17]

More and more springs were discovered, and each provided with a pump room and a name: the Old Well, Montpellier, Alstone, Essex, Orchard and Cambray were the major ones of Jane Austen's time. We do not know which was patronized by Jane, who in September 1816 wrote, 'The Duchess of Orleans, the paper says, drinks at my pump'. Presumably the waters had benefited not Jane but Cassandra, who returned to Cheltenham with Mary Austen that month. 'How very much Cheltenham is to be preferred in May!' exclaimed Jane on hearing from her, and 'Three guineas a week for such lodgings!'

There is more on that subject in Jane's next letter. 'I hope Mary will change her lodgings at the fortnight's end; I am sure, if you looked about well, you would find others in some odd corner, to suit you better. Mrs Potter charges for the *name* of the High Street.' Nevertheless, 'I am very glad you find so much to be satisfied with at Cheltenham. While the waters agree, everything else is trifling.'

8

The Midlands and the North:
In Search of the Picturesque

What man of taste my right will doubt,
To put things in, or leave things out?
'Tis more than right, it is a duty,
If we consider landscape beauty:
He ne'er will as an artist shine
Who copies nature line by line;
Whoe'er from nature takes a view
Must copy and improve it too:
To heighten ev'ry work of art,
Fancy should take an active part.
William Combe, *The Tour of Dr Syntax
in Search of the Picturesque*, 1809

From Gloucestershire, in the summer of 1806, the Austens planned to proceed north into Staffordshire, where another relation was waiting to receive them in his rectory. But first, an event of great moment in the family, occurring at this very time, gave to their travels an intriguing detour.

The Leigh family consisted of two branches, descended from two sons of Sir Thomas Leigh, Lord Mayor of London in Queen Elizabeth's reign, and his wife Alice, niece and heiress of another wealthy London merchant, Sir Rowland Hill. One branch of the family had lived for generations at Adlestrop; the other, who had acquired a barony by giving hospitality to Charles I when the gates of Coventry were shut against him, at Stoneleigh Abbey in Warwickshire.[1]

The last Lord Leigh of this line had died, childless and insane, in 1786, whereupon Stoneleigh passed to his unmarried sister, Mary Leigh. Her death occurred at the beginning of July 1806, while the Austens were at Clifton, and they arrived at Adlestrop to find great excitement and confusion in the family. The Stoneleigh branch being now extinct, the property reverted to the Adlestrop Leighs – to the Reverend Thomas Leigh for his life, and then to James Leigh Perrot (Mrs Austen's brother) for his life, and then to James Henry Leigh of Adlestrop Park.

Since the two former were childless old men, it was clear that James Henry Leigh and his children would eventually inherit. Mr Leigh Perrot, content with his fine home at Scarlets, was ready to waive his claim in return for a financial settlement, but Thomas Leigh, who had all his life been a poor relation, obliged to live in an indifferent rectory while first his brother and then his nephew occupied the great house next door, was eager to take occupation of Stoneleigh. He had already visited his new home once, briefly, before his Austen cousins arrived at Adlestrop; at the beginning of August he set off again, taking them with him.

It was a fascinating deviation for Jane, introducing her to a new county and to two other extremely 'ancient edifices' besides Stoneleigh itself, which, with its combination of old and new, was curiously like her own Northanger – but even more magnificent.

Stoneleigh was a Cistercian abbey, belonging to that order notable for their careful husbandry. The foundation stone had been laid in 1155 after the assent of the priors and canons of Kenilworth, to whom the parish church of Stoneleigh belonged, had been granted. The monks agreed not to diminish in any way the rights of that church and to pay tithes to Kenilworth for all the land they should till within the parish.

Like Northanger, Stoneleigh was ranged about a quadrangle, acquiring, in the course of nearly 400 years of prosperity and growth, all the usual appurtenances of an abbey – chapter-house and cloister, warming room and dormitory, gatehouse and hospitium.

After the Dissolution Stoneleigh was granted in 1538 to Charles Brandon, Duke of Suffolk, and sold by his heirs jointly to Sir Rowland Hill and Sir Thomas Leigh, whose mutual descendant, a second Sir Thomas Leigh, made it his home. (His brother Rowland was given Aldestrop.) The Leighs continued the process of adding to and rebuilding parts of the abbey, so that there was scarcely a century not represented in the rambling buildings which confronted Jane Austen at Stoneleigh. But by far the most impressive – and indeed oppressive – of the additions was the great west range, erected between 1714 and 1726. Out of scale and out of character with all that had gone before, it was a mighty, rectangular edifice of dark grey stone, uncompromisingly symmetrical, uncompromisingly Baroque; stunning the observer with its pedimented fenestration and obliterating, from this aspect, all signs that Stoneleigh was of medieval origin.

Interestingly the estimate for the great west wing survives, at £545 for three storeys or £463 for two – but it adds 'My Lord to find all materials and bring them convenient to the building, to find all scaffolding, ladders, tressels, tackle, ropes and to pull down the old building and to dig the foundations and clear the rubbish'.[2] Interior finishing, which was very sumptuous, was also excluded.

That the Austens found Stoneleigh the most amazing house they had ever stayed in is evident from a wonderfully descriptive letter written by

Stoneleigh Abbey The great west wing of Stoneleigh was built before the rage for Gothic and completely obscures from this side the genuine medieval remains of a property which had been in Jane Austen's mother's family for generations

Mrs Austen a few days after their arrival to her daughter-in-law Mary. Dated Wednesday 13 August 1806, the letter begins by explaining the circumstances of their visit. (Mr Hill was Mary Leigh's man of business.)

The very day after I sent you my last letter Mr Hill wrote his intentions of being at Adlestrop (with Mrs Hill) on Monday the 4th and his wish that Mr Leigh and family would go with them to Stoneleigh the following day as he was hurried for time and there was much business for the executors awaiting them at the Abbey. All this accordingly took place and we all found ourselves on Tuesday (that is yesterday se'n-night) eating fish, venison and all manner of good things at a late hour, in a noble large parlour hung round with family pictures – everything is very grand and very fine and very large. The house is larger than I could have supposed. We can *now* find our way about it, I mean the best part; as to the offices (which were the old Abbey) Mr Leigh almost despairs of ever finding his way about them. I have proposed his setting up *directing posts* at the angles. I expected to find everything about the place very fine and all that, but I had no idea of its being so beautiful. I had figured to myself long avenues, dark rookeries and dismal yew trees, but here are no such melancholy things.

The Avon runs near the house amidst green meadows bounded by large and beautiful woods, full of delightful walks.

At nine in the morning we meet and say our prayers in a handsome Chapel, the pulpit etc., now hung with black. Then follows breakfast consisting of chocolate, coffee and tea, plum cake, pound cake, hot rolls, cold rolls, bread and butter, and dry toast for me. The House-Steward (a fine large respectable-looking man) orders all these matters. Mr Leigh and Mr Hill are busy great part of the mornings. We walk a great deal, for the woods are impenetrable to the sun even in the middle of an August day. I do not fail to spend some time every day in the kitchen garden where the quantities of small fruits exceed anything you can form an idea of. This large family with the assistance of a great many blackbirds and thrushes cannot prevent its rotting on the trees. The garden contains five acres and a half. The ponds supply excellent fish, the park excellent venison; there is also great plenty of pigeons, rabbits and all sorts of poultry, a delightful dairy where is made butter, good Warwickshire cheese and cream ditto. One man servant is called the Baker, he does nothing but brew and bake. The quantity of casks in the strong beer cellar is beyond imagination; those in the small beer cellar bear no proportion, tho' by the bye the small beer may be called ale without a misnomer.

This is an odd sort of letter. I write just as things come into my head. I will now give you some idea of the inside of this vast house, first premising that there are forty-five windows in front (which is quite straight with a flat roof) fifteen in a row. You go up a considerable flights of steps (some offices are under the house) into a large hall: on the right hand the dining parlour, within that the breakfast room, where we generally sit, and reason good 'tis the only room (except the Chapel) that looks towards the river. On the left hand of the hall is the best drawing-room, within that a smaller; these rooms are rather gloomy brown wainscot and dark crimson furniture, so we never use them but to walk through them to the old picture gallery. Behind the smaller darwing-room is the state bedchamber, with a high dark crimson velvet bed: an *alarming* apartment just fit for a heroine; the old gallery opens into it; behind the hall and parlours is a passage all across the house containing three staircases and two small back parlours. There are twenty-six bedchambers in the new part of the house and a great many (some very good ones) in the old. There is also another gallery fitted up with modern prints on a buff paper and a large billiard room: every part of the offices kept so perfectly nice, that were you to cut your finger I do not think you could find a cobweb to wrap it up in.

I need not have written this long detail, for I have a presentiment that if these good people live till next year you will see it all with your own eyes. Our visit has been a most pleasant one. We all seem in good humour, disposed to be pleased, endeavour to be agreeable and I hope succeed. Poor Lady Saye and Sele to be sure is rather tormenting, though sometimes amusing, and affords Jane many a good laugh, but she fatigues me sadly on the whole. Tomorrow we depart, Hamstall is thirty-eight miles from hence. We have seen the remains of Kenilworth Castle which afforded us much entertainment, I expect still more from the sight of Warwick Castle which we are going to see today. . . .'[3]

From this letter it is apparent that Northanger was by no means modelled on Stoneleigh, where the new west wing provided all of the state, and most of the family, accommodation. Nevertheless, in its quadrangular form, its Gothic remains, its neat arrangements, its huge kitchen garden, and its armies of servants – Mrs Austen speaks elsewhere of eighteen menservants to be put into mourning – there were echoes of her own creation which must have amused and interested Jane. Her mother's remark, 'an alarming apartment just fit for a heroine' shows the way their minds ran.

With so much to see and enjoy at Stoneleigh itself, and with so much business to occupy Thomas Leigh, it is significant that nevertheless two sightseeing expeditions were made during a visit which lasted little more than a week. The Austens' interest in the historic buildings of their country was evidently keen – and was inspired, perhaps, by Gilpin. The route he had followed northwards on his *Lakes Tour* (published in 1786) passed through exactly those places named in *Pride and Prejudice* as forming the Gardiners' journey: Oxford, Blenheim, Warwick, Kenilworth and Birmingham; while he returned via Matlock, Chatsworth and Dovedale, which they also planned to see. It could be that the early version of *Pride and Prejudice* had been something of a skit on Gilpin's northern tour, an idea to which we will be returning in this chapter. Meanwhile, Jane was now able to visit two of these places for herself, and see with her own eyes what she had long been familiar with from Gilpin's description.

The great ornament of Warwick is the *castle*. This place, celebrated once for its strength, and now for its beauty, stands on a gentle rise, in the midst of a country not absolutely flat. The River Avon washes the rock, from which its walls rise perpendicularly. You see its grand foundation to most advantage from the windows of the great hall; from which you look down a considerable height, upon the river.

This noble castle having appeared in the different capacities, first of a fortress, and afterwards of a county-jail, was at last converted by its proprietor, the Earl of Warwick, into a habitable mansion. The old form is still preserved; at least it may everywhere be traced; and each addition is in symmetry with what is left.

The old entrance is still in use. A bridge is thrown over the ditch, and leads into the inner area of the castle, through a grand turreted gate. This gate is placed in the middle of a curtain, at the extremities of which stand two round towers, known by the names of Guy's and Caesar's.

On entering this venerable gate and surveying, from its inner arch, the area or court of the castle, which contains about an acre, you see the ground-plot, and plan of the whole fortress. On the left is the habitable part. In front rises a woody mount, probably artificial, where formerly stood the citadel, part of which remains. The area itself is covered with turf, and surrounded by a broad gravel walk, as a coach-ring: and the whole is encompassed by a wall, adorned with the ruins of towers, and other mural projections, which being shattered in many places, and covered with ivy, catch little breaks of light, and often make a picturesque appearance.

The house is grand, and convenient: the rooms spacious, and comfortable. Some of the offices, particularly the kitchen, are hewn out of the solid rock on which the castle is founded.

The garden consists only of a few acres, and is laid out by Brown in a close walk, which winds towards the river, and somewhat awkwardly

Warwick Castle (1814) Visited by Jane Austen in the footsteps of William Gilpin. The river is Shakespeare's Avon

reverts into itself, taking no notice, except in one single point, of the noble pile it invests.

The armour and tilting spear of the celebrated Guy, Earl of Warwick, a rib of the dun-cow, and other monuments of the prowess of that hero, are shown at the porter's lodge. These remains, though fictitious, no doubt, are not improper appendages of the place, and give the imagination a kind of tinge, which throws an agreeable, romantic colour on all the vestiges of this venerable pile.

The Earl of Warwick, who had commissioned 'Capability' Brown in 1759, also filled the house – part of which was Jacobean – with treasures brought back from continental Grand Tours. His successor, inheriting in 1773, saw Gilpin's remarks in manuscript some years before publication and resolved to make improvements accordingly. Gilpin became personally acquainted with him and found his taste 'wholly of the sublime kind, formed upon the mountains and lakes of Switzerland and Cumberland' and considered his projected changes 'will out-Brown anything that is done there'.[4] This was the earl in residence at the time of Jane's visit: his the improvements that she saw.

If Warwick was impressive for being extravagantly cared for, Kenilworth was awe-inspiring for being in ruins. (Of the two Warwickshire castles one has no doubt which Catherine Morland would have preferred.) Gilpin termed Kenilworth 'one of the most magnificent piles of ruin in England' though, somewhat oddly, pronouncing it 'not picturesque'. The reddish-brown stone he allowed to be 'beautiful to the eye' but so friable that 'another century will probably bring it all to the ground'. The charm of Kenilworth, to Gilpin as to later observers, was the idea of decayed grandeur it evoked, the piquant contrast to the mind between its present and past states. This was a concept moralists loved to dwell on, and we can be confident it afforded no small part of the 'entertainment' enjoyed by the Austens. Jane, knowledgeable in history, may have amused herself by visualizing the scene when, in the thirteenth century, a hundred knights, watched by a hundred ladies, gathered for three days of jousting; or more solemnly, when Edward II signed his abdication there; or with a return to gaiety and extravagance, when Dudley, Earl of Leicester, fêted Elizabeth with a round of dancing, plays, contests and pageantry lasting nineteen days – during which all clocks were stopped so that 'time might stand still' – at a cost, reputedly, of £1,000 a day. Leicester it was who built the great gatehouse to receive the Queen (Jane's least favourite character in history) and inserted the incongruously large windows in the Norman masonry.

Gilpin quoted an Elizabethan account of Kenilworth Castle:

Every room was spacious, and high-roofed within; and every part seemly to the sight, by due proportion, without; in the daytime, on every side glittering with glass: at night, transparent by continual brightness of candle, fire and torch light.

He then described its change of fortune.

After the civil wars of Charles I, the pride of this noble mansion was humbled. Its owner was a favourer of the royal cause; and Cromwell, in revenge, tore it to pieces, and set everything to auction, that could be severed from the walls. These rapacious hands left it in a state from which it has never recovered; yet even still it is a splendid ruin.

Another writer, of Jane's own generation, was to find inspiration for a whole novel at Kenilworth. 'The massive ruins of the castle only serve to show what their splendour once was and to impress on the musing visitor the transitory values of human possessions and the happiness of those who enjoy a humble lot in virtuous contentment', wrote Sir Walter Scott in *Kenilworth*, published four years after Jane's death. In 1806, as a 'musing visitor' herself, how interested she would have been could she have foreseen all the literary connections that were to arise between herself and

Kenilworth Castle (1814) During Jane Austen's lifetime ruins came to be viewed with a new romantic reverence for the past. She saw Kenilworth in 1806

him. He was to be one of her earliest and warmest admirers and reviewers, while her letters and novels abound with references to his work.

At this point, 1806, he had only just begun to publish poetry, including *The Lay of the Last Minstrel* the previous year. Jane knew this poem well enough to quote from it twice in *Mansfield Park*. One is merely a verbal borrowing, showing how readily his phraseology came to her mind. The other is more illustrative of Scott's influence on the way people were beginning to regard old customs and old objects. The excessive sensibility of the eighteenth-century Gothic novel, so ably burlesqued by Jane in her earliest works, is maturing to a more thoughtful and romantic reverence for the past. This Jane endorses in the very character of Fanny Price, whose cast of mind could scarcely have existed before Scott. Visiting the chapel at Sotherton, Fanny is disappointed to see 'no banners, cousin, to be "blown by the night wind of Heaven". No signs that a "Scottish monarch sleeps below".' (The chapel at Sotherton, incidentally, recalls the similar post-Reformation domestic chapel at Stoneleigh, where, as Mrs Austen affirms, daily prayers had not yet been 'left off' – nor were likely to be, with the new owner a clergyman.)

Altogether there is ample evidence to suggest that Jane Austen followed Scott's career, first as poet and then as novelist, with intense interest; that, exact contemporaries though they were, he was the innovator, and she absorbed from him ideas that drew her into the nineteenth century; that her imagination became to some extent coloured by his very powerful one. From Marianne Dashwood in the first published novel, to Captain Benwick in the last, with Fanny Price in between, the pensive and ardent characters of Jane Austen find in Scott a favourite poet – and are only a little laughed at for their preference.

The foremost literary association of Warwickshire of course was Shakespeare, 'part of every Englishman's constitution' as Jane Austen said in *Mansfield Park*. It was hardly possible she could find herself in his county without sometimes thinking of him. She may even have passed through Stratford-upon-Avon *en route* from Adlestrop to Stoneleigh. Certainly the half-timbered buildings of Warwickshire, of which the village of Stoneleigh itself afforded some remarkably pretty examples, were constant reminders to her that she was now in the west Midlands, territory of lush orchards, snug farmsteads and well-wooded valleys. And when she left Stoneleigh it was to travel into the hillier county of Staffordshire, where she could feel herself to be on the very brink of the north country.

Here she stayed at the rectory of Hamstall Ridware, home of Mrs Austen's nephew Edward Cooper, his wife Caroline, and their large family. They had moved there from Harpsden in Oxfordshire, as Jane had informed Cassandra in January 1799:

> Yesterday came a letter to my mother from Edward Cooper to announce, not the birth of a child, but of a living; for Mrs Leigh [i.e. Mary Leigh of Stoneleigh Abbey, the lady whose death set off the 1806 scramble for the inheritance] has begged his acceptance of the Rectory of Hamstall Ridware in Staffordshire, vacant by Mr Johnson's death. We collect from his letters that he means to reside there, in which he shows his wisdom. Staffordshire is a good way off; so we shall see nothing more of them till, some fifteen years hence, the Miss Coopers are presented to us, fine, jolly, handsome, ignorant girls. The living is valued at £140 a year, but perhaps it may be improvable. How will they be able to convey the furniture of the dressing-room so far in safety?

This sarcastic comment is followed by a rather callous one – pompous, self-satisfied Edward Cooper always called out the worst in Jane. 'Our first cousins seem all dropping off very fast. One is incorporated into the family [Eliza, who had recently married Henry] another dies [Jane, Lady Williams, née Cooper, with whom Jane and Cassandra Austen had been at school, and who had been tragically killed in a carriage accident amid the peaceful English countryside while her naval captain husband survived all the hazards of fighting at sea] and a third goes into Staffordshire'. Here then, in one letter, are three jokes, if they may be so called, deriving from Jane's idea of Staffordshire as impossibly distant.

However, her prophecy was wrong. Two years later she wrote to Cassandra, 'Edward Cooper is so kind as to want us all to come to Hamstall this summer, instead of going to the sea, but we are not so kind as to mean to do it. Another year, if you please, Mr Cooper, but for the present we greatly prefer the sea to all our relations.' He persevered, and in April 1806 Mrs Austen was informing Mary, wife of James,

> I had a letter the other day from Edward Cooper; he wrote to congratulate us on Frank's victory and safety [at the battle of St Domingo] and to invite us to Hamstall in the ensuing summer, which invitation we seem disposed to accept; he says they are all well, expresses himself much gratified by James's visit, only it was too short, and hopes he got to Steventon safe. . . .

One doubts if Jane was keen even in 1806 to go so far out of their way to visit Edward Cooper, but she as always fell in with her mother's wishes. Jane evidently found his eldest son growing up in the father's image, for three years later she told Cassandra, 'A great event happens this week at

Hamstall in young Edward's removal to school; he is going to Rugby and is very happy in the idea of it; – I wish his happiness may last, but it will be a great change, to become a raw schoolboy from being a pompous sermon-writer and a domineering brother. It will do him good I dare say.'

Unfortunately no letters exist to record the length of Jane's visit to Staffordshire, which other places in the county she saw, or what opinion she formed of this, the northernmost point she ever – to our knowledge – reached. At Hamstall Ridware the Austens' long progression north was halted, and they turned round, and headed for the south coast. This journey must have been performed in many stages, and unfolded to them a fascinating view of the changing English countryside: but of the route they took, and the impressions they received, we are again, most unfortunately, ignorant.

For someone who had actually been to Staffordshire, where the famous works of Josiah Wedgwood were located, Jane showed a strange carelessness of geography when in June 1811 she wrote to Cassandra,

> On Monday I had the pleasure of receiving, unpacking and approving our Wedgwood ware. It all came very safely, and upon the whole is a good match, though I think they might have allowed us rather larger leaves, especially in such a year of fine foliage as this. One is apt to suppose that the woods about Birmingham must be blighted.

Perhaps like Gilpin the Austens had 'wished for time to have visited the potteries of Mr Wedgwood, where the elegant arts of old Etruria are revived. It would have been pleasing to see all these works in their progress to perfection. . . .' Factories and mills, which had begun to appear in the northern landscape, were still exciting, even awe-inspiring novelties, proof of the ingenuity of man. (Birmingham is part of the Gardiners' itinerary; but in *Emma* Jane Austen has some fun with it at Mrs Elton's expense. ' "How they got their fortune nobody knows. They came from Birmingham, which is not a place to promise much, you know, Mr Weston. One has not great hopes from Birmingham. I always say there is something direful in the sound." ')

Jane Austen's sense of the northern part of England being very far distant recurs in her letters. In 1801 'Mr Peter Debary has declined Deane curacy; he wishes to be settled nearer London. A foolish reason! as if Deane were not near London in comparison of Exeter or York.' In 1814, advising Anna about her novel, 'What can you do with Egerton to increase the interest for him? I wish you could contrive something . . . to take him mysteriously away, and then heard of at York or Edinburgh.'

In her own novels, the 'northern extremities' of England are mentioned only occasionally, but always to good effect. (Catherine Morland, it is well known, was not even quite certain that 'the laws of the land and the manners of the age prevailed' there.) The Churchills own a great estate in Yorkshire, conveniently for the plot of *Emma* beyond the range of easy, though not of possible, travel to the south. Somehow the county of their property bestows on them a grandeur akin to that of the real-life Howards, as well as a suitable remoteness and chilliness both physical and social. Mary King, escaping from Wickham's designs on her fortune, seeks refuge with an uncle in Liverpool – aptly, since she is newly rich but vulgar; and it is to that great entrepreneurial port that Sir Thomas Bertram returns, in a private vessel, from visiting the source of his wealth, his plantations in Antigua. Wickham himself, newly married, is banished as far away as possible, to Newcastle.

His sister-in-law also finds her destiny in the north. Why did Jane Austen site Pemberley in Derbyshire, a county of which she had no personal knowledge? Could it be that one of the themes of *First Impressions*, as the original version of *Pride and Prejudice* was called, was a burlesque on a favourite book, *The Lakes Tour* of William Gilpin?

Of the handful of writers who 'discovered' and enthused about the Lake District in the last quarter of the eighteenth century, Gilpin, with his very visual approach and accompanying drawings, was undoubtedly the most popular and influential. People of leisure began to travel northwards, into regions hitherto considered bleak and barbaric, to be thrilled by the dramatic scenery so different from anywhere else in England. Jane Austen had already had some fun at the expense of this movement in *Catharine*, the fragment written when she was just sixteen. The foolish Camilla Stanley gushes:

'We are going to the Lakes this autumn, and I am quite mad with joy. . . . I assure you I have done nothing for this last month but plan what clothes I should take with me, and I have at last determined to take very few indeed besides my travelling dress, and so I advise you to do, when ever you go; for I intend in case we should fall in with any races, or stop at Matlock or Scarborough, to have some things made for the occasion.'

' "You intend then to go into Yorkshire?" ' enquires Catherine, to be answered, ' "I believe not – indeed I know nothing of the route, for I never trouble myself about such things. I only know that we are to go from Derbyshire to Matlock and Scarborough, but to which of them first, I neither know nor care." '

Jane's earliest impulse to write came from perceiving what was ridiculous in the various movements and literary moods prevalent in her youth. Not only the juvenilia but the first three novels betray their origins in burlesque. While the plot of *Northanger Abbey* parodies the Gothic novel,

Matlock Bridge (1802) One of the picturesque sights of Derbyshire described by Gilpin and visited by Elizabeth Bennet

and the plot of *Sense and Sensibility* the sentimental novel, both contain passages in direct response to Gilpin's strictures on the picturesque. With *First Impressions* Jane indulged in a fuller treatment of the theme, shaping the action as she had shaped that of the other two novels, but this time to mock the fashion for northern tours: her heroine is deliberately sent in Gilpin's footsteps. The novel grew into something considerably greater than this, of course, and much of the fun had to be sacrificed when the manuscript was 'lop't and crop't' into *Pride and Prejudice*: but the design remains.

As in the passage from *Catharine*, Jane Austen's humour is directed not against 'him who first defined what picturesque beauty was' but against those who take up a fashion mindlessly, bringing to the privilege of travel neither sense nor taste.

Elizabeth, at the end of the first, 'Hertfordshire', section of the novel, having met with disappointment on all sides,

> had the unexpected happiness of an invitation to accompany her uncle and aunt in a tour of pleasure which they proposed taking in the summer.

'We have not quite determined how far it shall carry us,' said Mrs Gardiner, 'but perhaps to the Lakes.'

No scheme could have been more agreeable to Elizabeth and her acceptance of the invitation was most ready and grateful. 'My dear, dear aunt,' she rapturously cried, 'what delight! what felicity! You give me fresh life and vigour. *Adieu* to disappointment and spleen. What are men to rocks and mountains? Oh! what hours of transport shall we spend! And when we *do* return, it shall not be like other travellers, without being able to give one accurate idea of anything. We *will* know where we have gone – we *will* recollect what we have seen. Lakes, mountains and rivers shall not be jumbled together in our imaginations; nor, when we attempt to describe any particular scene, will we begin quarrelling about its relative situation. Let *our* first effusions be less insupportable than those of the generality of travellers.'

In the event,

they were obliged to give up the Lakes, and substitute a more con-tracted tour. They were to go no farther northwards than Derbyshire. In that county, there was enough to be seen to occupy the chief of their three weeks.

That is, 'all the celebrated beauties of Matlock, Chatsworth, Dovedale and the Peak.'

All these places were described at length by Gilpin. Two passages will suffice to show the elevated tone of his response to scenes of which Elizabeth's *First Impressions* may have been prosaically different.

Matlock Vale, wrote Gilpin, was

a romantic and most delightful scene, in which the ideas of sublimity and beauty are blended in a high degree. . . . It is impossible to view such scenes as these without feeling the imagination take fire. . . . Every object here is sublime and wonderful. Not only the eye is pleased, but the imagination is filled. We are carried at once into the fields of fiction, and romance. Enthusiastic ideas take possession of us, and we suppose ourselves among the inhabitants of fabled times.

And of Dovedale Gilpin wrote,

the whole composition is chaste, and picturesquely beautiful, in a high degree. . . . Among all the picturesque accompaniments of rocks there is nothing which has a finer effect [than the] variation and contrast of colour between the cold, grey hue of a rocky surface, and the rich tints

of herbage. . . . Dovedale is a calm, sequestered scene; and yet not wholly the haunt of solitude and contemplation. It is too magnificent, and too interesting a piece of scenery, to leave the mind wholly disengaged.

Jane Austen herself could not be quite comfortable with such wildness. Derbyshire for her, and for her heroine, is Pemberley, and a return, after seeing 'the principal wonders of the country', to civilization and the controlling hand of late eighteenth-century taste.

It was a large, handsome, stone building, standing well on rising ground, and backed by a ridge of high woody hills; and in front, a stream of some natural importance was swelled into greater, but without any artificial appearance. Its banks were neither formal, nor falsely adorned. Elizabeth was delighted. She had never seen a place for which nature had done more, or where natural beauty had been so little counteracted by an awkward taste. They were all of them warm in their admiration; and at that moment she felt, that to be mistress of Pemberley might be something!

Dovedale (1802) Another beauty spot mentioned in *Pride and Prejudice* as among the 'principal wonders' of Derbyshire

9

Southampton and Portsmouth:
Two Naval Households

Clouds, gold and purple, o'er the western ray
Threw a bright veil, and catching lights between,
Fell on the glancing sail, that we had seen
With soft, but adverse winds, throughout the day
Contending vainly.
Charlotte Smith, *Elegiac Sonnets*, 1784

From the autumn of 1806 to the spring of 1809 Jane Austen made her home in Southampton. Here she lived not only with her mother and sister, but with her brother Frank and his new wife, Mary, and with Martha Lloyd, recently rendered homeless by the death of her mother. The idea was to lessen all household expenses by sharing them, and to provide companionship for Mary when her husband was away at sea. The five females and Frank, who was 'considerate and kind, all gentleness to those around, and eager only not to wound', appear to have got on very amicably together.

Jane already knew Southampton, from having been briefly at school there; she had also danced at a public ball in the town when she was eighteen, though the circumstances of that visit are unknown. That she greatly preferred it to Bath, even to Canterbury, is evident – and not hard to explain. It was in her home county, and on the coast – two very powerful recommendations. Its pretensions to fashion were slight, compared with Bath's, and its air agreed with her better. Sea breezes successfully counteracted the 'stinking fish of Southampton' she had once joked about in a childish fragment. Within a compact area, the city was intensely built up, with a network of narrow medieval streets and tall overhanging buildings, but there was little sense of confinement, with the sea dancing virtually on three sides, and the countryside immediately beyond the ancient city walls. Best of all, perhaps, in Southampton the Austens were able once again to have a garden, essential to Jane's well-being.

Unlike Bath, the city of Southampton was found worthy to make part of a landscape, and by no less an authority than Gilpin himself:

A little beyond Redbridge, at a place called Milbroke, a beautiful view opens of Southampton. Before us lay Southampton bay, spreading into a noble surface of water. The town runs out like a peninsula on the left, and, with its old walls and towers, make a picturesque appearance. On the right, forming the other side of the bay, appear the skirts of New Forest, and the opening in front is filled with a distant view of the Isle of Wight.

Southampton is an elegant, well-built town. It stands on the confluence of two large waters; and when the tide is full, is seated on a peninsula. It is a town of great antiquity, and still preserves its respectable appendages of ancient walls and gates. The country around is beautiful.

This description was written in 1775, though not published in Gilpin's *Western Tour* until 1798. Of course the town had grown somewhat since the year of Jane's birth – that quarter of a century which saw so many English towns improve themselves in elegance and cleanliness, and so many coastal places attempt to become fashionable resorts. By 1801 the population was almost 8000. But that Southampton had by no means lost its character and charm is confirmed by a letter written to a friend by Mary Russell Mitford as late as 1812:

Have you ever been at that lovely spot which combines all that is enchanting in wood and land and water, with all that is 'buxom, blythe and debonair' in society – that charming town which is not a watering-place only because it is something better? . . . Southampton has in my eyes an attraction independent even of its scenery in the total absence of the vulgar hurry of business or the chilling apathy of fashion. It is indeed, all life, all gaiety, but it has an airiness, an animation. . . .[1]

A more substantial picture is given in the *Guide to all the Watering and Sea-Bathing Places* of 1810 to which we have already had recourse.

The lovely situation of Southampton, the elegance of its buildings, the amenity of its environs, and the various other attractions which it possesses, in a very high degree, will always render it a place of fashionable residence, as well as of frequent resort. The beach, on which there are several bathing machines, is very favourable for the purpose; and the sea-water here is as salt as that at the Needles. The air is soft and mild, and sufficiently impregnated with saline particles to render it agreeable, and even salutory, to those who cannot endure a full exposure to the sea, on a bleak and open shore.

Equally adapted for health, pleasure and commerce, Southampton . . . occupies a kind of peninsula, the soil of which is a hard gravel; and, as the buildings rise from the water with a gentle ascent, the streets are

Southampton (1810) Here Jane Austen made her home from the autumn of 1806 to the spring of 1809. Southampton's proximity to the water made amends to her for living in a town

always clean and dry. The approach from London is uncommonly striking; in fact, it is almost unparalleled in the beauty of its features, for the space of two miles. At first appear an expanse of water, and the distant Isle of Wight, the charming scenery of the New Forest, and Southampton itself in pleasing prospect. Elegant seats and rows of trees, nearer the town, line the road on both sides; and on entering the place, by one of its most fashionable streets, that venerable remain of antiquity the Bargate, gives a finish to the scene, and fixes the impression of the objects through which we have passed.

Gilpin, incidentally, also mentions the 'beauty of this avenue' leading out of Southampton, allowing that 'the idea of an avenue as a connecting thread between a town and a country, is a good one'.

The Austens took furnished lodgings in the town while they looked about for a more permanent home to rent. Their choice fell on 'a commodious old-fashioned house in a corner of Castle Square' with 'a pleasant garden, bounded on one side by the old city walls; the top of this wall was sufficiently wide to afford a pleasant walk, with an extensive view, easily accessible to ladies by steps.'[2]

Their view was to the west, across the bay to the New Forest. At high tide water lapped a narrow foreshore at the very foot of the wall: 'watching the flow and ebb of the river' became a favourite occupation.

Their landlord was the Marquis of Lansdowne. 'We hear that we are envied our house by many people, and that the garden is the best in town,' wrote Jane, shortly before they took occupation. The fact that the garden required 'improvement' only added to its attraction:

> Our garden is putting in order, by a man who bears a remarkably good character, has a very fine complexion, and asks something less than the first. The shrubs which border the gravel walk he says are only sweetbriar and roses, and the latter of an indifferent sort; we mean to get a few of a better kind therefore, and at my own particular desire he procures us some syringas. I could not do without a syringa, for the sake of Cowper's line. We talk also of a laburnam. The border under the terrace wall is clearing away to receive currants and gooseberry bushes, and a spot is found very proper for raspberries.

The line she refers to is from 'The Task', and describes the beauties to be looked forward to with spring,

> . . . Laburnam rich
> In streaming gold, syringa, ivory pure.

Jane also desired Cassandra 'to bring away some flower-seeds from Godmersham, particularly mignionette'.

Castle Square was situated in the north-west quarter of the city, not far from the medieval Bargate, through which all traffic entering the city by land had to pass. From the Bargate the High Street, running south the length of the city to the sea, was one of the most attractive streets in the south of England, with a crop of new bow windows adding variety to the Elizabethan timber-fronted shops and houses ('If there is one thing more than another my aversion,' declared General Tilney, 'it is a patched-on bow.')

There had been a castle in Southampton since the eleventh century, standing on a tall motte and improved and strengthened over the years. By the seventeenth century it was ruinous, however, and in 1804, just two years before the Austens' arrival in the city, the remains were romantically incorporated by the Marquis of Lansdowne into a new mock-Gothic castle which became his home. Like Beckford's Fonthill, this extravaganza must have been very badly built, or very inconvenient for living in, or both, for after only fifteen years of existence it was pulled down. But while it stood it provided the city with yet another 'enchantment' as a nephew of Jane Austen's, who visited his relations in Southampton as a boy, described:

At that time Castle Square was occupied by a fantastic edifice, too large for the space in which it stood, though too small to accord well with its castellated style, erected by the Second Marquis of Lansdowne. . . . The Marchioness had a light phaeton, drawn by six, and sometimes by eight little ponies, each pair decreasing in size, and becoming lighter in colour, through all the grades of dark brown, bay and chestnut, as it was placed farther away from the carriage. The two leading pairs were managed by two boyish postillions, the two pairs nearest to the carriage were driven in hand. It was a delight to me to look down from the window and see this fairy equipage put together; for the premises of this castle were so contracted that the whole process went on in the little space that remained of the open square.[3]

One disadvantage of living in a place which jutted out into the sea was the wind: 'Castle Square-weather' Jane called the north-west gales to which they were susceptible. Luckily there was no wind to fan the flames Jane witnessed in October 1808: the damage which fire could do in the close-built, timber-framed towns and cities of medieval origin was all too well known, for several of them had been burnt to the ground in the preceding century. Her account describes the fear and panic vividly:

On Tuesday evening Southampton was in a good deal of alarm for about an hour; a fire broke out soon after nine at Webbes, the pastrycook, and burnt for some time with great fury. I cannot learn exactly how it originated, at the time it was said to be their bakehouse, but now I hear it was in the back of their dwelling house, and that one room was consumed. The flames were considerable, they seemed about as near to us as those at Lyme, and to reach higher. One could not but feel uncomfortable, and I began to think of what I should do, if it came to the worst; happily however the night was perfectly still, the engines were immediately in use, and before ten the fire was nearly extinguished – though it was twelve before everything was considered safe, and a guard was kept the whole night. . . . I am afraid the Webbes have lost a great deal – more perhaps from ignorance or plunder than the fire; they had a large stock of valuable china, and in order to save it, it was taken from the house, and thrown down anywhere. The adjoining house, a toyshop, was almost equally injured – and Hibbs, whose house comes next, was so scared from his senses that he was giving away all his goods, valuable laces etc, to anybody who would take them. The crowd in the High Street I understand was immense. . . . Such are the prominent features of our fire. Thank God! they were not worse.

A spring containing compounds of both iron and sulphur had been discovered at Southampton in 1755, and the town possessed the usual accoutrements of a spa: Pump Room, two sets of Assembly Rooms, and several Baths, which by retaining the sea-water at high tide provided bathing throughout the day. There was also a theatre, the interior of which Jane Austen did not consider worth a second visit. She rarely joined in the evening amusements the town provided, but in December 1808 she attended a public ball – either at the Dolphin Assembly Rooms in the High Street, or near the West Quay in the Long Rooms, which, with their 'magnificent pier glasses' and 'music judiciously disposed down the centre' catered for dancing, card-playing and promenading.[4] Whichever it was, the place prompted Jane to write, 'It was the same room in which we danced fifteen years ago! – I thought it all over – and in spite of the shame of being so much older, felt with thankfulness that I was quite as happy now as then.'

Rural pleasures were not lost to the family at Southampton. 'We did not take our walk on Friday, it was too dirty, nor have we yet done it; we may perhaps do something like it today, as after seeing Frank skate, which he hopes to do in the meadows by the beech, we are to treat ourselves with a passage over the ferry' wrote Jane in January 1807. (She misspelt the word; 'The Beach' was the land between the walled town and the River Itchen.)

One of their regular walks was to Chiswell, 'about a mile and three-quarters from Southampton to the right of the new road to Portsmouth', where some acquaintance occupied one of the houses 'which are to be seen almost anywhere among the woods on the other side of the Itchen. It is a handsome building, stands high, and in a very beautiful situation.' On at least one occasion 'we went by the ferry and returned by the bridge'.

In November 1808 Jane wrote, 'The furniture of Bellevue is to be sold tomorrow, and we shall take it in our usual walk if the weather be favourable'. Bellevue was one of the sights recommended in the 1810 *Guide*:

'This delightful seat stands within a mile of Southampton on the road towards Winchester. It is a superb building within itself, but the scenery is so various and beautiful that no language can do it adequate justice. There are several fine buildings and commanding situations contiguous, but this eclipses them all.'

The proximity of the water provided a constant source of refreshment to body and mind. In October 1808, when Edward's two sons were visitors at Castle Square, 'We had a little water party yesterday; we agreed to be rowed up the river; both the boys rowed great part of the way, and their questions, and remarks, as well as their enjoyment, were very amusing.'

Excursions to Netley, Beaulieu and the Isle of Wight (in her letters Jane, like Fanny Price, calls it *the island*), were all possible from Southampton, and were often arranged for the pleasure of visiting nephews and nieces. A visit from James Austen and his son – the same little boy who loved to look at the 'fairy equipage' in the castle grounds – 'will be a good time for our scheme to Beaulieu'. On another occasion, when Jane was at Godmersham, James' daughter Anna accompanied Cassandra to the island: 'We give you credit for your spirited voyage, and are very glad it was accomplished so pleasantly, and that Anna enjoyed it so much. I hope you are not the worse for the fatigue – but to embark at four you must have got up at three, and most likely had no sleep at all.' Although there is no reference to Jane's visiting the island herself, the tone of her remarks makes it highly probable that she did; and that her opinion, given in *Persuasion*, that the scenery around Lyme 'may more than equal any of the resembling scenes of the far-famed Isle of Wight' was based on observation.

'Every visitor of Southampton makes an excursion to Netley, and generally by water,' says the 1810 *Guide*. 'The picturesque and still beautiful ruins of Netley Abbey . . . lie about six miles from Southampton by land and four by water. They are so surrounded by venerable woods as to be scarcely discovered. . . .'

Among the visitors to Netley Abbey had been Alexander Pope; both George Keate and William Sotheby were inspired to write a poem about

Netley Abbey (1805) These ruins inspired several writers in the eighteenth century and were visited by Jane Austen on a 'water party'

Netley in the 1790s. But when they visited Netley the Austens were following chiefly in Gilpin's footsteps, and his description helps us to see with Jane's eyes:

At Southampton we took a boat to see the ruins of Netley Abbey, which lie about three miles below on the bay. As we approached, nothing could be seen from the water; the bank is high and woody, and screens everything beyond it. Having landed and walked up the meadows about a quarter of a mile, we entered a circular valley, which seems to be a mile in circumferance. . . . In a dip, near the centre of this valley, stands Netley Abbey. . . . You enter a large square, which was formerly known by the name of the Fountain-court. The side on which you enter seems to have been once chambered, and divided into various offices. Such also was the left side of the court, where the bakery and ovens may still be traced. But in general, whatever the rooms may have been which occupied these two sides, the traces of them are very obscure. On the third side, opposite to the entrance, the court is bounded by the south wall of the great church; and along the fourth side range different apartments, which are the most perfect of any that remains in this whole mass of ruin.

The first you enter seems to have been a dining-hall. It is twenty-five paces long and nine broad, and has been vaulted, and chambered above. Adjoining to it, on the right, are the pantry and kitchen. You still see in the former the aperture, or buttery-hatch, through which victuals were conveyed into the hall. The kitchen of Netley Abbey is . . . a spacious and lofty vaulted room; and what is peculiar, from one side of it leads a subterraneous passage to the river, which some imagine to have been a common sewer, but is too ample, I should suppose, to have been intended for that purpose.

At the other end of the dining-hall, you pass through a small vaulted room, into the chapter-house, which is ten paces square. This room is beautifully proportioned, and adorned on each side by three arches, which uniting at the top in ribs, support a vaulted roof. To this adjoin two smaller rooms, from whence there is an entrance to the great church by the cross aisle.

The great church has been a very elegant piece of Gothic architecture; and is almost the only part of the whole ruin, which is picturesque. All traces of the aisles and pillars are lost; but the walls are entire, except half the cross-aisle, which is gone. The east and west windows remain; the former has not yet lost all its ornaments; and both are very beautiful without, as well as within. . . .

We can imagine the delight with which Catherine Morland would have explored all this – and the enjoyment, different in kind but hardly inferior in degree, with which Jane would have explained it to her eager, enquiring nephews. Their journey home was also captured in print by Gilpin: 'As we set sail from Netley Abbey, we had a beautiful view of Southampton, running from us in a point directly opposite to that view which we had from Redbridge. The indentations made by the River Itchen, and other creeks, are great advantages to the view.'

In contrast to these ruins, so overgrown with ivy and brushwood that Gilpin (wrongly) thought that 'in twenty years you may look for Netley Abbey in vain,'[5] Beaulieu Abbey was the abode of a wealthy family, the Dukes of Montagu, who loved and cherished their ruins very properly. If Jane approached Beaulieu by water, she would also have seen Buckler's Hard, a village created by the second Duke and consisting of one broad, grass-verged street of late eighteenth-century cottages running down to the Beaulieu River. Here, she may have pondered, had been built many warships of Nelson's navy – her brothers' navy – from good Hampshire oak.

Jane Austen had, to some extent, come home in returning to Hampshire, although the fact that she wrote no fiction at Southampton implies she was still not wholly settled in her mind and habits. Fanny Price, too, feels that she is going home to Hampshire – albeit a very distinctive part of the county. 'When she had been coming to Portsmouth, she had loved to call it her home, had been fond of saying that she was going home. . . .'

Portsmouth, eighteen miles from Southampton, was evidently well-known to Jane. 'Admiral Foote was surprised that I had the power of drawing the Portsmouth scenes so well,' she noted amongst the 'Opinions of *Mansfield Park*' she preserved as the response of family, friends and acquaintances reached her following its publication in 1814.

Long established as a military and naval town, Portsmouth possessed a character very different from Southampton's. It was not a place to be visited by the idle rich for pleasure. Mrs Price cannot understand how a fine gentleman like Mr Crawford 'should be come down to Portsmouth neither on a visit to the port-admiral, nor the commissioner, nor yet with the intention of going over to the island, nor of seeing the dockyard'. It was a thoroughly workaday town, and, as Fanny was to find, exceptionally noisy, dirty, crowded and smelly in consequence. But yet it was not unpleasing to the eye. No Georgian town could be so. They were incapable of building anything ugly. Portsmouth had its share of fine buildings and attractive streets.

With a population at the turn of the century four times that of Southampton, Portsmouth was just beginning to spread beyond the defensive ramparts which enclosed the old town on a line established in the Middle Ages, though much fortified in the intervening centuries. Portsmouth was a city on an island: on Fanny's arrival she passes the 'drawbridge' and on her exit, with a sense of release, the 'barriers'. The drawbridge was the outer barrier and the Landport Gate the inner, a tunnel-vaulted passage through the landward ramparts dating from 1760.

Within the ramparts a long, comparatively wide and gently curving High Street was the main thoroughfare. At No 85 was Turners, where William Price's mess things were bought. Fanny and Susan too did their shopping in the High Street, off which the narrow side street containing their father's house directly led. The architectural flavour of the areas has been recently described by David Lloyd in a paragraph so peculiarly pertinent to the present study that it must be quoted here:

> There are still plenty of eighteenth century houses in Old Portsmouth and Portsea, some quite demure with locally characteristic shallow segmental bow windows on the first floor, so different from the bold, usually semicircular bows characteristic of Southampton. It is strange that so much of late-Georgian Portsmouth, with its martial tradition, should have looked so Jane Austenish, while peacable Southampton, then a spa, should have developed a domestic architectural tradition that was much more robust.[6]

An opening in the ramparts on the seaward side was known as the sallyport – the word means a gate wide enough for troops to sally through – and gave access to the foreshore from the town and garrison. On the first evening of Fanny's visit the male part of the Price family walk to the sallyport from where William is rowed out to the *Thrush*, lying at anchor at Spithead, just to the eastward of the 'sheer hulk' – a floating dockyard.

North of the residential quarter was the true dockyard, which Fanny visits with Henry Crawford. Surrounded at that period by a red brick wall, the dockyard contained numerous storehouses constructed of the same material in the prosperous decades between 1760 and 1800: large edifices, in a town of small houses, but sacrificing nothing of Georgian elegance and proportion merely because they were functional and not for show.

At the south-east corner of the dockyard Fanny might have seen the Royal Naval Academy, built in 1729–32 and remodelled in 1808 as the Royal Naval College, when a large octagonal wooden cupola, surmounted by a ball used for teaching the sextant, was added to the handsome early Georgian building of dark red brick, three storeys high, with symmetrical wings forming a shallow open-fronted courtyard. Here two of Jane Austen's brothers had been educated, Frank in the late 1780s and

Charles in the early 1790s. It is possible that her own acquaintance with Portsmouth dated from then: at the very least she must often have heard them talking about the town. (Both men were to rise to the rank of Admiral; and Sir Francis Austen, at the outbreak of the Crimean War, was to be offered the top post in the navy, that of Port Admiral at Portsmouth, with his flag on HMS *Victory* – an honour which, at eighty years of age, he felt unequal to accepting.)[7]

Jane Austen is quite specific about which of the two medieval churches lying close to the High Street the Prices attend, sending them not to the cathedral but to 'the Garrison Chapel'. This was originally the God's House or *Domus Dei*, founded in 1212, as an almhouse and hospice for travellers, the sick and the aged, and administered by Southwick Priory. Unlike its counterpart in Southampton, it did not escape the Dissolution; the buildings were converted first to military stores and later to the residence of the military governor of Portsmouth. The chancel remained in use as the Garrison Chapel, which Mr Price, belonging to the Marines, was entitled to use – and where we may imagine Fanny Price worshipping.

After church it was Mrs Price's habit to walk on the seaward ramparts, where exercise, air and gossip 'wound up her spirits for the six days ensuing'. From the Garrison Church to the ramparts was only a question of crossing the Grand Parade, an open space used for military parades before and after service.

On the ramparts Fanny too draws sustenance, physical and spiritual, to see her through another week of confinement in her father's noisy, narrow house. The passage is vibrant with Jane Austen's own love of the sea, and with a new surrender to the emotional effects of nature:

> The day was uncommonly lovely. It was really March, but it was April in its mild air, brisk soft wind, and bright sun, occasionally clouded for a minute; and everything looked so beautiful under the influence of such a sky, the effects of the shadows pursuing each other, on the ships at Spithead and the island beyond, with the ever-varying hues of the sea now at high water, dancing in its glee and dashing against the ramparts with so fine a sound, produced altogether such a combination of charms for Fanny, as made her gradually more careless of the circumstances under which she felt them. . . . [She has been obliged to accept Henry Crawford's arm.] The loveliness of the day, and of the view, he felt like herself. They often stopt with the same sentiment and taste, leaning against the wall, some minutes, to look and admire; and considering he was not Edmund, Fanny could not but allow that he was sufficiently open to the charms of nature, and very well able to express his admiration. She had a few tender reveries now and then. . . .

Portsmouth is Jane Austen's only portrait of a town which is stultifying not for being a heartless, fashionable resort, but for almost the very opposite, its vulgarity, dirtiness and confusion. Much is due to the mismanagement of the Price household: in *Persuasion* the Harvilles, another naval family in a seaside town, are equally short of money and space, but theirs is a charming home. So undoubtedly was the Austens' own, formed under somewhat similar conditions. But urban reality plays its part in Fanny's discomfort.

The sun's rays falling strongly into the parlour, instead of cheering, made her still more melancholy; for sunshine appeared to her a totally different thing in a town and in the country. Here, its power was only a glare, a stifling, sickly glare, serving but to bring forward stains and dirt that might otherwise have slept. There was neither health nor gaiety in sunshine in a town.

Fanny's longings for the country surely echo her creator's own:

It was sad to Fanny to lose all the pleasures of spring. She had not known before what pleasures she *had* to lose in passing March and

Portsmouth where the sea dashing against the ramparts was the only alleviation of Fanny Price's misery in the confinement of a town

April in a town. She had not known before, how much the beginnings and progress of vegetation had delighted her. What animation both of body and mind, she had derived from watching the advance of that season which cannot, in spite of its capriciousness, be unlovely, and seeing its increasing beauties, from the earliest flowers, in the warmest divisions of her aunt's garden, to the opening of the leaves of her uncle's plantations, and the glory of his woods – to be losing such pleasures was no trifle; to be losing them, because she was in the midst of closeness and noise, to have confinement, bad air, bad smells, substituted for liberty, freshness, fragrance and verdure, was infinitely worse. . . .

Jane Austen could not have written so while she herself was confined, against her inclination, to a town, however pleasant that town. It was only when she was once again settled in the country that she allowed herself to explore and express some of her deepest feelings.

10

Chawton:
Home Ground

May my humble dwelling stand
Upon some chosen spot of land:
A pond before full to the brim,
Where cows may cool, and geese may swim;
Behind, a green, like velvet neat,
Soft to the eye and to the feet,
Where odorous plants in evening fair
Breathe all around ambrosial air.
                    Matthew Green, *The Spleen*, 1737

As a woman, and as a writer, Jane Austen could find complete fulfilment only in the country. It offered her both 'animation' and repose. Her joy on finding, towards the close of 1808, that circumstances were once more to place her in a small Hampshire village, was immense. Among other effects it produced an immediate revival of interest in her three unpublished novels. Her creative powers were reawakened, never to fail her again.

Like her own Anne Elliot, since leaving Steventon her private wishes had always centred on a 'small house in their own neighbourhood'. Chawton Cottage, seventeen miles south-east of Steventon, was almost exactly that. It belonged to her brother Edward, who had inherited the estates of Steventon and Chawton in addition to that of Godmersham from the Knights. Both Hampshire manor houses were let to tenants, but the cottage occupied by his steward in the village of Chawton became available, and it was this which he offered now to his mother and sisters.

They did not ask to see it before accepting, so confident were they that it would suit them, and that they would be happy there. They had been thinking of leaving Southampton anyway. The exigencies of Frank's profession made it often more convenient for his wife to take lodgings elsewhere – we hear of the couple at Portsmouth, Yarmouth, Deal and Cowes – and a smaller house became desirable to the others. At one time they were considering the country town of Alton, where Henry's banking firm had a branch, and which was only a mile from Chawton. But Edward's offer of Chawton Cottage was replete with every advantage.

'Everybody is acquainted with Chawton and speaks of it as a remarkably pretty village,' Jane wrote from Southampton when their plans became known. The next few months were filled with happy anticipation of the move. Their last night in Southampton was Easter Sunday, 2 April 1809. The following day Jane saw her new home for the first time. However, it was not yet ready for occupation. Edward wanted to know what alterations his mother required to make the cottage comfortable to her. The Austens spent the night at an inn at Alton, proceeded for a week's visit to relations in Great Bookham, Surrey, and thence to Godmersham, where they stayed until July.

Returning from the east, they approached their new home through the vale between Farnham and Alton, which Arthur Young, the eighteenth century traveller and agricultural writer, called 'the finest ten miles in England', and which Cobbett, whose birthplace it was, described affectionately: 'Here is a river with fine meadows on each side of it, and with rising grounds on each side of the meadows, those grounds having some hop gardens and some pretty woods.'[1] Jane was indeed come to a part of the world which those who knew intimately, loved deeply. Three and a half miles south lay Selborne; Gilbert White's description of the country around his beloved parish, 'an assemblage of hill, dale, woodlands, heath and water', serves to indicate the nature of the scenery on that side of Chawton.[2] It indicates, too, one of the special charms of England, the variation to be found within a small area. Though relatively near to Steventon, this was a different landscape, more lush and undulating, fertile and woody. Chawton had been enclosed early – in the 1740s – and had had ample time to mature.[3] Even Gilpin allowed that 'From Farnham to Alton, the road passes through pleasant lanes'.[4]

A mile beyond Alton, a busy little town owing much of its prosperity to the brewing industry, began the village street of Chawton, winding between pretty cottages in a mixture of styles, some of them thatched. At the far end lay the village pond, around which the road forked: left past the woods and lawns of Chawton Park, past the ancient church and grey stone manor house, and on towards Gosport; right to Winchester. In this curve of the road, and only feet from it, protected from runaway vehicles by a little paled enclosure, stood Chawton Cottage.

A timber-framed house which had since been clad in red brick, the cottage had an air of great solidity and squareness, but without that perfect symmetry indicative of Georgian origin. It was evidently an older building which had been improved and altered over the years, in a somewhat piecemeal fashion, but it was no less comfortable and charming for that. Only the front windows were sash; the little casements remained at the back, which sprawled away into a collection of outbuildings, including a room which doubled as a bakehouse and wash-house. There were six bedchambers, none of them large, and two garret windows pierced the roof.

Formerly both the dining-room and the drawing-room faced the road, one either side of the front door, but Edward's contribution to the process of modernization had been to stop up the old drawing-room window – turning it, with great ingenuity, into a most useful bookcase – and to cut a new one, complete with the Gothic glazing bars fashionable in 1809, in the side wall of the house, where it enjoyed pleasant garden views, and complete privacy.[5] The dining-room could not be given a different aspect; travellers could peep in, and see the occupants at table; conversely, the occupants could look out, and enjoy the little comings and goings of the village scene, and the occasional stirring sight of the stagecoach and six horses sweeping by.

To screen the garden, which lay to the side and rear of the house, from the Winchester road, a high wooden fence was erected, and planted inside with trees and shrubs, forming a pleasant walk around the perimeter of their property. Among Jane's first enquiries from Southampton had been, 'What sort of kitchen garden is there?' Now again the family could indulge in the exquisite delight of 'improvements'. From the 'two or three little enclosures, thrown together', which they inherited from Edward's steward, they created a garden suitable to their own more ladylike tastes, with seclusion, space for exercise, and room for all their favourite fruit and flowers.[6] Over the next few years they made an orchard and a lawn, a kitchen garden and a shrubbery, a gravel walk and flower beds.

'Our young peony at the foot of the fir-tree has just blown and looks very handsome, and the whole of the shrubbery border will soon be very gay with pinks and sweet williams, in addition to the columbines already in bloom', reported Jane to her absent sister in May 1811. 'The syringas, too, are coming out. We are likely to have a great crop of Orleans plums, but not many greengages – on the standard scarcely any, three or four dozen, perhaps, against the wall.' Later that month she added, 'You cannot imagine, it is not in human nature to imagine what a nice walk we have round the orchard. The row of beech look very well indeed, and so does the young quickset hedge in the garden – I hear today that an apricot has been detected on one of the trees.' Other crops mentioned in her letters from Chawton include 'strawberries, gooseberries, currants and pease'.

Cassandra, in a letter written in August 1811 to their newly married cousin Philadelphia, furnishes further insight into the concerns and pleasures of life in Chawton cottage.

What delightful harvest weather we have and how thankful we ought to be for it! You are now a farmer I think and will I trust have the pleasure of seeing your first crop got in in capital order. I quite envy you your farm, there is so much amusement and so many comforts attending a farm in the country that those who have once felt the advantages cannot easily forget them. We have not now so much as a cow. Pembury [in Kent] is I suppose in a fine fruit country, I hope you are better off in that respect than we are this year. We have a few orchards round us but scarcely an apple. The hops look better than they have ever done since we have been settled here. My mother is remarkably well this summer, her garden, in which she works a great deal, furnishes her both with amusement and health.[7]

There were lovely walks in every direction from the cottage, not least in Edward's woods and groves. (A visitor from London 'admired the trees very much, but grieved that they should not be turned into money'.) The Great House, as it was called by Jane, dated back to Tudor times. Its irregular shape, its clusters of tall chimneys, its stone mullioned windows topped by drip-moulds, and its broad, ogee-arched porch, were in complete contrast to Edward's fine classical mansion in Kent. But such houses as Chawton would soon be desirable again, as everything historic gained on the public imagination; and meanwhile it inspired its own brand of respect. Jane, like Emma Woodhouse, may surely have

felt all the honest pride and complacency which her alliance with the present and future proprietor could fairly warrant, as she viewed the respectable size and style of the building, its suitable, becoming, characteristic situation, low and sheltered – its ample gardens . . . and its abundance of timber. . . .

The presence of his mother and sisters in Chawton endeared Edward to his property there, and he suffered the tenancy of the Great House to lapse, reserving it for his occasional occupation, and intending it for his eldest son when he should marry. Edward and his family adopted the surname of Knight in 1812, on Mrs Knight's death. The following summer they spent five months at Chawton while Godmersham was redecorated. In 1814 Frank and Mary became Edward's tenants at the Great House – their sixth child, born there in 1815, was the first baby to be born in the house for 100 years. Chawton was reviving as a family home, and the village was becoming the centre of the Austen world. Henry frequently stayed either at the Great House or at the cottage when down on business to Alton, and from 1811 another regular visitor was Charles, who had been absent from England on service seven years, during which time he had acquired a wife and two daughters. (He was too poor to afford lodgings, and they all lived on board his ship.) From Steventon James often rode over on horseback to see his mother, and his three children were sometimes visitors in their own right. The eldest, Anna – the aspiring novelist – married in 1814 and from 1815 rented part of Wyards, a redbrick farmhouse just outside Alton. Frank and Mary moved to lodgings in Alton in 1816.

With her extended family all about her, or constantly visiting, Jane was deeply content. Neither she nor the other inhabitants of the cottage felt the need for much other company, and in any case, they could afford to keep no carriage (at least, only a humble donkey cart for daytime use). The tone of their life at Chawton was therefore much quieter, less sociable, more self-contained than it had been at Steventon. This was the result of circumstances – of growing older and poorer, and of being only a party of ladies – as well as of preference, but it was curiously representative of the change of century. 'Society' had been all-important in the eighteenth; home and family were the gods of the nineteenth.

A passage from a letter which Jane wrote to Frank in the summer of 1813, when he was away at sea, and Edward in the middle of his long visit to Chawton, gathers together all the interests and satisfactions of her life there and seems to glow with contentment:

July begins unpleasantly with us, cold and showery, but it is often a baddish month. We have had some fine dry weather preceding it, which was very acceptable to the holders of hay and the masters of meadows. In general it must have been a good haymaking season. Edward has got in all his, in excellent order; I speak only of Chawton; but here he has had better luck than Mr Middleton ever had in the five years he was tenant. Good encouragement for him to come again; and I really hope he will do so another year. The pleasure to us of having them here is so great, that if we were not the best creatures in the world we should not deserve it. We go on in the most comfortable way, very frequently dining together, and always meeting in some part of every day. Edward is very well and enjoys himself as thoroughly as any Hampshire-born Austen can desire. Chawton is not thrown away upon him. He talks of making a new garden; the present is a bad one and ill-situated, near Mr Papillon's; he means to have the new at the top of the lawn behind his own house. We like to have him proving and strengthening his attachment to the place by making it better. . . .

Her own attachment could not have been greater. At Chawton she had everything she valued about her: family, garden, the Hampshire countryside – and the products of her imagination. She had begun to revise her early novels almost as soon as she moved in, and determined to risk

Chawton House (1831) The property of Jane Austen's brother Edward, who took the surname Knight

publication at her own expense; *Sense and Sensibility* appeared in 1811, followed by *Pride and Prejudice* in 1813. Even as she was working on these manuscripts she was creating fresh worlds in her mind, and the great, original works of her maturity were conceived and brought to perfection at Chawton Cottage. *Mansfield Park* was published in 1814, *Emma* in 1815, and *Persuasion*, together with the earlier work *Northanger Abbey*, in 1817.

The Chawton years were the settled, fulfilling, productive years – but the years and the travels which had preceded them were not wasted. All that she had seen and read, all that she had learnt to feel for the English landscape, was there for her to draw on now that she had found the right conditions in which to exercise her genius.

11

London:
Bustle and the World

Oh! when shall I 'scape to be truly my own
From the noise, and the smoke, and the bustle of town?
Then I live, then I triumph, whene'er I retire
From the pomp and parade that the many admire.

Isaac Hawkins Browne,
The Fire Side. A Pastoral Soliloquy, 1746

Although village life suited Jane Austen so well, familiarity with London formed an important part of her cultural background and contributed to her assurance as a commentator on society. In this respect she was particularly fortunate in having at her disposal, for most of her adult life, the London home of her brother Henry. Secure in her country base, she could relish the occasional visit to the capital. But she would have agreed wholeheartedly with her mother's verdict on London, given as early as 1770: ' 'Tis a sad place; I would not live in it on any account. One has not time to do one's duty either to God or man.'

The London of Georgian good society, which forms the background of much of *Sense and Sensibility*, but which also makes its presence felt in *Pride and Prejudice* and *Mansfield Park*, is the area of regular streets and squares lying immediately north and south of Oxford Street. Laid out speculatively during the middle years of the eighteenth century by the great noblemen on whose estates they lay, and bringing in an immense profit as the demand for 'a house in town' steadily rose, Mayfair and Marylebone were characterized by formality, grandeur, regular Palladian architecture and total absence of individual gardens: only the railed-in greenery of the occasional spacious square providing relief from brick, cobble and stone. These were streets and houses for the highly ritualized, highly exclusive, highly unnatural style of life which Jane Austen deplored.

It took a foreigner to express the absurdity of it.

The trade of London is carried on in the east part of the town, called, *par excellence*, the City,

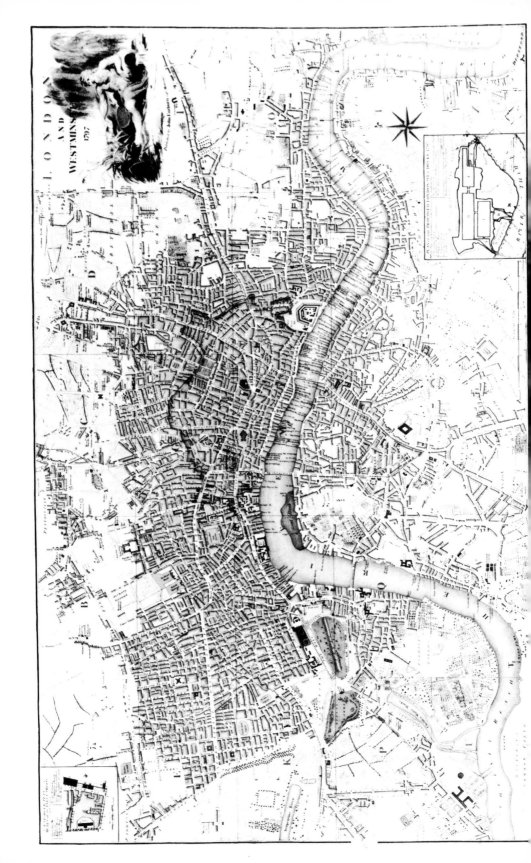

LONDON
AND
WESTMINSTER
1797

wrote Louis Simond.[1]

> The west is inhabited by people of fashion, or those who wish to appear such; and the line of demarcation, north and south, runs through Soho Square. Every minute of longitude east is equal to as many degrees of gentility minus, or minutes west, plus. To have a right to emigrate from east to west it is requisite to have an income of at least £3,000 a year; and £6,000 would be safer.

He was also amused by the English predilection for vertical living, which these early upper-class town houses established as the desirable norm. In continental cities available space was divided into flats; but Englishmen, even when *choosing* to live at close quarters with one another, demanded their own front door and portion of roof. Simond wrote,

> These narrow houses, three or four storeys high – one for eating, one for sleeping, a third for company, a fourth underground for the kitchen, a fifth perhaps at top for the servants – and the agility, the ease, the quickness with which the individuals of the family run up and down, and perch on the different storeys, give the idea of a cage with its sticks and birds.

Conforming to the taste and ideas of a generation or two before her own, this then was the heartless heart of Jane Austen's London. As the city expanded, other areas were developed which pleased her better; and she delighted in praising yet others which never had been nor ever would be fashionable; but this was what was generally meant by 'Town' both by her characters and by her acquaintance.

Her first known visit to London was in the summer of 1788, when, with her parents and sister, she dined at Orchard Street, the lodgings of her aunt Philadelphia and cousin Eliza, on both the outward and return journeys between Steventon and Kent. On this occasion the family probably put up at a hotel, perhaps the same one in Cork Street which they regularly used and from which Jane wrote in 1796, *en route* to Kent, 'Here I am once again in this scene of dissipation and vice, and I begin already to find my morals corrupted'.

London, at this stage in her life, seemed good for a joke. On her return journey, 'My father will be so good as to fetch home his prodigal daughter from Town, I hope, unless he wishes me to walk the hospitals, enter at the Temple, or mount guard at St James'. She was hoping to find an overnight resting-place with some acquaintance at Greenwich, or 'I should inevitably fall a sacrifice to the arts of some fat woman who would make me drunk with small beer'. The allusion is to the first plate of Hogarth's

London in 1797

Harlot's Progress, showing an innocent country girl being cajoled by a greedy procuress.[2] Bawdy, licentious eighteenth-century London is immediately before us, reminding us that this was Jane Austen's inheritance as well as the grim proprieties of Mayfair.

From 1801 there was no need to make use of hotels, or the homes of slight acquaintance, on the frequent journeys of the family in and out of Kent. In that year Henry resigned from the militia and with a former fellow officer set up as army agents and bankers with offices at Cleveland Court. Henry had married his widowed cousin, the pleasure-loving, sociable Eliza, some three years previously, and now, as Philadelphia Walter reported, 'They live quite in style in Upper Berkeley Street, Portman Square'.[3] When Jane visited them here she was in the centre of the fashionable district.

Henry, if not Eliza, retained a taste for the country which his sister thoroughly approved, and striking a happy compromise, the couple made their next two homes in a semi-rural setting. From 1805 to 1809 they lived at 16, Michael's Place, Brompton, and from 1809 to 1813 at 64, Sloane Street, Knightsbridge. Both were on the west route out of London, separated from Hyde Park Corner (where Wellington's Apsley House was known as No 1, London) by marshy, undeveloped land, riddled by creeks

View of London (1808) Jane Austen often stayed in London with her brother Henry, and all of her novels contain references to the capital, though only *Sense and Sensibility* is partially set there

from the Thames and occupied only by market gardens. Jane was a frequent visitor at both addresses and wrote from there of walking *into* London.

Brompton then had the character of an outlying village; Sloane Street was a little different, being part of the speculative 'Hans Town' designed by Henry Holland, architect of the Prince of Wales' home Carlton House, on eighty-nine acres of land leased from Sir Hans Sloane, in the 1770s. Built of red brick, these houses did not aim very high on the social scale, but appealed to people whose professional lives kept them in London, while their tastes were still those of the country. The green spaces on this side of the capital certainly made city life bearable to Jane, who wrote of taking a pleasant walk in Kensington Gardens in April 1811, noting that the lilacs were in bloom, the horse-chestnuts quite out, and the elms almost.

But of course it was the theatres, galleries and museums of London which were of unique value in broadening her experience. With Henry she visited Drury Lane, Covent Garden and the Lyceum (where they took a private box: 'one is infinitely less fatigued than in the common way'. Audiences, drawn from all the social classes, were much less decorous then!) In 1796 she attended Astley's equestrian theatre – where nearly twenty years later she was to place Harriet Smith's reconciliation with Robert Martin. Henry took her to the Liverpool Museum, the British Gallery, and an exhibition of paintings at Spring Gardens.

From 1811, when her first novel was published, the necessity of checking proofs and dealing with the final traumas of publication made it especially useful that she could command a London base with Henry, whose business acumen was also invaluable to her. And after Eliza's death in the spring of 1813 the childless Henry became particularly grateful for the companionship of one or other of his sisters, and Jane's visits became more frequent and longer.

Henry's bank had expanded and moved twice, first to the Albany and then to 10, Henrietta Street, Covent Garden. On Eliza's death he decided to give up the house in Sloane Street and move into rooms above the bank, suitably improved to receive him. In May 1813, still at Sloane Street, Jane reported that No 10 was 'all dirt and confusion, but in a very promising way'. Henry was planning to tour Scotland with a nephew during the summer, and Jane added,

He will not want either of us again till he is settled in Henrietta Street. This is my present persuasion. And he will not be settled there, really settled, till late in the autumn; he will not be 'come to bide' till after September. There is a Gentleman in treaty for this house. Gentleman himself is in the country, but Gentleman's friend came to see it the other day and seemed pleased on the whole. Gentleman would rather prefer an increased rent to parting with five hundred guineas at once; and if that is the only difficulty, it will not be minded. Henry is indifferent as to the which.

In fact Henry was settled in his new quarters by September, when, at the end of Edward's long summer visit to Chawton, he, his family and Jane, who was accompanying them to Godmersham, broke their journey in London. 'This house looks very nice, it seems like Sloane Street moved here,' Jane informed Cassandra, characteristically making the best of things, and to Frank at sea she sent a lengthier report in the same vein:

We were accommodated in Henrietta Street. Henry was so good as to find room for his three nieces and myself in his house. Edward slept at an hotel in the next street. No 10 is made very comfortable with cleaning and painting and the Sloane Street furniture. The front room upstairs is an excellent dining and common sitting-parlour – and the smaller one behind will sufficiently answer his purpose as a drawing-room. He has no intention of giving large parties of any kind. His plans are all for the comfort of his friends and himself.

Edward, incidentally, made use of this opportunity to take his daughters to a dentist; there was also a visit to Wedgwood's showroom, where he chose a dinner service, and much female shopping for fabrics and trimmings: 'We must have been three-quarters of an hour at Grafton House, Edward sitting by all the time with wonderful patience'. Shopping was an important element in all Jane's visits to London; besides her own requirements, a visitor from the country was always charged with commissions by friends and relations left behind. On another occasion Jane was sent to order the family's tea supply from Twinings in the Strand. The obverse to all this shopping was the flow of provisions to Henry from his connections in the country – a turkey from Steventon, a hamper of apples from Kintbury, a hare and four rabbits from Godmersham, nine gallons of mead brewed for him at Chawton. The interdependence of town and country could not be better illustrated than by this two way traffic which surfaces at points throughout Jane's correspondence.

Her next visit to Henry coincided with one from James and his son Edward. 'Their business is about teeth and wigs.' The family's observant habits, and farming interests, are revealed in her comment, on this journey to London, 'The wheat looked very well all the way, and James says the same of *his* road.'

This visit, of August 1814, was to yet another address. Presumably

Henry found himself cramped in Henrietta Street, either indoors or out – it was an area of tightly packed streets, without gardens, and of course in the heart of the business district – for he stayed there less than a year. The space, air and greenery of Hans Town drew him back, and he took No 23 in Hans Place, a charming little enclave tucked behind Sloane Street and designed by Holland to imitate, though on a much smaller scale, the shape of the Place Vendôme in Paris.

Hans Place was 'nearly surrounded by fields,' according to the writer Mary Russell Mitford, who happened to spend a fortnight visiting friends in the house next door to Henry's this same summer of 1814. At the southern end of Hans Place, into which its gates opened, Holland had constructed for himself a summer abode in extensive gardens, which he called Sloane Place, but which later became known as the Pavilion, perhaps because of his association with the Prince Regent's famous building in Brighton. By 1814 the Pavilion belonged to a Lady Charlotte Dennis. Whether Jane Austen walked into her grounds we do not know, but Mary Russell Mitford certainly did.

'What do you think,' she wrote to her mother,

> of a dozen different ruins, half-a-dozen pillars, ditto urns, ditto hermitages, ditto grottoes, ditto rocks, ditto fortresses, ditto bridges, ditto islands, ditto live bears, foxes and deer, with statues wooden, leaden, bronze and marble past all count? What do you think of all this crammed into a space of about ten acres, and at the back of Hans Place? It is really incredible.[4]

Jane thoroughly approved of her brother's new house. To Cassandra she wrote,

> It is a delightful place – more than answers my expectation. Having got rid of my unreasonable ideas, I find more space and comfort in the rooms than I had supposed, and the garden is quite a love. I am in the front attic, which is the bedchamber to be preferred. Henry wants you to see it all. . . . I live in his room downstairs, it is particularly pleasant from opening upon the garden. I go and refresh myself every now and then, and then come back to solitary coolness.

And to Martha she wrote,

> I am extremely pleased with this new house of Henry's, it is everything that could be wished for him, and I have only to hope he will continue to

like it as well as he does now, and not be looking out for anything better.
. . . I shall have spent my twelve days here very pleasantly, but with not
much to tell of them; two or three *very* little dinner-parties at home,
some delightful drives in the curricle, and quiet tea-drinkings with the
Tilsons, has been the sum of my doings.

Mr Tilson, a partner in Henry's bank, also lived in Hans Place, and the
Austens could talk to him 'across the intermediate gardens'. Among its
charms 23 Hans Place possessed a balcony and a conservatory, where
Henry could sit out when it was too cool for the garden.

Jane was with Henry again in November. Her niece Anna married that
month and with her husband, Ben Lefroy, went first to live at his brother's
house in Hendon, from where she wrote to her aunt. 'I think I understand
the country about Hendon from your description', Jane replied. 'It must
be very pretty in summer. Should you guess you were within a dozen miles
of the Wen from the atmosphere?' She was able to judge for herself when
only a week later she visited Hendon from Hans Place, but her verdict
went unrecorded.

During her next visit to London in October 1815, the purpose of which
was to see *Emma* through the press, Henry fell seriously ill, and in addition
to her tussles with the printer, Jane took on the office of nurse. One of the
doctors who attended her brother was physician to the Prince Regent, and
through him Jane was invited to visit the sumptuous library of Carlton
House. The Prince let it be known that he was an admirer of her work and
that she might dedicate her forthcoming novel to him.

This was her only brush with the Court, and her brush with the literary
life of the capital was yet slighter, for while she felt obliged to accept the
invitation to Carlton House, she positively declined one from 'a noble-
man, personally unknown to her . . . desirous of her joining a literary circle
at his house', and at which the celebrated Madame de Staël was to be
present.[5] With the exception perhaps of Egerton Brydges, a very minor
figure and one whom she knew only when she was young and unpublished, she never spoke to another writer in her life.

This visit to London, lasting nearly two months and full of varying
anxieties, though not without its pleasures once Henry's danger had
passed, was Jane's last. The following spring his business, through no
fault of his own, went bankrupt, and, 'dreams of affluence' over, he was
obliged to begin all over again. He decided, within weeks of the catas-
trophe, to become a country clergyman, like his father and eldest brother,
though without their expectation of a comfortable living. 'London,' Jane
wrote, 'is become a hateful place to him.'

It is interesting to trace the treatment of London as a thread running through all Jane Austen's novels. It is present, to a greater or lesser degree, in them all, and is, generally speaking, the thread of evil surfacing every so often in an otherwise 'light and bright and sparkling' fabric. From Mrs Percival's description of it as 'a hothouse of vice' in the early fragment *Catharine*, to Mrs Smith's unhappy revelations at the end of *Persuasion*, some twenty years later, the tone is remarkably consistent. Only in the happiest of all the novels, *Emma*, is London let off lightly.

Almost without exception, Jane's really reprehensible characters embrace London values, and were either brought up there, or choose to make their homes there, or retreat there to indulge in wrong-doing. Much of this happens either in the past or off-stage, in accordance with her distaste for dwelling on 'odious subjects'. But in her first novel Jane Austen perhaps felt obliged to tackle London head-on, and the London chapters of *Sense and Sensibility* conveniently set the scene and decide the tone for most of the allusions which come after.

The action is mainly confined to the streets of Mayfair and Marylebone; the atmosphere is oppressive. The physical constriction of tall narrow houses and noisy cobbled roads underlines the social constriction of being always surrounded by people, people who are neither strangers to whom one owes no duty, nor friends whose company one has chosen. The two principal gatherings attended by Elinor and Marianne illustrate the distresses of such a meaninglessly sociable life, though these are distresses which pass for pleasures with the majority. Accompanying Lady Middleton to a party, they

> entered a room splendidly lit up, quite full of company, and insufferably hot. When they had paid their tribute of politeness by curtseying to the lady of the house, they were permitted to mingle in the crowd, and take their share of the heat and inconvenience, to which their arrival must necessarily add. After some time spent in saying little, and doing less, Lady Middleton sat down to Casino. . . .

At the Dashwoods' dinner party, where Mrs Ferrars, who prides herself on good breeding, is so rude to Elinor,

> No poverty of any kind, except of conversation, appeared – but there, the deficiency was considerable. John Dashwood had not much to say for himself that was worth saying, and his wife had still less. But there was no particular disgrace in this, for it was very much the case with the chief of their visitors, who almost all laboured under one or other of these disqualifications for being agreeable – want of sense, either

natural or improved – want of elegance – want of spirits – or want of temper.

In the fashionable London life, time and money can be frittered selfishly away, as exemplified by Robert Ferrars' deliberations in the jeweller's, Grays – a real shop in Sackville Street. This is bad enough, but beneath the modish surface there is a yet more horrifying London, where women who have taken one false step can be left rotting in sponging houses, or be abandoned to give birth friendless and alone.

London as a hiding-place for the guilty rather than the unfortunate is one of the three aspects of the city depicted in *Pride and Prejudice* – it takes a great deal of ingenuity, not to mention 'bribery and corruption', to find those who do not wish to be found, Wickham and Lydia. The other two aspects of London are – once again – polite society, personified in Bingley's snobbish sisters; – and – something confined to this novel – good, honest trade. The Gardiners, whose home is in Cheapside, east of the City, are wholly estimable, not only in their hearts, but in their manners. 'The Netherfield ladies would have had difficulty in believing that a man who lived by trade, and within view of his own warehouses, could have been so well bred and agreeable.' No social intercourse is possible between Grosvenor and Gracechurch Streets, separated not so much by physical as by social distance. ' "Mr Darcy may perhaps have *heard* of such a place as Gracechurch Street," ' says Elizabeth, ' "But he would hardly think a month's ablution enough to cleanse him from its impurities, were he once to enter it. . . ." ' In fact, of course, Darcy is to enter a much less respectable, though unnamed, London street for love of Elizabeth.

In *Northanger Abbey* London is seen as the incubus of everything harmful and 'horrid': be it sensational novel, public riot or corrupted values. The Thorpes come from Putney, and betray the vulgarity from which the Gardiners are so remarkably free. Isabella Thorpe has all the pseudo-sophistication and worldliness of a 'town miss'. But as a heartless flirt interested only in money and conquests, she is surpassed by the older and better-born Lady Susan, in the short undated piece of that name. Cleverer and wickeder than Isabella, Lady Susan conceals beneath a surface of great charm all the faults of avarice, duplicity, vanity and self-centredness which, though occurring everywhere, are shown to be particularly prevalent in London – either because London breeds such traits, or because people who possess them gravitate there.

Jane Austen's third study of this type of character is much more

Cheapside (1808) The commercial quarter of London, where Mr Gardiner, in *Pride and Prejudice*, lived within sight of his warehouse

complex and subtle. She gives Mary Crawford every good quality and then shows it all spoilt by a London education. Without the scheming of Lady Susan, Mary possesses the same power to corrupt the integrity of a country community, to undermine its determination to do right. So too does her brother, who *is* a heartless schemer – capable of wishing to reform, but incapable of denying himself gratification.

The theme of the novel is how such a threat to integrity, in its most seductive form, is withstood and overcome. ' "I shall understand all your ways in time," ' Mary says shortly after her arrival at Mansfield; ' "but coming down with the true London maxim, that everything is to be got with money, I was a little embarrassed at first by the sturdy independence of your country customs." ' She and Henry find that everything worth having is *not* to be got with money, and in the end the 'sturdy independence' of the country triumphs over the superficial attractiveness of town.

Mary's London friends and London background are sketched in with economy and absolute conviction. They are part of the same world which Lady Susan and the Bingley sisters inhabit. Mary dreams for a moment of a double wedding at St George's, Hanover Square – the early Georgian square where Mr Palmer, MP, of *Sense and Sensibility* has his town house, and yards from Mr Hurst's in *Pride and Prejudice*. Even if Edmund and Fanny were to marry the Crawfords, can one imagine them doing so anywhere other than Mansfield Church?[6]

Jane Austen does not need to take her heroine, or the narrative, to London, in order to illustrate the dichotomy between town and country. It is there in speech, action and character throughout the novel. Mary's first comparison of the Bertram brothers comes down in favour of Tom, and not *only* because he is the elder: '*He* had been much in London, and had more liveliness and gallantry than Edmund'. (Of course it is greatly to her credit – we wouldn't be interested in her if it were not so – that she soon recognizes Edmund's 'endowments of a higher stamp'.) Edmund himself draws a comparison when he asserts that London does not reflect 'the proportion of virtue to vice throughout the Kingdom. We do not look in great cities for our best morality.'

The Bertram sisters are defined by their attitude to London. Maria enters into her engagement with Mr Rushworth to 'ensure her the house in town, which was now a prime object', and marries him, having learnt to despise him, and having been disappointed in her hopes of Mr Crawford, intending to 'find consolation in fortune and consequence, bustle and the world, for a wounded spirit'; while 'Julia was quite as eager for novelty and pleasure as Maria, though she might not have struggled through so much to obtain them'. Maria obtains 'one of the best houses in Wimpole Street,' preferred by Mary Crawford to almost any she knows in London, and considered by both women as *almost* compensating for the loss of Henry.

Twickenham (1808) This charming spot on the Thames in Middlesex, where early in the eighteenth century the poet Alexander Pope created his revolutionary and influential garden, was a favourite retreat with Londoners. Among many villas and cottages built here was one belonging to Admiral Crawford

' "This is what the world does. For where, Fanny, shall we find a woman whom nature had so richly endowed? – Spoilt, spoilt! –" ' cries Edmund when his eyes are opened to Mary's true nature; while Fanny herself soberly reflects her creator's opinion, we feel, in being 'disposed to think the influence of London very much at war with all respectable attachments'.

In *Emma*, which comes immediately after, the pressure is relented. This is the only novel in which London is not felt as an evil presence lurking in the background, ready to corrupt if country standards are relaxed. A London education has not spoilt Jane Fairfax. It has given her accomplishments and elegance without subverting her conscience or her heart. We glimpse two London households in *Emma*, those of the Campbells and of the John Knightleys. Both are notable for their family affection and good principles.

It is as if Isabella Knightley's effusions about the air of Brunswick Square could stand for the treatment of London in this novel: ' "Our part of London is so very superior to most others! – You must not confound us with London in general, my dear sir." ' Brunswick Square, one feels, might have been designed expressly for the Knightleys to live in, just as *Lovers Vows* might have been written for the company at Mansfield – so well do both fit. In the first place, Brunswick Square is not in the usual fashionable quarter, a point which would recommend it to John Knightley, whose dislike of meaningless socializing and love of his own fireside are plain. Then, it was conveniently close to the legal quarter of London where his work lay, being just north of the Inns of Court and west of Gray's Inn Road. Probably it was cheaper to rent than a comparable house in the West End; and there are hints that he was careful about money. And finally, Brunswick Square was both modern and airy, having been built early in the new century on the open land surrounding, and in the possession of, the Foundling Hospital.

In 1780 when it had been first proposed to build there, the governors had commissioned a report from Samuel Pepys Cockerell – the same man who built Warren Hastings' splendid house at Daylesford – which recommended the formation of two open-ended planted squares, facing each other with the hospital and its gardens in between. The object of these squares – Brunswick and Mecklenburgh Squares, as they eventually became – was to retain for the hospital 'the advantages of its present open situation' and provide it with an architectural setting 'rather to raise than depress the Character of this Hospital itself as an Object of National Munificence'.[7] (Did Mr Wingfield attend the foundlings, one wonders?)

London is only sixteen miles from Highbury, but seems to offer no threat of contamination. Easily reached by gentlemen on horseback, it is rather an amenity, a place for pleasant errands: Mr Elton takes Harriet's picture to be framed in Bond Street, Frank Churchill goes there nominally to have his hair cut, really to purchase a piano for the woman he loves. As with many of Jane Austen's plots, a little action off-stage in London assists the *dénouement*; but in *Emma* it is characteristically in the comic vein: the reconciliation between those simple country lovers, Robert Martin and Harriet Smith.

With *Persuasion* there is a return to the London of scheming and wickedness, with a new element of culpable extravagance superadded. The annual London visits of Sir Walter and Elizabeth Elliot have probably helped make them the cold, vain, snobbish creatures they are, and have certainly helped to run them into debt. 'A foolish, spendthrift baronet, who had not had principle or sense enough to maintain himself in the situation in which Providence had placed him,' Sir Walter is guilty of no mean crime in neglecting, even jeopardizing, his country estate for London pleasures. When obliged to leave it, he 'had at first thought more of London, but Mr Shepherd felt that he could not be trusted in London'.

London too has been the ruin of Charles Smith. 'We were a thoughtless, gay set, without any strict rules of conduct. We lived for enjoyment,' recalls his widow, describing the same society which has bred Mary Crawford. The Smiths' living beyond their means was encouraged by Mr Elliot, who turns out to be little less than a male Lady Susan, 'a disingenuous, artificial, worldly man,' who marries for money and has no heart for anybody's suffering. All this is imputed to the world in which he moved as a young man with chambers in the Temple, 'scarcely able to support the appearance of a gentleman' yet habituating such resorts of the privileged male as Tattersal's and the lobby of the House of Commons. Acquiring a taste for expensive pleasures he soon 'had one object in view – to make his fortune, and by a rather quicker process than the law'.

Disliking London, then, and not wishing to 'dwell on guilt and misery', Jane Austen set most of her work in the country houses and villages with which she felt happiest. But to have ignored London as an aspect of life for the cultivated classes would have been, in the late eighteenth century, unthinkably parochial. The provincial novel as such had not yet evolved. So she introduced London into her work as a background presence, a constant threat to country life, a range of shades on her moral spectrum, an aid to the fine discriminations she calls on her readers to make. Her portrayal of the capital is no less realistic for that.

12

Northamptonshire:
The Improver's Hand

Whatever charms the ear or eye,
All beauty and all harmony;
If sweet sensations these produce,
I know they have their moral use;
I know that nature's charms can move
The springs that strike to virtue's love.

John Langhorne, *Fables of Flora*, 1779

As far as is known, Jane Austen never travelled north or east of London into East Anglia or the East Midlands. However, that did not prevent her enlisting the 'fine open sea' of Cromer or the 'mud' of Southend into the high comedy of *Emma*; nor of setting a fair portion of *Pride and Prejudice* in Hertfordshire (though Barnet and Hatfield are the only real places mentioned) and almost all of *Mansfield Park* in Northamptonshire.

It is well known that in her search for verisimilitude she made enquiries of Northamptonshire among her family, in January 1813 requesting Cassandra, then at Steventon, to find out if it were 'a county of hedgerows', and a fortnight later writing to Martha, 'I am obliged to you for your enquiries about Northamptonshire, but do not wish you to renew them, as I am sure of getting the intelligence I want from Henry, to whom I can apply as some convenient moment *sans peur* and *sans reproche*'. Henry was on visiting terms with at least one gentleman whose country seat was in Northamptonshire.

It is just one aspect of Jane's mature artistry that *Mansfield Park* is geographically well organized. Henry Crawford, whose estate is in Norfolk, and who lives most of the time with his uncle in London, is very plausibly educated at Westminster and Cambridge; Edmund's ground is a little to the west, at Eton and Oxford. He is ordained in his native county, at Peterborough.

The county town, Northampton, is where Mansfield residents expect to attend public assemblies, and where harps, necklaces and visiting Prices await collection. Sir Thomas Bertram finds his wife in the neighbouring county town: Miss Maria Ward of Huntingdon, niece of a local attorney, certainly has good luck in captivating him. And while Tom, one gathers, is familiar with all the pleasure resorts of the kingdom, it is appropriately at Newmarket where the illness which changes his life is brought on.

In connection with a novel so much concerned with the countryside and the responsibilities, moral and financial, of those in whose stewardship it lies, it is worth noticing that Northamptonshire was relatively late in completing its enclosure.[1] Jane mentions Mansfield Common, and her accuracy is endorsed by the *General View of Northamptonshire* produced for the Board of Agriculture in 1809, which reported that 'even the open common fields increase the variety and add to the general appearance of beauty and utility'.

Attitude to the land is an important yardstick in measuring the characters of *Mansfield Park*. Sir Thomas is properly aware of his duties towards it. On the first morning after his return from Antigua, 'he had to reinstate himself in all the wonted concerns of his Mansfield life, to see his steward and his bailiff . . . and in the intervals of business, to walk into his stables and his gardens, and nearest plantations'. His heir, Tom, only looks to the land for sport and plunder – shooting and hunting. Mrs Norris plunders in a more underhand way, whether it is roses from the park or a heather from Sotherton.

Northampton (1810) The local town of *Mansfield Park*, and where we may imagine Mary Crawford's harp and Fanny Price's necklace being collected

Fostered and shared by Edmund, Fanny's love of nature is intense, as we saw when she was deprived of it in Portsmouth. Early in the novel, travelling a road new to her, 'in observing the appearance of the country, the bearings of the road, the difference of soil, the state of the harvest, the cottages, the cattle, the children, she found entertainment that could only have been heightened by having Edmund to speak to of what she felt'. Mary's deficiencies of character are revealed on the same journey: 'She had none of Fanny's delicacy of taste, of mind, of feeling; she saw nature, inanimate nature, with little observation'. Her brother is different again – capable of appreciating nature but not of accepting his responsibilities towards it. At Portsmouth he looks at the sea with 'the same sentiment and taste' as Fanny, who 'could not but allow that he was sufficiently open to the charms of nature'; but that does not prevent his neglecting his property in the country.

'To a mind richly stored, almost every object of nature or art, that presents itself to the senses, either excites fresh trains and combinations of ideas, or vivifies and strengthens those which existed before', wrote Richard Payne Knight in 1805 in *An Analytical Enquiry into the Principles of Taste*. 'The pleasures of vision . . . find endless gratification, at once exquisite and innocent, in all the variety of productions, whether animal, vegetable or mineral, which nature has scattered over the earth.' That Fanny Price has a mind thus richly stored we know from her star-gazing, her rhapsodies on the evergreen, her quotation of Cowper's lines, 'Ye fallen avenues, once more I mourn your fate unmerited'. Her declaration, 'One cannot fix one's eyes on the commonest natural production without finding food for a rambling fancy,' almost echoes Payne Knight's words.

'Improvement' runs through *Mansfield Park* as a theme comparable and indeed related to the town versus country theme – for the younger generation at Mansfield, those who are about to inherit both power and responsibility, have to decide whether the adoption of London values would be an improvement in itself.

Jane Austen's mind too was richly stored with, among much else that contributed to her portrayal of the English countryside, gardening history and theory, and with all the grounds and gardens, representative of the developments of the preceding century, which her travels had brought within her view. In *Mansfield Park* she draws on this material to consider how her society have refashioned and are refashioning their environment.

'Our old gardens were formed by the rule and the square, with a perpetual uniformity and in a manner more fit for architecture than for pleasure grounds,' Joseph Spence had written in 1751. 'Nature never plants by the line, or in angles.'[2] The innovation which released the garden from its slavish attachment to the house and allied it rather to the countryside beyond was the sunk fence, or the ha-ha. Invented by the royal gardener Charles Bridgeman, the device was first exploited to the full by William Kent, as Horace Walpole described in his *History of Modern Taste in Gardening*, published in 1771.

> No sooner was this simple enchantment made, than levelling, mowing and rolling followed. The contiguous ground of the park without the sunk fence was to be harmonized with the lawn within; and the garden in its turn was to be set free from its prim regularity, that it might assort with the wilder country without. The sunk fence ascertained the specific garden, but that it might not draw too obvious a line of distinction between the neat and the rude, the contiguous outlying parts came to be included in a kind of general design: and when nature was taken into the plan, under improvements, every step that was made, pointed out new beauties and inspired new ideas. At that moment appeared Kent, painter enough to taste the charms of landscape, bold and opinionative enough to dare and to dictate, and born with a genius to strike out a great system from the twilight of imperfect essays. He leaped the fence, and saw that all nature was a garden.

Oddly, perhaps, the only ha-ha mentioned by Jane Austen is at Sotherton Court, which by 1814 or thereabouts is considered hopelessly old-fashioned. The house is Elizabethan, but the grounds sound as if they were partially remodelled eighty or ninety years before the action of *Mansfield Park*, perhaps according to the ideas of Batty Langley, whose *New Principles of Gardening*, published in 1728, occupied a middle position between the old formality and the extreme simplicity that was to follow under the influence of 'Capability' Brown. Whilst expressing his distaste for 'that abominable mathematical regularity and stiffness' and advocating 'that all gardens be grand, beautiful and natural', he yet retained many of the straight lines and fussy details that Brown was to sweep completely away. Jane Austen must have known gardens which, for one reason or another, from indifference, conservatism or lack of money, remained in the Batty Langley mould. Among his 'Directions' are several that draw the hot day at Sotherton, with its avenue, bowling green, wilderness and grassy knoll, irresistibly to mind:

> That grand avenues be planted . . . with a breadth proportionable to the building, as well as to its length of view. . . . The entire breadth of every avenue should be divided into five equal parts: of which the middle, or grand walk, must be three-fifths; and the side, or counter-walks on each side one-fifth each. But let the length of avenues fall as it will, you

must always observe, that the grand walk be never narrower than the front of the building.

Did the avenue at Sotherton observe these rules? – we only know that it was half a mile in length, led to the west front of the house, and was of 'oak entirely'.

The lawn at Sotherton was presumably square, as it was bounded by walls, and the bowling green would have formed another geometrical feature: 'The most beautiful and grand figures for fine large open lawns, are the triangle, semicircle, geometrical square, circle or ellipsis'.

Sotherton did not quite satisfy this rule of Langley's: 'In the disposition of the several parts of gardens in general, always observe that a perfect shade be continued throughout, in such a manner as to pass from one quarter to another, etc., without being obliged at any time to pass through the scorching rays of the sun'.

But it is interesting to learn how the 'grassy knoll' may have been created: 'That hills and dales of easy ascents, be made by art, where nature has not performed that work before. That earths cast out of foundations, etc., be carried to such places for raising of mounts, from which fine views may be seen.'

Finally Langley advocated

That all those parts which are out of view from the house be formed into wildernesses, labyrinths etc. . . . That the walks of a wilderness be never narrower than ten feet, or wider than twenty-five feet. . . . In the planting of a wilderness, be careful of making an equal disposition of the several kinds of trees, and that you mix therewith the several sorts of evergreens.

Sotherton's wilderness, so important in the action of *Mansfield Park*, is 'a planted wood of about two acres, and though chiefly of larch and laurel, and beech cut down, and though laid out with too much regularity, was darkness and shade, and natural beauty, compared with the bowling green and the terrace'.

When the projected improvement of Sotherton first becomes a topic of conversation at Mansfield, Mary Crawford speaks of the discomfort experienced during her uncle's improvement of a cottage at Twickenham. It was at Twickenham, almost 100 years before, that the most famous of small gardens was created along lines far more revolutionary than Langley's by the poet Alexander Pope, whose influence on the gardening movement was immense.

He gains all ends, who pleasingly confounds,
Surprises, varies, and conceals the bounds,

he wrote, summing up not merely gardening philosophy, perhaps, but the art of the novelist. Together with Addison's essays in the *Spectator*, Pope's garden and poetry gave the movement the impetus and publicity necessary to disseminate the new ideas widely. By Jane Austen's time, both writers were part of every educated person's mental equipment.

But though the respective contributions of Kent and Pope were invaluable, both were guilty of absurdities of the sort Jane Austen delighted in ridiculing. Walpole says of Kent, 'In Kensington gardens he planted dead trees, to give a greater air of truth in the scene – but he was soon laughed out of this excess'; and in 1746 the poet Thomson 'mentioned that Pope had a scheme in his head of planting trees to resemble a Gothic cathedral'.[3]

Wholly free from such questionable taste, 'Capability' Brown dealt only in wood, water and lawn, curves and contours. For a quarter of a century or more the simplicity and purity of his ideas dictated the fashion. But he had his detractors. Walpole, unable perhaps to visualize the 'clumps' of trees when they had attained their full stature and magnificence, thought Brown's work spotty and trivial. The estate where this criticism was made was Moor Park. The improvement of house and grounds together cost its owner £80,000.[4] Huge amounts of earth were moved to create the correct gently swelling lawns and a lake. Later in the century Moor Park was to become famous for its fruit trees – including the apricot bought by Sir Thomas for Mansfield Parsonage.

Mary Crawford says that Fanny had been 'brought up' to improvements, implying that she is used to living in a place while they are being carried out. Very probably Mansfield Park had been fully refashioned or created along Brownian lines much earlier, and in the period of Fanny's childhood, some time in the first two decades of the nineteenth century, had undergone the comparatively minor updating which the shrubbery, gravel walk and flower garden suggest. These are all Reptonian, contemporary ideas. By this date people had become bored with the simplicity of Brown:

> Oft when I've seen some lonely mansion stand,
> Fresh from th'improver's desolating hand,
> 'Midst shaven lawns, that far around it creep
> In one eternal undulating sweep;
> And scattered clumps, that nod at one another,
> Each stiffly waving to its formal brother;
> Tir'd with th'extensive scene, so dull and bare,
> To Heav'n devoutly I've address'd my pray'r,
> Again the moss-grown terraces to raise,
> And spread the labyrinth's perplexing maze;

Replace in even lines the ductile yew,
And plant again the ancient avenue.
Some features then, at least, we should obtain,
To mark this flat, insipid, waving plain;
Some vary'd tints and forms would intervene,
To break this uniform, eternal green.[5]

As for Mansfield Parsonage, although Mrs Norris boasts about how much was done there in *her* time, when the Bertram children were too young to remember, it was left to Dr Grant to carry on the garden wall, and make a plantation to shut out the churchyard; and to his wife to create a shrubbery walk with a simplicity of taste which Fanny admires:

'Every time I come into this shrubbery I am more struck with its growth and beauty. Three years ago, this was nothing but a rough hedgerow along the upper side of the field, never thought of as anything, or capable of becoming anything; and now it is converted into a walk, and it would be difficult to say whether most valuable as a convenience or an ornament.'

Unlike Fanny, Mary is never carried out of herself in this 'exquisite and innocent' way. She can 'see no wonder in this shrubbery equal to seeing myself in it'. Money is never far from her thoughts. In an earlier discussion she confesses, 'I have no eye or ingenuity for such matters, but as they are before me; and had I a place of my own in the country, I should be thankful to any Mr Repton who would undertake it, and give me as much beauty as he could for my money.'

Henry Crawford does possess 'eye and ingenuity' – too much. With unconscious portent he declares, 'I am inclined to envy Mr Rushworth for having so much happiness yet before him. I have been a devourer of my own.' With no proper channel for his energy and inventiveness, he idly interferes in other people's concerns, without thought for the consequences. He may have taste and 'genius' and be 'a capital improver' but his doings improve nobody's comfort. Having ruined Mr Rushworth's chances of happiness by the day at Sotherton, he would financially ruin Edmund Bertram by his designs on the parsonage at Thornton Lacey.

'The farm-yard must be cleared away entirely, and planted to shut out the blacksmith's shop. The house must be turned to front the east instead of the north – the entrance and principal rooms, I mean, must be on that side, where the view is really very pretty; I am sure it may be done. And *there* must be your approach – through what is at present the garden. You must make you a new garden at what is now the back of the house; which will be giving it the best aspect in the world – sloping to the south-east. The ground seems precisely formed for it. I rode fifty yards up the lane between the church and the house in order to look about me, and saw how it might all be. Nothing can be easier. The meadows beyond what *will be* the garden, as well as what now *is*, sweeping round from the lane I stood in to the north-east, that is, to the principal road through the village, must be all laid together of course; very pretty meadows they are, finely sprinkled with timber. They belong to the living, I suppose. If not, you must purchase them. Then the stream – something must be done with the stream; but I could not quite determine what. I had two or three ideas.'

It has been noted how close this description is to what Humphry Repton had done for Harlestone House, itself in Northamptonshire, and described by him in his *Fragments on the Theory and Practice of Landscape Gardening*:

The house was formerly approached and entered in the south front, which was encumbered by stables and farm yards; the road came through the village, and there was a large pool in front; this pool has been changed to an apparent river, and the stables have been removed. An ample garden has been placed behind the house, the centre of the south front has been taken down, and a bow added with pilasters in the style of the house: the entrance is changed from south to the north side, and some new rooms to the west have been added.

These improvements were made around 1808 but the *Fragments* were not published until 1816, two years after *Mansfield Park*. Henry Crawford's 'ideas' prove not so much that Jane Austen set out to satirize Humphry Repton, as that she understood precisely what was fashionable at the time. Edmund's objections to the plan are grounded in what is appropriate to his income and position in life; a parsonage is quite a different proposition from a mansion. ' "I must be satisfied with rather less ornament and beauty. I think the house and premises may be made comfortable, and given the air of a gentleman's residence without any very heavy expense, and that must suffice me; and I hope may suffice all who care about me." '

Having so greatly enjoyed making 'improvements' herself, Jane knew it was a pleasure not lightly to be resigned to a professional. Tastes and talents ought to be exercised – so long as they are exercised responsibly. So when Edmund says, " 'Had I a place to new fashion, I should not put myself into the hands of an improver. I would rather have an inferior degree of beauty, of my own choice, and acquired progressively. I would

Improvements Humphry Repton's Bookplate showing improvements in progress – one of the major themes of *Mansfield Park*. Mr Rushworth considered employing Repton to improve Sotherton

rather abide by my own blunders than his" ', she shares his feelings without implying any criticism of Repton, who had remarked, in his description of Harlestone, that 'the more essential part of landscape gardening is apt to be overlooked in the general attention to the picturesque, which has often little affinity with the more important objects of comfort, convenience and accommodation.'

The question Jane Austen addresses in *Mansfield Park* is to what degree 'improvement' may be progress; and to what degree despoliation. She knew that the issue went wider than the laying out of grounds, to embrace the philosophy of a whole society. When Mary Crawford says 'Every generation has its improvements,' she is not speaking of gardening. Nor was the statesman Edmund Burke, when in his *Reflections on the Revolution in France* he used its imagery to sound a warning:

Lest the temporary possessors and life-renters . . . unmindful of what they have received from their ancestors, or of what is due to their posterity, should act as if they were the entire masters: . . . think it amongst their rights to . . . commit waste on the inheritance, by destroying at their pleasure the whole original fabric of their society: hazarding to leave to those who came after them, a ruin instead of a habitation – and teaching these successors as little to respect their contrivances, as they themselves had respected the institutions of their forefathers. By this unprincipled facility of changing the state as often, and as much, and in as many ways as there are floating fancies or fashions, the whole chain and continuity of the commonwealth would be broken.

Fanny would probably have said 'certainly' to this 'with gentle earnest-ness': and so would her creator; but Jane Austen had as always a balanced view and was not usually greatly out of tune with her times. Despite Fanny's lamentations over the avenue, Jane Austen made her own sensible Edmund decide that it is right to give Sotherton 'a modern dress'.

13

Surrey and Sussex:
Landscape into Fiction

It is the soul that sees; the outward eyes
Present the object, but the mind descries . . .
When minds are joyful, then we look around,
And what is seen is all on fairy ground.
        George Crabbe, *The Lover's Journey*, 1812

'The garden of England' Mrs Elton insisted on calling Surrey. Jane
Austen hardly disagreed with her. From her letters it is evident that she
loved the lush beauty of this county, and she paid it the compliment of
using it as the setting of that most idyllic and pastoral and *English* of her
novels, *Emma*.

She was acquainted with Surrey from her earliest travelling days, often
passing through it on her way between Hampshire and London or Kent.
She was also a guest at two Surrey rectories: Great Bookham, home of her
mother's cousins, the Cookes, and Streatham, home of her friend Mrs
Hill.

Travelling back from Kent with her parents in 1798, she wrote, 'Our
route tomorrow is not determined. We have none of us much inclination
for London, and . . . I think we shall go to Staines through Croydon and
Kingston, which will be much pleasanter than any other way.'

Her father had been asked by some village people, Robert and Nanny,
to recommend them for a tenancy of an alehouse. Mr Austen applied to
Mr May, a brewer. Jane told Cassandra that May expected to have an
empty alehouse soon at Farnham, 'so perhaps Nanny may have the
honour of drawing ale for the Bishop'. A passage from Gilpin's *Western
Tour* explains her reference, and brings Farnham before us in all its
hop-growing glory and picturesque associations; Gilpin even quotes the
same lines from Cowper that spring to Fanny Price's mind.

> Farnham consists chiefly of one long, thorough-fare street, and is
> principally remarkable for its being the summer residence of the
> Bishop of Winchester.
>
> Farnham Castle stands high, and was formerly a fortress of consider-
> able reputation. It was built by a Bishop of Winchester in the time of
> King Stephen, when castles were much in fashion, and made some

figure in the troubled reign of that prince. It afterwards figures in the times of Lewis the Dauphin, in the insurrections of the barons, and in the civil wars of the last century. During these last troubles it was blown up by Sir William Waller; though not with that *picturesque judgment* with which many castles in those times were demolished. Very little is left that can make a pleasing picture. After the restoration it deposited its military character, and was changed again into an episcopal palace by Bishop Morley; but it has ever since been neglected. The present bishop is the first who has paid any attention, for many generations, to Farnham Castle. He has greatly improved the house, and has fitted it up in such a manner, as will probably make it an object to every future bishop. The keep, or inner castle, is left standing in its ruins, and is still a curious piece of antiquity. It is surrounded by a deep ditch, which, together with the area of the castle, containing about two acres, makes an excellent kitchen garden.

Shades of General Tilney?

Behind the house extends a park, about four miles in circumference, which the bishop found as much neglected and out of order as the house itself. It was cut with unlicensed paths, the trees were mangled to browse the deer, and a cricket ground had so long been suffered, that the people conceived they had now a right to it. This last was a great nuisance. Such a scene of riot and disorder, with stands for selling liquor, just under the castle windows, could not easily be endured. The bishop took the gentlest methods he could to remove the nuisance; and at length, though not without some difficulty, got it effected.

Having thus removed the nuisances from his park, he began to embellish it. He improved the surface, he laid out handsome roads and walks, he planted young trees, and protected the old trees from farther ill usage.

Across the park runs an avenue a mile long, of ancient elms. The bishop could not persuade himself to remove this monument of antiquity; and I think with great judgment hath left it in its old form; for though an avenue is neither a pleasing nor a picturesque arrangement of trees, yet the grandeur of this gives it consequence; and its connection with the antiquity of the castle gives it harmony. Here the poet, after mourning the loss of other avenues, may exult:

> Ye fallen avenues! once more I mourn
> Your fate unmerited; once more rejoice
> That yet a remnant of your race survives

About a quarter of a mile from the house arises in the park an eminence, on which stands a keeper's lodge. The situation is conspicuous, but the object unpleasing. A few acres, therefore, around it are enclosed, a greenhouse is built to screen the lodge, and walks are cut, and adorned with different kinds of curious shrubs in high perfection. . . .

From the terrace before the castle, the view is singular. We over-looked the town of Farnham, and a tract of country, which may properly be called the *vale of hops*: for we saw nothing but ranges of that plant, which was now in full leaf, and made a curious, though very unpleasing, appearance. The hop and the vine, in a *natural* state, are among the most picturesque plants. Their shoots, their tendrils, their leaves, their fruit, are all beautiful: but in their cultivated state they are perfect samples of regularity, stiffness, and uniformity; which are, of all ideas, the most alien to everything we wish in landscape.

Nothing shows so much the prejudice of names, as the value fixed on Farnham hops. Those produced in this parish sell at Weyhill, and all the great fairs, at a considerably greater price than those which grow even in the next parish, though divided only by a hedge. To keep up this idea of excellence, the Farnham farmers agree every year on a secret mark, which they affix to all their own bags. The value of the hops, spread under our eye from the terrace on which we stood, was supposed to be at least ten thousand pounds.

Quite how often Jane visited Great Bookham we do not know. As early as 1799 she mentioned a possible visit – and not in a way from which it would be inferred this was to be her first; in 1808, in anticipation of travelling with Henry from London to Southampton, she wrote, 'I shall be nearer to Bookham than I could wish, in going from Dorking to Guildford – but till I have a travelling purse of my own, I must submit to such things'. (That is, she felt it impolite to pass so near to her relations without calling on them – but the arrangements were not under her control.)

The Reverend Samuel Cooke, Rector of Great Bookham, had married Mrs Austen's cousin, Cassandra Leigh; he was Jane's godfather. The Cookes had three children, Theophilus, George and Mary. Another resident of the village in whom Jane Austen took a lively, if distant, interest – there is no suggestion that they met – was her 'sister author', Fanny Burney, who occupied a cottage called The Hermitage after her romantic marriage, at the age of forty, to a penniless French *emigré*, General D'Arblay. On the proceeds of her novel *Camilla*, Fanny built a cottage of the same name in the grounds of nearby Norbury Park on land leased to her by the owner, her friend William Locke. Their cottage was intended to be the inheritance of the D'Arblays' precious only son.[1] 'Perhaps I may marry young Mr D'Arblay,' joked Jane in 1813 when she had published *Pride and Prejudice*.

On leaving Southampton in 1809, the Austens planned to stay for a week at Great Bookham, before travelling on to Kent.

> Edward and Henry have started a difficulty respecting our journey, which I must own with some confusion, had never been thought of by us; but if the former expected by it, to prevent our travelling into Kent entirely, he will be disappointed, for we have already determined to go the Croydon road, on leaving Bookham, and sleep at Dartford – will not that do? – There certainly does seem no convenient resting place on the other road.

('The other road' is the Dorking to Maidstone road which she had travelled the previous autumn – in the other direction.)

In May 1811 she paid her first visit to the rectory at Streatham. Her friend Catherine Bigg had married the Reverend Herbert Hill in 1808, and two years later he had been appointed to Streatham. Catherine was twenty-four years younger than her husband – who was related to Robert Southey – and when she had children Jane remarked on the 'melancholy disproportion' between the ages of the father and his young brood. In April 1811, writing from London, she told Cassandra of her plans:

> I wrote to Mrs Hill a few days ago, and have received a most kind and satisfactory answer; my time, the first week in May, exactly suits her; and therefore I consider my goings as tolerably fixed. I shall leave Sloane Street on the 1st or 2nd and be ready for James on the 9th; and if his plan alters, I can take care of myself. I have explained my views here, and everything is smooth and pleasant; and Eliza talks kindly of conveying me to Streatham.

Two years later, shortly after Eliza's death, Jane travelled, with Henry, from Chawton to Sloane Street, and described the journey through Surrey quite at length.

> How lucky we were in our weather yesterday! This wet morning makes one more sensible of it. We had no rain of any consequence. The head of the curricle was put up three or four times, but our share of the showers was very trifling, though they seemed to be heavy all round us, when we were on the Hogs-back, and I fancied it might then be raining so hard at Chawton as to make you feel for us much more than we deserved. Three hours and a quarter took us to Guildford, where we stayed barely two hours, and had only just time enough for all we had to

Guildford (1813) 'I think most highly of the situation of Guildford,' wrote Jane Austen in 1813, adding that she considered the country between Guildford and Ripley 'particularly pretty'

do there; that is, eating a long comfortable breakfast, watching the carriages, paying Mr Herington, and taking a little stroll afterwards. From some views which that stroll gave us, I think most highly of the situation of Guildford. We wanted all our brothers and sisters to be standing with us in the bowling green, and looking towards Horsham. . . .

We left Guildford at twenty minutes before twelve (I hope somebody cares for these minutiae), and were at Esher in about two hours more. I was very much pleased with the country in general. Between Guildford and Ripley I thought it particularly pretty, also about Painshill, and everywhere else; and from a Mr Spicer's grounds at Esher which we walked into before our dinner, the views were beautiful. I cannot say what we did *not* see, but I should think that there could not be a wood, or a meadow, or palace, or a remarkable spot in England that was not spread out before us on one side or the other. Claremont is going to be sold: a Mr Ellis has it now. It is a house that seems never to have prospered.

At three we were dining upon veal cutlets and cold ham, all very good, and after dinner we walked forward to be overtaken at the coachman's time, and before he *did* overtake us we were very near Kingston. I fancy it was about half past six when we reached this house

– a twelve hours' business, and the horses did not appear more than reasonably tired. I was very tired too, and very glad to get to bed early, but am quite well today. Upon the whole it was an excellent journey and very thoroughly enjoyed by me; the weather was delightful the greatest part of the day. Henry found it too warm, and talked of its being close sometimes, but to my capacity it was perfection. I never saw the country from the Hogs-back so advantageously. . . .

I am very snug with the front drawing-room all to myself, and would not say 'Thank you' for any companion but you. The quietness of it does me good. Henry and I are disposed to wonder that the Guildford road should not be oftener preferred to the Bagshot. It is not longer, has much more beauty, and not more hills. If I were Charles I should choose it, and having him in our thoughts we made enquiries at Esher as to their posting distances. From Guildford to Esher fourteen miles, from Esher to Hyde Park Corner fifteen – which makes it exactly the same as from Bagshot to H.P. Corner, changing at Bedfont, forty-nine miles altogether each way.

This description may be compared with Gilpin's (travelling in the opposite direction):

Guildford is a town both of antiquity and curiosity; but it is in no part picturesque. It consists of one long street, running down precipitately to the River Wey; from whence the road on the other side rises still more abruptly. . . . From Guildford to Farnham the form of the country is singular. The road is carried through a space of eight miles, over a ridge of high ground with a steep descent on each side. This grand natural terrace, which the country people call the Hogs-back, presents on each hand extensive distances. On the right the distance is very remote, consisting of that flat country through which the Wey, the Mole and the Thames, though none of them objects in the scene, flow with almost imperceptible motion. On the left the distance is more broken with rising grounds interspersed through various parts of it. Though the distance on neither hand forms a picture, except in a few places, for want of foregrounds and proper appendages proportioned to the scene; yet on both sides we study a variety of those pleasing circumstances, which we look for in remote landscape.[2]

It is not difficult to decide whose response to a glorious and dramatic countryside is the more spontaneous and heartfelt.

In the autumn of that year Jane again travelled through Surrey – being delayed at Kingston for quarter of an hour about the horses – when she accompanied Edward, at the end of his long summer visit to Chawton, back to Kent. In November, anticipating her journey home, Jane wrote, 'My scheme is to take Bookham in my way home for a few days and my hope that Henry will be so good as to send me some part of the way thither. I have a most kind repetition of Mrs Cooke's two or three dozen invitations, with the offer of meeting me anywhere in one of her airings.' Cassandra, meanwhile, was to visit Streatham. 'On Monday I suppose you will be going to Streatham, to see quiet Mr Hill and eat very bad baker's bread.' That was written on Wednesday; on Saturday Jane wrote, evidently in reply to a change of plan by Cassandra – not to mention Henry: 'You, and Mrs Hill and Catherine and Alethea going about together in Henry's carriage seeing sights! I am not used to the idea of it yet. All that you are to see of Streatham, seen already! Your Streatham and my Bookham may go hang. The prospect of being taken down to Chawton by Henry, perfects the plan to me.'

The following March Jane again travelled up to London from Chawton with Henry, but this time the 'twelve hours' business' was spread more comfortably over two days. She wrote from Henrietta Street to Cassandra,

You were wrong in thinking of us at Guildford last night: we were at Cobham. On reaching Guildford we found that John and the horses had gone on. We therefore did no more there than we had done at Farnham – sit in the carriage while fresh horses were put in, and proceeded directly to Cobham, which we reached by seven, and about eight were sitting down to a very nice roast fowl, etc. We had altogether a very good journey, and everything at Cobham was comfortable. I could not pay Mr Herington! That was the only alas! of the business. . . . We left Cobham at half-past eight, stopped to bait and breakfast at Kingston, and were in this house considerably before two. . . . It is snowing. We had some snow-storms yesterday, and a smart frost at night, which gave us a hard road from Cobham to Kingston.

In June 1814, Jane wrote from Chawton to Cassandra in London,

The only letter today is from Mrs Cooke to me. They do not leave home till July and want me to come to them, according to my promise. And, after considering everything, I have resolved on going. . . . They will meet me at Guildford. In addition to their standing claims on me they admire *Mansfield Park* exceedingly, Mr Cooke says 'it is the most sensible novel he ever read,' and the manner in which I treat the clergy delights them very much. Altogether I must go, and I want you to join me there when your visit to Henrietta Street is over.

Another variation on the journey between Chawton and London

occurred in August 1814 when Jane travelled, unusually, by public coach, known as the Yalden.

> I had a very good journey, not crowded, two of the three taken up at Bentley being children, the others of reasonable size; and they were all very quiet and civil. We were late in London, from being a great load and from changing coaches at Farnham, it was nearly four I believe when we reached Sloane Street; Henry himself met me, and as soon as my trunk and basket could be routed out from all the other trunks and baskets in the world, we were on our way to Hans Place in the luxury of a nice large cool dirty Hackney coach. There were four in the kitchen part of Yalden – and I was told fifteen at top.

This was the journey during which Jane observed that 'the wheat looked very well all the way'.

In January 1817, writing to Alethea Bigg, who was staying with her sister at Streatham and who had friends and relations taking advantage of the peace to travel abroad (Alethea herself was to join them in a few months), Jane expressed the hope that 'your letters from abroad are satisfactory. They would not be satisfactory to *me*, I confess, unless they breathed a strong spirit of regret for not being in England.'

Her intense love of England found its most sustained and happy expression in *Emma*, begun in January 1814 and finished in March 1815. The novel is set wholly in Surrey – the only one of her novels to include no change of location. Yet there is nothing monotonous, nothing restrictive about *Emma*. Highbury is shown to be largely self-sufficient, but also to be connected to the world beyond culturally, socially, economically.

Highbury is specified as being sixteen miles from London and nine from Richmond and thus cannot be identified with any real 'large and populous village almost amounting to a town'. Real places are however mentioned in the novel: Mr Weston assures Mrs John Knightley that there is no scarlet fever at Cobham; Kingston is specified as the local market town, visited weekly by Robert Martin (and on one notable occasion by Mr Knightley, on horseback); the climax of the novel is the 'exploring party' which travels seven miles to Box Hill. Thus the part of Surrey is evidently in the general locality of Great Bookham, which we know Jane revisited in the summer of 1814, when she was halfway through her novel.

I believe that Jane Austen deliberately avoided, out of respect for her acquaintance and fear of identification, using her beloved Hampshire countryside as the setting for a novel: Surrey, the neighbouring county, and one she had travelled through with delight, took its place when she came to describe her ideal community. For Highbury is an ideal (though not idealized) place. Even at the end of the book it has its faults: a deplorable vicar, chicken-thieves, gypsies, hovels; but it has too its moral and physical beauties. And Emma herself has come to realize that while there is little she can do about its faults, her role in life is to assist Mr Knightley in preserving and extending its beauties.

For Mr Knightley is much more than the conventional hero of a novel. One of the many advances discernible between Jane Austen's early and mature fiction is the usefulness of the male characters, or rather, her emphasis that to be approved a man *must* be useful. Henry Crawford, Mr Rushworth, Frank Churchill, Charles Musgrove and Mr Elliot all are censured for failing to employ their time or exploit their positions for the advantage of others. Edmund Bertram may be compared with Henry Tilney as a portrait of a committed clergyman; William Price and Captain Wentworth are something wholly new in being men whose profession gives meaning to their lives and value to their characters.

As a landowner, the obvious comparison with Mr Knightley is Mr Darcy, whose treatment of his dependants is excellent – it is one of the reasons Elizabeth changes her mind about him – but who is not shown to have the same involvement with the daily life of his community that is so notable in Mr Knightley. A closer comparison is perhaps with Colonel Brandon – a bachelor of much the same age and income, and with a home of similar old-fashioned comfort. No criticism is voiced of Colonel Brandon, yet he wastes huge chunks of his time at Barton or in London, simply because he can find nothing better to do.

Mr Knightley is always busy – and if he goes to London, he completes his business, sees his brother, and hurries back to ' "his farm, and his sheep, and his library, and all the parish to manage" '. In his home, he is always ' "reading to himself or settling his accounts" '; out of doors, he is occupied on his farm, or in meetings of the parish council. Emma teases him about his value for the society of William Larkins, his bailiff, and rebukes him for being so little of the fine gentleman as to go almost everywhere on foot or on horseback.

Jane Austen's thorough approval of this unpretentious and truly gentle-manly character appears in the early passage when his brother, a lawyer obliged to live in London, visits Highbury.

John Knightley made his appearance, and 'How d'ye do, George?' and 'John, how are you?' succeeded in the true English style, burying under a calmness of manner that seemed all but indifference, the real attachment which would have led either of them, if requisite, to do everything for the good of the other. . . .

The brothers talked of their own concerns and pursuits, but principally of those of the elder, whose temper was by much the most
communicative, and who was always the greater talker. As a magistrate,
he had generally some point of law to consult John about, or, at least,
some curious anecdote to give; and as a farmer, as keeping in hand the
home-farm at Donwell, he had to tell what every field was to bear next
year, and to give all such local information as could not fail of being
interesting to a brother whose home it had equally been the largest part
of his life, and whose attachments were strong. The plan of a drain, the
change of a fence, the felling of a tree, and the destination of every acre
of wheat, turnips or spring corn, was entered into with as much equality
of interest by John, as his cooler manners rendered possible; and if his
willing brother ever left him any thing to enquire about, his enquiries
even approached a tone of eagerness.

The importance of farming in *Emma* is reflected in the many references
to food and especially the *giving* of food; this is what an interdepend-
ent community is all about, and food in this context represents also
mental succour. Mr Knightley gives his last apples to the Bateses, and
Emma sends them pork from Hartfield; Mrs Martin makes Mrs
Goddard, whose school her daughter attended, the gift of a goose,
while Robert Martin rides about the country collecting walnuts for the
girl he loves.

Robert Martin is one of the new breed of tenant farmers then emerging
from the revolution in farming methods, and as such his presence, albeit
in the background of *Emma*, proves Jane's awareness of contemporary
change. While some of the old yeomen farmers had gone under with
enclosure, a minority, those most adaptable and intelligent, had prospered, taking advantage of new methods and new markets opened up by
better roads. To survive and to establish themselves as men of some local
consequence – though, as they did not own the land they farmed, they
could never be on a footing of complete equality with the gentry – such
farmers had to be business-like, experimental and literate. Robert Martin's reading habits are just what they should be – chiefly agricultural
reports, with a sprinkling of novels, when he has leisure to spare, to give
him a broader view of the world. His sisters are educated, and do not have
to seek paid employment, though no doubt they perform about the home
the same sort of tasks which Jane herself performed at Steventon and
Chawton. As Arthur Young, in a report on the agriculture of Oxfordshire,
wrote in 1809, 'If you go into Banbury market next Thursday you may
distinguish the farmers from enclosures from those from open-fields;
quite a different sort of men; the farmers are as much changed as their
husbandry – quite new men, in point of knowledge and ideas.'[3] Jane

Austen and Mr Knightley showed themselves more progressive than Emma in welcoming these new men for the contribution they could make to the welfare of their communities and for the proof they represented of the increasing prosperity of the country at large.

This is one of several lessons which Emma eventually learns from wise and benevolent Mr Knightley. She is halfway to accepting it when, during the strawberry-picking party to Donwell Abbey, she looks with satisfaction on a scene which encompasses Robert Martin's farm.

It was so long since Emma had been at the Abbey, that as soon as she was satisfied of her father's comfort, she was glad to leave him, and look around her; eager to refresh and correct her memory with more particular observation, more exact understanding of a house and grounds which must ever be interesting to her and all her family.

She felt all the honest pride and complacency which her alliance with the present and future proprietor could fairly warrant, as she viewed the respectable size and style of the building, its suitable, becoming, characteristic situation, low and sheltered – its ample gardens stretching down to meadows washed by a stream, of which the Abbey, with all the old neglect of prospect, had scarcely a sight – and its abundance of timber in rows and avenues, which neither fashion nor extravagance had rooted up. The house was larger than Hartfield, and totally unlike it, covering a good deal of ground, rambling and irregular, with many comfortable and one or two handsome rooms. It was just what it ought to be, and looked like what it was – and Emma felt an increasing respect for it. . . .

It was hot; and after walking some time over the gardens in a scattered, dispersed way, scarcely any three together, they insensibly followed one another to the delicious shade of a broad short avenue of limes, which stretching beyond the garden at an equal distance from the river, seemed the finish of the pleasure grounds. It led to nothing; nothing but a view at the end over a low stone wall with high pillars, which seemed intended, in their erection, to give the appearance of an approach to the house, which never had been there. Disputable, however, as might be the taste of such a termination, it was in itself a charming walk, and the view which closed it extremely pretty. The considerable slope, at nearly the foot of which the Abbey stood, gradually acquired a steeper form beyond its grounds; and at half a mile distant was a bank of considerable abruptness and grandeur, well clothed with wood; and at the bottom of this bank, favourably placed and sheltered, rose the Abbey-Mill Farm, with meadows in front, and the river making a close and handsome curve around it.

It was a sweet view – sweet to the eye and to the mind. English verdure, English culture, English comfort, seen under a sun bright, without being oppressive.

Of all the scenes and homes described by Jane Austen, this surely comes closest to her ideal and embodies her sense of values. Fashion and extravagance have no place at Donwell, which has as much real respectability as Pemberley, if not such evidence of correct 'taste'. The close association of the great house and the farm is important. Abbey-Mill Farm, 'with all its appendages of prosperity and beauty, its rich pastures, spreading flocks, orchard in blossom, and light column of smoke ascending', is an integral part of the scene as of the community.

In this description, incidentally, Jane Austen, carried away by her approval of all that Donwell represents, makes the only factual mistake that has ever been discovered in her writing, when she has the orchard in blossom at strawberry-picking time. In all other detail *Emma* excels in the portrayal of the seasons. The year revolves palpably from the autumn of Mrs Weston's marriage to that of Emma's.

Only once in the novel does Emma stray beyond the confines of Highbury, and then she strays too beyond the confines of her own standards of politeness. Unforgivably rude to Miss Bates, she is rebuked by Mr Knightley, admits the justice of his words, and is reduced, uncharacteristically, to tears.

It happens at Box Hill, a famed beauty-spot commanding extensive views. Gilpin has this to say about the area:

The other side-screen of the vale consists of that boast of Surrey, the celebrated Box Hill; so called from the profusion of box which flourishes spontaneously upon it. This hill from its downy back and precipitous sides, exhibits great variety of pleasing views into the lower parts of Surrey; and the higher parts of the neighbouring counties. But we have here only to do with it, as itself an object in a retiring scene; in which it fills its station with great beauty; discovering its shivering precipices and downy hillocks, everywhere interspersed with the mellow verdure of box, which is here and there tinged, as box commonly is, with red and orange.

This hill, and the neighbouring hills, on which this beautiful plant flourishes in such profusion, should be considered as making a part of the natural history of Britain. Asser, in his *Life of Alfred the Great*, tells us, that Berkshire had its name from [this] wood. No trace of any such wood now remains; nor is there perhaps a single bush of indigenous box to be found in the whole country. All has been rooted up by the plough. If it were not therefore for the growth of box on the Surrey hills, whose precipitous sides refuse cultivation, it might perhaps be doubted, whether box was a native of England.

Insignificant as this shrub appears, it has been to its owner, Sir Henry Mildmay, a source of considerable profit. It is used chiefly in turning. But the ships from the Levant brought such quantities of it in ballast, that the wood on the hill could not find a purchaser; and not having been cut in sixty-five years, was growing in many parts cankered. But the war having diminished the influx of it from the Mediterranean, several purchasers began to offer: and in the year 1795 Sir Henry put it up to auction; and sold it for the immense sum of twelve thousand pounds. Box attains its full growth in about fifty years, in which time, if the soil be good, it will rise fifteen feet, and form a stem of the thickness of a man's thigh. The depredations made on Box Hill, in consequence of this sale, will not much injure its picturesque beauty; as it will be twelve years in cutting, which will give each portion a reasonable time to renew its beauty.'[4]

Jane Austen, incidentally, knew Sir Henry Mildmay's wife, having met her both at the Hackwood ball, and at Worting, in Hampshire, home of her sister Mrs Clarke. The sisters were co-heiresses of Carew Mildmay and Sir Henry had adopted his wife's surname on marriage.

Gilpin continues, 'The end-screen which shuts in the beautiful vale

Box Hill (1813) The renowned Surrey beauty spot which plays an important part in the plot of *Emma* and exemplifies Jane Austen's transformation of landscape into literature

just described, consists of the range of hills just beyond Dorking. . . . A little to the left of Dorking hills, the high grounds gradually falling, admit a distant catch of the South downs, which overhang the sea.'

On Box Hill Frank Churchill in his foolery declares, ' "Let everybody on the Hill hear me if they can. Let my accents swell to Mickleham on one side, and Dorking on the other." ' It is a day of 'questionable enjoyments'. There is 'a burst of admiration on first arriving' and, at the end of two hours, a desire by the weary Emma to be 'sitting almost alone, and quite unattended to, in tranquil observation of the beautiful views beneath her'. There is no enthusiastic authorial praise of this landscape comparable to Jane Austen's description of Lyme. Home scenes attract all the approbation in *Emma*: Donwell, Abbey-Mill Farm, and even the village street at Highbury, which Emma observes with 'a mind lively and at ease'. Box Hill is visited for the wrong reasons, with the wrong people – and Emma suffers from allowing herself to be 'betrayed' into such a scheme. With her thankful return home, there is a new, sincere and thoughtful commitment on her part to all the duties associated with home.

One further place in Surrey remains to be mentioned: Richmond, on the River Thames, so naturally beautiful a spot and so convenient for London that its popularity as a place to build one's country villa was quickly established in the eighteenth century. The area was fashionable enough for the arch-snob Mrs Churchill to seek her health there; Isabella Thorpe, newly engaged to a man she hopes is wealthy, declares, ' "Where people are really attached, poverty itself is wealth: grandeur I detest: I would not settle in London for the universe. A cottage in some retired village would be ecstasy. There are some charming little villas about Richmond." ' And Mr Crawford, by spending Easter at Richmond, puts himself in the way of temptation by Mrs Rushworth at Twickenham – though as it was at Twickenham that his uncle's villa was located, I cannot help but feel that Jane Austen made a little mistake and intended the two households to be the other way round. Both places, of course, were equally fashionable – which brings us to consideration of Sussex.

For if Surrey was used by Jane Austen to celebrate an England under good management, Sussex was used to confront the prospect of an England misguidedly managed in the name of fashion.

'I assure you that I dread the idea of going to Brighton as much as you do, but I am not without hopes that something may happen to prevent it,' wrote Jane in 1799, with extraordinary vehemence. As far as we know the family never did go to that *crème de la crème* of resorts, made fashionable by the Prince of Wales, and evidently associated by Jane with immorality. She made it the scene of Lydia's disgrace, and sent Maria Bertram, so soon to fall, on honeymoon there. In both cases, the effect of Brighton was to do away the remains of such decorum as the young women may have possessed in the country and to prepare for scenes of 'guilt and misery' in London.

The Sussex resort which Jane almost certainly did visit, in the autumn of 1805, was Worthing. A large family-party was planned there: Edward and Elizabeth, Henry and Eliza, Mrs Austen, Cassandra and Jane. Unfortunately no letters of theirs from Worthing survive.

Worthing was one of the many seaside resorts newly sprung up in competition with Brighton. The phenomenon interested Jane deeply, so much so that she took it as the subject of a new novel in January 1817. *Sanditon*, of which only twelve chapters were drafted before illness put a stop to her writing, is in this sense Jane's most direct commentary upon England, and the changes her generation were making to its physical and mental landscape.

Mr Parker's ambitions for Sanditon are founded on such case histories as Worthing, described here in the 1810 *Guide*:

> Never was there an instance of the effects of public partiality more strongly exemplified than at Worthing. In a short space of time, a few miserable fishing huts and smugglers' dens have been exchanged for buildings sufficiently extensive and elegant to accommodate the first families in the kingdom. The establishment of two respectable libraries (Spooner's and Stafford's) at each of which the newspapers are regularly received, and the erection of commodious warm baths (Wickes's) within a few years sufficiently prove how far it has risen in public estimation. Worthing is in the parish of Broadwater, a village about the distance of half a mile, which now looks contemptible when contrasted with the growing splendour of its neighbour.

Jane Austen builds up her imaginary resort of Sanditon with many details which prove how thoroughly she understood 'the spirit of the day'. The 'church and neat village' of the original Sanditon lie at the foot of a hill, a little way from the coast and hidden from it; while 'a small cluster of fisherman's houses' stand where a little stream issues into the sea. As with Broadwater and Worthing, so with old and new Sanditon. The fashionable quarter is being laid out on the 'health-breathing hill' with sea views. Here is Mr Parker's new home, with its ample Venetian window,

> a light elegant building, standing in a small lawn with a very young plantation round it, about an hundred yards from the brow of a steep, but not very lofty cliff – and the nearest to it, of every building, excepting one short row of smart-looking houses, called the Terrace, with a broad

Entrance to Hastings (1810) In the fragment *Sanditon*, the Parkers are travelling 'towards that part of the Sussex coast which lies between Hastings and Eastbourne' when their carriage accident occurs

walk in front, aspiring to be the Mall of the place. In this row were the best milliner's shop and the library – a little detached from it, the hotel and billiard room. Here began the descent to the beach, and to the bathing machines – and this was therefore the favourite spot for beauty and fashion.

Mrs Parker is inclined to regret the snug comfort of their old house 'in a sheltered dip within two miles of the sea' and 'rich in the garden, orchard and meadows which are the best embellishments of such a dwelling'. Is it a change for the better to move to windswept Trafalgar House, for all its fine sea views? Here as so often Jane Austen is marking the difference between the old and well-tried, and the smart and new. It was the same at Uppercross, where the 'substantial and unmodernized' mansion of the Musgroves, behind its high walls, is contrasted with Uppercross Cottage, 'with its verandah, french-windows and other prettinesses . . . quite as likely to catch the traveller's eye as the more consistent and considerable aspect and premises of the Great House'. Donwell and Delaford also being warmly praised for their old-fashioned snugness, can we doubt where Jane Austen's tastes lay?

The nomenclature of Sanditon is amusing. Mr Parker is half inclined to wish he had called his house after the victory of Waterloo rather than Trafalgar; but he consoles himself with the idea of reserving Waterloo for the crescent of lodging-houses he hopes to build next year. The name 'crescent', he says, 'always takes'. Crescents, by enabling the view to be shared by more houses, were very popular at seaside resorts. In Sanditon too there is a Prospect House and a Bellevue Cottage – the latter perhaps the 'tasteful little cottage *ornée* which Sir Edward Denham is 'running up' purely for speculation – that is, not to adorn any estate or shelter any dependant.

All this is the work of the great landowners of the place; but in the old village even the cottagers are catching on to the idea that money may be made from visitors, and are smartening up their premises, advertising lodgings, and, if they are shopkeepers, dealing in more fashionable wares. The mental outlook of the population of Sanditon is being transformed along with the appearance of their village – for better or worse.

The same year, 1817, that Jane Austen was composing *Sanditon*, William Wordsworth wrote in a letter to Daniel Stuart:

> I see clearly that the principal ties which kept the different classes of society in a vital and harmonious dependence upon each other have, within these thirty years, either been greatly impaired or wholly dissolved. Everything has been put up to market and sold for the highest price it would buy. . . . All . . . moral cement is dissolved, habits and prejudices are broken and rooted up, nothing being substituted in their place but a quickened self-interest.[5]

Sanditon sparkles with sunshine, sea breezes and freshness. The little place is as inviting in its way as any Jane Austen invented. She can see and enjoy its attractions: but she can also recognize it as a symptom of a malaise about to overspread England. Restlessness and dissatisfaction with home on the part of the travellers; avarice and loss of sense of community among those who receive them; and the countryside itself becoming covered with buildings – these are the consequences of too much travel. The enthusiastic speculator Mr Parker, and the stay-at-home gentleman farmer Mr Heywood, voice the two sides of the question when first they meet. Mr Parker – of course – begins:

> 'Everybody has heard of Sanditon – the favourite – for a young and rising bathing-place, certainly the favourite spot of all that are to be found along the coast of Sussex; the most favoured by nature, and promising to be the most chosen by man.'
>
> 'Yes, I have heard of Sanditon,' replied Mr Heywood. 'Every five years, one hears of some new place or other starting up by the sea, and growing the fashion. How they can half of them be filled is the wonder! *Where* people can be found with money or time to go to them! Bad things for a country; sure to raise the price of provisions and make the poor good for nothing – as I dare say you find, Sir.'

'Not at all, Sir, not at all,' cried Mr Parker eagerly. 'Quite the contrary, I assure you. A common idea – but a mistaken one. It may apply to your large, overgrown places, like Brighton, Worthing or Eastbourne, – but *not* to a small village like Sanditon, precluded by its size from experiencing any of the evils of civilization, while the growth of the place, the buildings, the nursery grounds, the demand for everything, and the sure resort of the very best company, those regular, steady, private families of thorough gentility and character, who are a blessing everywhere, excite the industry of the poor and diffuse comfort and improvement around them of every sort.'

This is the classic debate, surely, between the relative virtues of progress and the preservation of the *status quo*. Progress was to win – as it always does – and, accelerating with every decade, was to transform the England Jane Austen knew. In the last fragment she wrote, she addressed herself to this prospect, with no small degree of apprehension. She had been privileged to inhabit a particularly lovely England; was it now, from greed or thoughtlessness, to be lost?

14

Winchester:
Journey's End

> These beauteous forms,
> Through a long absence, have not been to me
> As is a landscape to a blind man's eye:
> But oft, in lonely rooms, and 'mid the din
> Of towns and cities, I have owed to them
> In hours of weariness, sensations sweet
> Felt in the blood, and felt along the heart.
> William Wordsworth, *Tintern Abbey*, 1798

In the early summer months of 1817, as Jane lay dying in a strange, rented room, languid and listless from her malady, the sounds of a bustling town outside her window, and only Cassandra's presence to make it all bearable, did visions of the beautiful England she had seen sweeten some of her final musings?

If she had to die, she would surely have preferred to do so at home, in her beloved Chawton, amid the peace of the countryside. But in May, after best part of a year of deteriorating health, she was advised to go to Winchester for the sake of the medical attendance there. The last letter which she wrote from Chawton – to a friend, Anne Sharpe, in Doncaster – is worth quoting at length for the picture it gives of the state of her mind, as well as her health, two days before the removal to Winchester, which took place on 24 May:

> Your kind letter, my dearest Anne, found me in bed, for in spite of my hopes and promises when I wrote to you I have since been very ill indeed. An attack of my sad complaint seized me within a few days afterwards – the most severe I ever had – and coming upon me after weeks of indisposition, it reduced me very low. I have kept my bed since the 13th of April, with only removals to a sofa. *Now*, I am getting well again, and indeed have been gradually though slowly recovering my strength for the last three weeks. I can sit up in my bed and employ myself, as I am proving to you at this present moment, and *really* am equal to being out of bed, but that the posture is thought good for me.
>
> How to do justice to the kindness of all my family during this illness, is quite beyond me! Every dear brother so affectionate and so anxious! –

and as for my sister! – Words must fail me in any attempt to describe what a nurse she has been to me. Thank God! She does not seem the worse for it *yet*, and as there was never any sitting up necessary, I am willing to hope she has no after-fatigues to suffer from.

I have so many alleviations and comforts to bless the Almighty for! My head was always clear, and I had scarcely any pain; my chief sufferings were from feverish nights, weakness and langour. This discharge was on me for above a week, and as our Alton apothecary did not pretend to be able to cope with it, better advice was called in. Our nearest *very good*, is at Winchester, where there is a hospital and capital surgeons, and one of them attended me, and *his* applications gradually removed the evil. The consequence is, that instead of going to Town to put myself in the hands of some physician as I should otherwise have done, I am going to Winchester instead, for some weeks to see what Mr Lyford can do farther towards re-establishing me in tolerable health.

On Saturday next I am actually going thither – my dearest Cassandra with me I need hardly say – and as this is only two days off you will be convinced that I am now really a very genteel, portable sort of an invalid. The journey is only sixteen miles, we have comfortable lodgings engaged for us by our kind friend Mrs Heathcote who resides in Winchester and are to have the accommodation of my elder brother's carriage which will be sent over from Steventon on purpose. . . .

Mrs Frank Austen has had a much shorter confinement than I have – with a baby to produce into the bargain. We were put to bed nearly at the same time, and she has been recovered this great while. . . . I have not mentioned my dear mother; she suffered much for me when I was at the worst, but is tolerably well. Miss Lloyd too has been all kindness. In short, if I live to be an old woman, I must expect to wish I had died now; blessed in the tenderness of such a family, and before I had survived either them or their affection. You would have held the memory of your friend Jane too in tender regret I am sure. But the Providence of God has restored me – and may I be more fit to appear before him when I *am* summoned, than I should have been now! – Sick or well, believe me ever your attached friend

J. Austen

Mrs Heathcote will be a great comfort, but we shall not have Miss Bigg, she being frisked off like half England, into Switzerland.

Xenophobic to the end! Mrs Heathcote, who *was* a comfort to the sisters in their loneliness and fear at Winchester, had been widowed since 1802 and lived with her unmarried sister in The Close.[1] They were the Elizabeth and Alethea Bigg of Manydown, and Mrs Heathcote's presence must have brought poignant reminders to Jane of their youth together, of

Winchester Cathedral (1805) Here Jane Austen was buried in July 1817.
As Rudyard Kipling wrote:

> Jane lies in Winchester
> Blessed be her shade;
> Praise the Lord for making her
> And her for all she made;
> And while the stones of Winchester –
> Or Milsom Street – remain,
> Glory, love and honour,
> Unto England's Jane.

the happy Steventon days, the Basingstoke balls, and the proposal of marriage she had declined from their brother. How different her life would have been had she accepted it! But with six 'darling children' brought into the world, to give happiness to herself and others, there was nothing to regret.

The journey to Winchester, the last journey she ever made, was performed in rain, blotting out her last view of the countryside, and matching the anxious spirits and sombre purpose of the travellers. The carriage containing the two sisters was attended all the way by two riders on horseback: Henry, and one of Edward's sons, William. Jane grieved to see them getting wet.

Their destination was No 8, College Street, Winchester. 'Our lodgings are very comfortable. We have a neat little drawing-room with a bow window overlooking Dr Gabell's garden,' Jane wrote cheerfully to a nephew. Beyond the garden rose the precinct wall, above which Jane could look out every day on the towers of the cathedral. It was to be her final resting-place.

She went out on at least one occasion in a sedan chair into the town, but her strength continued to ebb away, and she was mainly confined indoors. Her life at Winchester lasted a little less than two months. On 18 July she died, aged forty-one. Cassandra, in a long heartbroken letter to her niece Fanny Knight, wrote,

The last sad ceremony is to take place on Thursday morning, her dear remains are to be deposited in the Cathedral – it is a satisfaction to me to think that they are to lie in a building she admired so much. Her precious soul I presume to hope reposes in a far superior Mansion.

Notes

(where full details are not given, see Bibliography)

Introduction

1. *Letters from England; by Dom Manuel Alvarez Espriella*, 1807.
2. *Austen Papers*.
3. Anne-Marie Edwards, *In The Footsteps of Jane Austen* is a good present-day guide to many of the places referred to in this book.
4. Margaret Drabble, *A Writer's Britain*.

Chapter 1: The England of Jane Austen's Time

1. Daniel Defoe, *A Tour Thro' The Whole Island of Great Britain*, 1724.
2. Anthony Ashley Cooper, 3rd Earl of Shaftesbury, *The Moralists*, 1709.
3. Horace Walpole, *The History of the Modern Taste in Gardening*, 1771.
4. Horace Walpole's phrase, invaluable for describing the level which Jane Austen and her characters chiefly occupy and for which 'middle class' sounds too bourgeois.
5. Louis Simond, *Journal of a Tour and Residence in Great Britain 1810/1811*, published Edinburgh, 1817.
6. For the statistics in this chapter I am indebted to Michael Reed, *The Georgian Triumph*.
7. The phrase is Humphry Repton's (*Red Book for Blaise Castle*, 1796).
8. Quoted in John Barrell, *The Idea of Landscape and the Sense of Place*.
9. Ibid.
10. Richard Payne Knight, *The Landscape, A Didactic Poem*, 1794.
11. This and the following remarks by Repton are quoted in Edward Hyams, *Capability Brown and Humphry Repton*.
12. William Gilpin, *Lakes Tour*.
13. Letter to a friend, quoted in Carl Paul Barbier, *William Gilpin*.
14. Alice Harford, *Annals of the Harford Family*.
15. In 1812 John Scandrett Harford built the ten cottages of Blaise Hamlet for 'upwards of £3,000'. Nigel Temple, *John Nash and the Village Picturesque*.
16. *The Gothick Taste*.
17. William Gilpin, *Lakes Tour*.
18. *Biographical Notice* appended to the posthumously published *Northanger Abbey* and *Persuasion* and believed to have been composed by Jane's brother Henry.

Chapter 2: Steventon

1. *Austen Papers.*
2. *Western Tour.*
3. James Edward Austen-Leigh, *Memoir of Jane Austen.*
4. Ibid.
5. Ibid.
6. Unpublished manuscript at Chawton Cottage.
7. Constance Hill, *Jane Austen, Her Homes and Her Friends.*
8. *Memoir*
9. Ibid.
10. *Austen Papers.*

Chapter 3: Oxfordshire and Berkshire

1. For a full account of the family history see my *Jane Austen's Family*, Robert Hale, 1984.
2. Quoted by R. W. Chapman in his Notes to *Jane Austen's Letters.*
3. *Austen Papers.*
4. Caroline Austen, *Reminiscences*
5. Elizabeth Jenkins, *Some Banking Accounts of the Austen Family*, Annual Report of the Jane Austen Society, 1954.
6. Quoted in *Jane Austen, Her Homes and Her Friends.*
7. Unpublished manuscript at Chawton Cottage.
8. George Sawtell, *Sons of the Parsonage* (unpublished manuscript).
9. Caroline Austen, op. cit.
10. *Memoir.*

Chapter 4: Kent

1. *Austen Papers.*
2. Ibid.
3. Ibid.
4. Edward Hyams, op. cit.
5. William Austen-Leigh and Montagu George Knight, *Chawton Manor and Its Owners*, 1911.
6. John Summerson, *Architecture in Britain 1530–1830*
7. *Chawton Manor and Its Owners*, op. cit.
8. David Waldron Smithers, *Jane Austen in Kent.*
9. Egerton Brydges, *Autobiography*, 1834.

Chapter 5: Bath

1. *Journal of a Tour and Residence in Great Britain 1810/1811*
2. Tobias Smollett, *Humphrey Clinker*, 1771.
3. Ibid.
4. Piers Egan, *Walks Through Bath*, 1819.

Chapter 6: Devon and Dorset

1. Quoted in Ruth Manning-Sanders, *Seaside England*.
2. *Diary and Letters of Madame D'Arblay*, 7 vols., 1842–6.
3. *Austen Papers*.
4. Quoted in *Seaside England* by Ruth Manning Sanders.
5. *Austen Papers*.
6. *Memoir*.
7. *Austen Papers*.
8. 'Roll on, thou deep and dark blue Ocean – roll!' follows shortly after the lines quoted at the head of this chapter.
9. *Lord Tennyson, A Memoir By His Son*, 1897.
10. Article by T. F. Palgrave in *The Grove*, 1891.

Chapter 7: Bristol and Gloucestershire

1. *Felix Farley's Bristol Journal*, 1806.
2. Samuel Rudder, *History of Gloucestershire*, 1779.
3. Robert Atkyns, *History of Gloucestershire*, 1712.
4. Alice Harford, *Annals of the Harford Family*.
5. Humphry Repton's *Red Book For Blaise Castle* is a leather bound manuscript volume illustrated with 'before and 'after' watercolour sketches such as he habitually produced on being commissioned to landscape a park.
6. Quoted at the head of this chapter. But Milton had used a very similar phrase as early as 1632 in 'L'Allegro':
   > Towers and battlements it sees
   > Bosom'd high in tufted trees,
   > Where perhaps some beauty lies,
   > The Cynosure of neighbouring eyes.
7. The last phrase of Edward Thomas's evocative poem, 'Adlestrop'.
8. Samuel Rudder, op. cit.
9. David Verey, *The Buildings of England: The Cotswolds*.
10. E. W. Brayley and J. Britton, *A Topographical and Historical Description of the County of Gloucester*, 1815.
11. Keith Feiling, *Warren Hastings*.
12. Sir Robert Clive, quoted in Mark Bence-Jones, *Clive of India*, 1974.
13. *Austen Papers*.
14. Ibid.
15. *Warren Hastings*, op. cit.
16. Bryan Little, *Cheltenham*.
17. *Austen Papers*.

Chapter 8: The Midlands and the North

1. The Leigh family are well-chronicled in George Holbert Tucker, *A Goodly Heritage*.
2. Quoted in *The Buildings of England: Warwickshire*.

3. *Austen Papers.*
4. Quoted in Barbier, *William Gilpin.*

Chapter 9: Southampton and Portsmouth

1. Quoted in *Jane Austen, Her Homes and Her Friends.*
2. *Memoir.*
3. Ibid.
4. Quoted in Kathleen Denbigh, *A Hundred British Spas.*
5. Letter to a friend, quoted in Barbier, *William Gilpin.*
6. *The Buildings of England: Hampshire.*
7. John and Edith Hubback, *Jane Austen's Sailor Brothers*, 1904.

Chapter 10: Chawton

1. William Cobbett, *Rural Rides*, 1825. (Cobbett quotes Arthur Young.)
2. Gilbert White, *The Natural History of Selborne*, 1789.
3. *Chawton Manor and Its Owners.*
4. *Western Tour.*
5. Caroline Austen, *My Aunt Jane Austen*, published by the Jane Austen Society, 1952.
6. Ibid.
7. *Austen Papers.*

Chapter 11: London

1. Op. cit.
2. Identification made by George Holbert Tucker in *A Goodly Heritage.*
3. *Austen Papers*
4. Quoted in *Jane Austen, Her Homes and Her Friends.*
5. *Memoir.*
6. Surely not in the church where Sir William Hamilton had married his Emma!
7. Quoted in John Summerson, *Georgian London.*

Chapter 12: Northamptonshire

1. John Barrell, op. cit., where the enclosure of Northamptonshire is discussed in relation to the poetry of John Clare.
2. *Observations, Anecdotes and Characters of Books and Men*, first published 1820, but known and widely quoted in the eighteenth century. See *The Genius of the Place* by John Dixon Hunt and Peter Willis.
3. 'Account of an Interview between Shenstone and Thomson' published in *The Edinburgh Magazine*, 1820. See *The Genius of the Place* by John Dixon Hunt and Peter Willis.
4. Edward Hyams, op. cit.
5. Richard Payne Knight, *The Landscape*, 1794.

6. By R. W. Chapman and Alistair M. Duckworth; Edward Hyams and Nikolaus Pevsner both offer Harlestone as a possible 'original' for Mansfield Park.

Chapter 13: Surrey and Sussex

1. Jane's opportunities for meeting Fanny Burney in Surrey were limited to the years between 1793, when the D'Arblays settled in The Hermitage, and 1802, when Fanny followed her husband to France to which he had immediately returned on the Peace of Amiens. The sudden renewal of war trapped the couple in France for another dozen years. (The Henry Austens, who had travelled at much the same time and for much the same purpose – in an attempt to retrieve French property – very nearly suffered the same fate.) Camilla Cottage had to be sold in 1814 on the sale of Norbury Park, when it was found that the D'Arblays had no proper lease on the ground on which they had built. Joyce Hemlow, *Fanny Burney*, 1958.
2. *Western Tour.*
3. Quoted in John Barrell, op. cit.
4. *Western Tour.*
5. Quoted in *The Improvement of the Estate.*

Chapter 14: Winchester

1. *Memoir.*

Bibliography

Jane Austen Studies

Austen, Caroline, *Reminiscences* (Jane Austen Society, 1986)

Austen-Leigh, James Edward, *Memoir of Jane Austen* (Richard Bentley, 1870)

Austen-Leigh, Richard Arthur (editor), *Austen Papers 1704–1856* (Spottiswoode, Ballantyne and Co Ltd, 1942)

Bradbrook, Frank W., *Jane Austen and her Predecessors* (Cambridge University Press, 1966)

Chapman, R. A. (editor), *The Works of Jane Austen* and *The Letters of Jane Austen to her Sister Cassandra and Others* (Oxford University Press, 1954 and 1972)

Duckworth, Alistair, M., *The Improvement of the Estate: A Study of Jane Austen's Novels* (John Hopkins Press, 1971)

Edwards, Anne-Marie, *In the Steps of Jane Austen* (Arcady Books, 1985)

Gillie, Christopher, *A Preface to Jane Austen* (Longman, 1974)

Hill, Constance, *Jane Austen, Her Homes and Her Friends* (John Lane, 1902)

Lane, Maggie, *Jane Austen's Family: Through Five Generations* (Robert Hale, 1984)

Pinion, F. B., *A Jane Austen Companion* (Macmillan, 1973)

Smithers, David Waldron, *Jane Austen in Kent* (Hurtwood, 1982)

Tucker, George Holbert, *A Goodly Heritage* (Carcanet, 1983)

Landscape and the Eighteenth Century

Barbier, Carl Paul, *William Gilpin, His Drawings, Teachings and Theory of the Picturesque* (Oxford University Press, 1963)

Barrell, John, *The Idea of Landscape and the Sense of Place 1730–1840* (Cambridge University Press, 1972)

Davis, Terence, *The Gothick Taste* (David and Charles, 1974)

Denbigh, Kathleen, *A Hundred British Spas* (Spa Publications, 1971)

Drabble, Margaret, *A Writer's Britain, Landscape in Literature* (Thames and Hudson, 1979)

Feiling, Keith, *Warren Hastings* (Macmillan, 1954)

Gadd, David, *Georgian Summer: Bath in the Eighteenth Century* (Moonraker, 1977)

Gilpin, William, *Observations on the English Lakes Relative Chiefly to Picturesque Beauty* (Cadell, 1786, republished Richmond Press, 1973)

Gilpin, William, *Observations on the Western Parts of England Relative Chiefly to Picturesque Beauty* (Cadell, 1798, republished Richmond Press 1973)

Hadfield, John (editor) *The Shell Book of English Villages* (Michael Joseph, 1980)

Hunt, John Dixon, and Willis, Peter, *The Genius of the Place: The English Landscape Garden 1620–1820* (Elek, 1975)

Hyams, Edward, *Capability Brown and Humphry Repton* (Dent, 1971)

Lang, Andrew, *Poets' Country* (T. C. & E. C. Jack, 1907)

Little, Bryan, *Cheltenham* (Batsford, 1952)

Lansdale, Roger (editor), *The New Oxford Book of Eighteenth Century Verse* (Oxford University Press, 1984)

Mullins, Edwin, *A Love Affair with Nature* (Phaidon, 1985)

Pevsner, Nikolaus, and others, *The Buildings of England* (Penguin)

Pilcher, Donald, *Regency Style* (Batsford, 1947)

Piper, David, *London* (Collins, 1980)

Plumb, J. H., *Georgian Delights* (Weidenfeld and Nicolson, 1980)

Reed, Michael, *The Georgian Triumph 1700–1830* (Routledge and Kegan Paul, 1983)

Sanders, Ruth Manning, *Seaside England* (Batsford, 1951)

Summerson, John, *Georgian London* (Barne and Jenkins, 1970)

Summerson, John, *The Pelican History of Art: Architecture in Britain 1530–1830* (Penguin, 1953)

Temple, Nigel, *John Nash and the Village Picturesque* (Alan Sutton, 1979)

Watson, J. R., *Picturesque Landscape and English Romantic Poetry* (Hutchinson, 1970)

Whitlock, Ralph, *The Shaping of the Countryside* (Robert Hale, 1979)

Williams, E. N., *Life in Georgian England* (Batsford, 1962)

Index

To distinguish members of the Austen family, in which Christian names were often shared, relationships to Jane are given in brackets